EUSTACE MULLINS

COLLECTED ESSAYS

[signature]

OMNIA VERITAS

EUSTACE CLARENCE MULLINS
(1923-2010)

COLLECTED ESSAYS

1978-1981

Published by
OMNIA VERITAS LTD

www.omnia-veritas.com

ABOUT THE AUTHOR	9
MY STRUGGLE	11
THE WAR AGAINST CHRISTIANITY	36
F.D.R.	44
DOUGLAS MACARTHUR	48

    HE WANTED TO WIN ... HIS GOVERNMENT DID NOT 48

WHY GENERAL PATTON WAS MURDERED	60
BEHIND THE FALKLAND ISLANDS STORY	66
THE $5 TRILLION COLD WAR HOAX	75

    Introduction 75
    "Scare the hell out of the country" 75
    Churchill launches cold war 76
    The conversion of senator Arthur Vandenberg 78
    The floozies of Washington 79
    Harriman's reply 80
    The first victims of the Cold War 81
    The eggheads 82
    A phony war 83
    A meteoric career 83
    Remarkable heritage 84
    The policy of "containment" 85
    The men behind containment 86
    Techniques of the cold war 87
    The cia rides to the rescue 87
    Effects of the Cold War 88

THERE'S A GULAG IN YOUR FUTURE	90
THE HOLOCAUST EXPLAINED	99
GENOCIDE IN AMERICA	111
PHONEY WARS FOR PHONEY PEACE AND THE MINISTRY OF FEAR	114
THE ADL-FBI CONSPIRACY EXPOSED	118

BOYCOTT: THE JEWISH WEAPON 149
SIGMUND FREUD – ANTICHRIST DEVIL 160

> *BIBLIOGRAPHY:* *181*
> *Psychiatrists' testimony said worthless in court* *182*

WHO OWNS THE TV NETWORKS 184
THE REUTERS CONNECTION(S) 194
THE GENTLE ART OF THOUGHT CONTROL............. 198
MONEY AND FREEDOM A BOOK BY HANS SENNHOLZ
REVIEWED BY EUSTACE MULLINS............................... 203
AMERICA'S NEW ROBBER BARONS............................. 208
WARNING — THE DEPARTMENT OF JUSTICE IS
DANGEROUS TO AMERICANS... 220
HOW TO BE A UNITED STATES SENATOR 231

> THE HIDING PLACE 231

THE DAY VIRGINIA DIED 241
ELEGY FOR A STATE 249
THE SCANDAL UNVEILED 258
THE SECRET HISTORY OF THE ATOMIC BOMB - WHY
HIROSHIMA WAS DESTROYED 265

> THE UNTOLD STORY 265
>
> > *A new mission* *265*
> > *Criminals on display* *266*
> > *Atomic terrorism* *267*
> > *A United Nations project* *269*
> > *The jewish hell-bomb* *271*
> > *The buck passes to truman* *272*
> > *Lipman siew* *273*
> > *Will Japan surrender before the bomb is dropped?* *273*
> > *The horror of Hiroshima* *274*

- *Mass murder* 275
- *A pilot's story* 278
- *Did the atomic bomb win the war against Japan?* 281
- *The Nagasaki bomb* 281
- *American military authorities say atomic bomb unnecessary* 282
- *Another Eisenhower speaks* 284
- *Macarthur's warning* 286
- *The new atomic age* 286
- *The rebirth of Israel* 287
- *The legal aspects of nuclear warfare* 289
- *Gandhi speaks* 290
- *Cast of Characters:* 290
- *BIBLIOGRAPHY:* 291
- *The Court of International Justice* 292

WASHINGTON DC CITY OF FEAR 299
THE LINDBERGH MURDERS HAUPTMANN WAS INNOCENT THE PROSECUTION AND DEFENSE COMBINED TO FRAME HIM 310
THE FOUR HORSEMEN OF THE APOCALYPSE 329

PROPAGANDISTS FOR ISRAEL, HARGIS, GRAHAM, FALWELL AND ROBERTSON, POSE AS CHRISTIANS 329

OTHER BOOKS BY EUSTACE MULLINS 339

ABOUT THE AUTHOR

Eustace Mullins is a veteran of the United States Air Force, with thirty-eight months of active service during World War II. A native Virginian, he was educated at Washington and Lee University, New York University, Ohio University, the University of North Dakota, the Escuelas des Bellas Artes, San Miguel de Allende, Mexico, and the Institute of Contemporary Arts, Washington, D.C.

The original book, published under the title *Mullins On The Federal Reserve,* was commissioned by the poet Ezra Pound in 1948. Ezra Pound was a political prisoner for thirteen and a half years at St. Elizabeth's Hospital, Washington, D.C. (a Federal institution for the insane). His release was accomplished largely through the efforts of Mr. Mullins.

The research at the Library of Congress was directed and reviewed daily by George Stimpson, founder of the National Press

Club in Washington, whom *The New York Times* on September 28, 1952 called, "A highly regarded reference source in the capitol. Government officials, Congressmen, and reporters went to him for information on any subject."

Published in 1952 by Kasper and Horton, New York, the original book was the first nationally-circulated revelation of the secret meetings of the international bankers at Jekyll Island, Georgia, 1907-1910, at which place the draft of the Federal Reserve Act of 1913 was written.

During the intervening years, the author continued to gather new and more startling information about the backgrounds of the people who direct the Federal Reserve policies. New information gathered over the years from hundreds of newspapers, periodicals, and books give corroborating insight into the connections of the international banking houses.[1]

While researching this material, Eustace Mullins was on the staff of the Library of Congress. Mullins later was a consultant on highway finance for the American Petroleum Institute, consultant on hotel development for Institutions Magazine, and editorial director for the Chicago Motor Club's four publications.

---

[1] The London Acceptance Council is limited to seventeen international banking houses authorized by the Bank of England to handle foreign exchange.

MY STRUGGLE

My life will be judged worthwhile to the extent that it is of use to others. For this reason, I wish to tell of the things which have happened to me in my struggle against the forces of darkness. It is my hope that others will be forewarned of what to expect in this fight.

During the past thirty years of this struggle, many of the great patriots who gave me, instinctively, their valuable guidance and inspiration, were themselves heavily immobilized by the machinations of international Jewry. They considered their personal losses relatively unimportant, however, compared to the sufferings of the Gentile people who have been enslaved by the Jews.

In the same way, it might seem idle carping for me to mention the murder of my parents by government agents working for the Jews, who wanted revenge against me for my work; *not when we consider that sixty-six million Christians have been killed in Russian concentration camps since 1917*, all of them murdered by the Jewish Communists who built and operated these camps.

These millions lie nameless and unmourned. But they were no less the victims of the Jews than my parents were — or many other Americans whose sacrifices have gone unrecorded by those who are next on the death list.

No one who has been martyred by the Jews should remain unknown. And no one who has been martyred by the Jews will remain unavenged.

I became the object of the Jews hatred by events which moved in a straight line. Successively, I became the protégé of George

Stimpson, the most respected journalist in Washington, who founded the National Press; and of Ezra Pound, the world-famous poet; and of H. L. Hunt, one of the world's richest men.

Of the three, only Ezra Pound fought the Jews openly. And he suffered grievously as a consequence, spending thirteen years in a hideous, urine-soaked madhouse in Washington D.C.

George Stimpson passed on to me many of the secrets of Washington, including the fact that Felix Frankfurter founded the Harold Ware Cell of Communists and the nature of the Jewish control over J. Edgar Hoover and the FBI. H.L. Hunt fought valiantly to preserve the values of Christian civilization. But he was unable to deploy his money effectively in a battle which was outside of his experience.

I was to visit Ezra Pound several times in the cell in which he was held as a political prisoner and which he aptly termed "the hellhole."

"Ezra Pound fought the Jews openly. And he suffered grievously as a consequence, spending thirteen years in a hideous, urine-soaked madhouse..."

In 1942, when I joined the United States Army Air Force, I had no thought that thirty-six years later, I would still be engaged in a life-or-death struggle with a tenacious and relentless enemy.

I regarded World War II as an unavoidable hiatus in my chosen career as an artist and writer. The war would be over in a couple of years, and I would resume the writing of books which I had already begun. I had no personal desire to 'slap the Jap,' or 'stun the Hun,' or any of the 'Tin Pan Alley' slogans which the Jews had conjured up to herd the Gentile cattle to the slaughter.

Like many of my fellow soldiers, I sensed that the enemy was not really overseas, but was more likely entrenched here on the home front. But also like my fellow soldiers, I knew there was little I could do about it. Almost a year later, I read some material which gave me enlightenment.

Although it seems unbelievable now, during the height of World War II, there was more widespread dissemination of patriotic material on the Jewish conspiracy than there is today. Many dedicated patriots turned out small papers which printed the hard facts. They had long since learned how to survive the daily harassment by FBI agents, ADL agents, and hordes of other 'home front' guardians. They were frequently denounced by the paid press.

After reading one of these hysterical attacks, I sent Gerald L. K. Smith twenty-five dollars for some material. This was a large sum at that time, as my pay was only fifty dollars a month. By return mail, I received a large box containing several hundred copies of 'The Cross and the Flag.'

Theis was the first material I had ever encountered on the Jewish problem. It contained many astounding revelations.

I realized at once that this was not the type of material to be quoted in the usual barracks discussions. Several soldiers had commented that there were informers in the barracks. Although I did not then make the connection, there was to be found in almost every barracks, a particularly obnoxious Jew, usually with a Brooklyn accent. It never occurred to me that these Jews were being as obnoxious as possible in order to goad the other soldiers into making an anti-Semitic remark. Nor did it occur to me that these Brooklyn Jews often had college degrees.

At that time, everyone with college background was ordered to try out for the Officer Candidate School. I did not realize that these Brooklyn Jews remained with the enlisted men for surreptitious reasons. This type of political supervision of the troops is axiomatic in Communist strategy. It was meticulously observed in the American Armed Forces during World War II. In combat zones, officers and enlisted men who had previously voiced doubts about the wisdom of Roosevelt's crusade to save Communism, were shot in the back by these same intelligence agents who had followed them into the front lines.

While General Eisenhower was cosily tucked away with his British Secret Service 'Chauffeur', Kay Summersby, the real decisions were made by his Liaison Officer, Captain Warburg of the Kuhn, Loeb Banking house — a Jewish concern.

The Communist control over the United States Army surfaced during World War II with the selection of General George C. Marshall as Chief of Staff. As Senator Joseph McCarthy later pointed out, Marshall was under Communist Party discipline at all times. This did not interfere with his direction of our war effort, since the goals of the Washington Marxists were the same, the total defeat of the German anti-Communist forces. In the Korean and Vietnam wars, Communists direction of our Armed Forces remained unchanged, even though we were then fighting against

'Communist' forces. When General Douglas McArthur tried to oppose this Communist betrayal of our men, he was fired by David Niles, the Jewish Communist who was President Truman's 'Aide.'

The Communist recognized that final political control always resided in the military. In Moscow and in Washington, every officer is absolutely responsive to the current ideological line, regardless of any military consideration. This was recently demonstrated when every officer on active duty was ordered to support the giveaway of the Panama Canal, while many retired officers openly opposed it. The most stringent measures are carried out to ensure that no officer is able to form a group to discuss and possibly take action against the high treason of his superiors. When Commander George Lincoln Rockwell surfaced at the Pentagon, there was consternation throughout the high command. At the least sign of any independence or patriotic speech from any officer, the Jewish controlled media immediately raises a hue and cry about 'Fascism' and the offender is quickly neutralized.

After receiving the supply of Smith's magazine, I distributed them in the day rooms to see who would read them. The next day, I toured the day rooms to see if anyone was reading them, and perhaps, to strike up a conversation. Every issue had disappeared. Not once did I see a copy while I remained on the base.

Apparently, I had been followed, and the papers picked up as fast as I had left them.

During my remaining years of military service, I encountered no one with strong political views. My own opinions were those of any young man of the period, hardly committed to any strong ideology. After the war, I enrolled at Washington and Lee University, intending to study law. After two years, I decided I should go to art school, and enrolled at the Institute of Contemporary Arts in Washington, D.C. The school had the usual mongrel types in its student body and a number of ardent Communists on the staff. But it attracted many of the leading writers as speakers. Like others among the ten million veterans, my main concern was in getting on with my career, and I had little concern with politics.

Over night my lack of concern changed.

One of the teachers at the Institute had been visiting Ezra Pound. He suggested I accompany him one afternoon, an offer which rather disturbed me. I thought it unlikely that the man who had edited T. S. Eliot and Ernest Hemingway would be interested in talking to me. But I went along.

The moment I entered the gloom of the insane ward, my former complaisance vanished, never to return.

I suddenly realized that a great writer had been punished by being confined in a madhouse, solely for his political views. In an instant, Pound filled the ideological gap in my life. Never again would I remain silent in the face of injustice.

EZRA POUND.

The famous American poet had been convicted of treason for revealing in radio broadcasts that World War Two had been started by International Jewry to further its own ends of world domination. He was kept thirteen years in a lunatic asylum in a urine-soaked cell, originally in solitary confinement and forced to wear a straitjacket. Only much later was he allowed to receive visitors such as Mullins.

Pound apparently considered me a kindred spirit, and offered to give me 'my own day.' That is, an afternoon to visit him alone each week. I accepted. And by the time the next week rolled around, he was waiting for me with food, assignments for research, and errands to run.

Shortly afterwards, he brought up the Federal Reserve System, which I had never heard of. From that day, my work was cut out for me. His concern for his country had been aptly expressed by Charles Dickens in his American Notes, written a century earlier: "I do fear that the heaviest blow ever dealt at liberty, will be dealt by this country, in the failure of its example to the earth."

The loss of liberty in America, which is occurring before our eyes, means the autocracy will be enthroned throughout the world, and that the freedom which was ours at our birth will never be known by future generations. Olga Ivinskaya, a Russian writer, writes of her years in a Soviet prison camp:

"Sanagian (a fellow inmate) had put down the story of her life in her awkward, uneven handwriting. She came from a working-class family and her father—long since dead—had taken part in the Revolution in 1917, for this she heaped curses on his memory."

In the usual hogwash about aristocrats, we never stop to think that it was the working people of Russia, not aristocrats, who were enslaved by the Communist Revolution. Similarly, in this country, it is the Jewish intellectuals, bankers, and industrialists who are in the forefront of the battle to enslave all Americans and take away their freedom forever. Should we allow this, future generations in the concentration camps will begin their days not with prayers, but with curses on our memory.

I soon began to visit Ezra Pound every day, a routine which I kept up for three years. During this time, I was thoroughly grounded in every aspect of the International Communist conspiracy. Pound said to me: "I am telling you things I didn't know until I was fifty. You are twenty-five, which means you are getting an extra twenty-five years to do something about it."

When I went to New York, bankers on Wall Street told me:– "I was here during the crash, but I didn't know what was going on until I read your book." I explained that I had had the benefit of Pound's experience, and his access to much information in Europe which had already been banned in the United States.

To support myself while writing the history of the Federal Reserve System, I obtained a job at the Library of Congress as a stack attendant. This was the same job J. Edgar Hoover had held for several years while he completed his law studies at George Washington University night school.

A few weeks later, because I had done advanced photographic studies at the Institute, I was promoted to the Photography Department. In the next several months, I received two more promotions, as I had studied with one of the finest Japanese photographers. During these months, I was able to see Pound only on weekends, and he suggested I send some of my writings to 'The Social Crediter,' a small weekly published in England. I sent them some articles, which they printed, sending me enthusiastic comments.

One day, while going into the National Press Club for my daily luncheon with George Stimpson, a man was handing out copies of 'Common Sense' at the front door. I showed it to Pound, an issue containing the Hermann Goering Testament. He suggested I send them articles, and they printed some excerpts from the Federal Reserve research.

One afternoon, a Jew came to the Library of Congress, asking for me. I was called out of the darkroom to see a Jew who was a caricature out of *Der Stürmer*. He immediately began to cross question me, saying he had been sent from 'Common Sense,' and he asked, 'Who is giving you your material? Where is this information coming from?'

Not wishing to involve Pound, who always faced the possibility of having his daily visitors turned away and being held incommunicado, I explained that I was doing research at the Library of Congress. It was obvious that he didn't believe me. A gawky small town boy could hardly be privy to the machinations of the worlds most powerful and secretive bankers!

A team of FBI agents was now sent to the Library of Congress to question everyone who had worked with me.

Senator Herbert Lehman, of the Lehman Brothers Banking house, and National Chairman of the Anti-Defamation League, had sent a demand to Luther Evans, Librarian of Congress, that I be fired because of an article I had written for the Social Creditor.

The demand, written on ADL stationery, had been drawn up by the ADL operator, Edelstein, and signed by Lehman without reading it, as he accepted anything which Edelstein brought to him. The article exposed the fact that one Katz, Marshall Plan Administrator, presided over the most of the Marshall Plan material to Communist countries, instead of sending it to the non-Communist countries for which Congress had designated it.

LD: In other words, because of Jewish machinations, money intended by Congress to help non-Communist countries, was secretly diverted to Communist countries where the sole beneficiaries were international Jewry. This was of course fraud and peculation on an unimaginable scale — comparable to the mysterious disappearance of $3 trillion when Rabbi Dov Zakheim was in charge of financial affairs at the Pentagon in 2001.

However, neither of them dared to publicly argue the point, as it would have exposed the fact that Marshall Plan Aid was going to the Communists.

Although I as yet knew nothing of the ADL order that I be fired, I had had a previous contact with Senator Lehman. Pound had noticed an advertisement in the Washington Post that Lehman would be speaking at Howard University on behalf of 'home rule,' a plan to wrest control of the District of Columbia from a group of White businessmen and turn it over to the Negroes. Howard University was the Communist training school for Ralph Bunche and many other Negro Marxists. Through the dogged influence of Eleanor Roosevelt, it was the only college in the United States whose entire budget was provided by the Federal Government.

Pound mentioned that Lehman, a typical Jewish degenerate, had a nervous tic, and suggested it would be amusing to see it in action.

When Dave Horton and I arrived at the Howard University auditorium, we found a group of Negroes, eight or ten, the entire audience for the August Senator. Rather put out by the poor attendance, Lehman, a short squat ole clothes dealer type, made a short speech about home rule and opened the floor to questions.

Immediately, Horton and I were on our feet.

"Would Lehman Brothers consider the District of Columbia a safe investment?"—asked Horton. "Will you support Alger Hiss as the first mayor of Washington?"—I asked. Lehman, a rather stupid Jew, was completely bewildered by our questions.

We continued to fire questions at him, as his aides, two young city College Jews, shook their fists at us.

The famed Lehman tic now made its appearance. It was not merely a tic of the eye, the entire left side of his face was twitching steadily and violently.

The audience of Negroes was glaring at us, muttering, 'Shame,' as Lehman's aides rushed him away.

I LATER LEARNED THAT IN THE FOYER OF THE LEHMAN MANSION IN NEW YORK, A SPLENDID FOURTEENTH CENTURY STATUE OF THE VIRGIN MARY, LOOTED FROM ONE OF THE GREAT CATHEDRALS OF EUROPE, STOOD NEAR THE DOOR. FOR THE TITILLATION OF VISITORS, A CIGARETTE WAS PLACED DANGLING FROM HER MOUTH. (Emphasis in original

A JEW S IDEA OF THE HOLY VIRGIN MARY

A few days after our Howard University evening, I was handed a letter of dismissal from the Library of Congress. The FBI interrogations had turned up nothing which could be used against me, and had caused considerable angry comment among the other employees. The letter stated I was being dismissed because I had written an article for the Social Creditor. I was given the option of making a personal appeal to the Librarian, which I did. In Evans office, he asked me, 'Did you write this article?'

'Yes,' I replied. 'Can you show me one false statement in it?'

'I'm not competent to do that.' said Evans. 'This is not out of my hands. Your dismissal stands.'

'But I am not a member of any political group.' I protested. 'I've never voted in my life. You have many staff members who are activist members of militant racial organizations. You have two staff members who do nothing but go through the stacks writing numbers bets all day. Why am I being singled out?'

Evans, who never once looked at me in the eye, jerked open the bottom drawer of his desk, where I glimpsed a half empty bottle of Country Gentleman bourbon. He looked longingly at it, turned to me, and said, 'Well, that's all.'

The Library of Congress where Eustace Mullins was employed briefly as a shelf stacker

<u>MY NEXT JOB</u>: At the Chicago Motor Club, I became editor of Motor News, with a circulation of 250,000. During the next two years, I willingly took on additional duties as editor of the 'Industrial Editors News Service,' public relations counselor, and

special events organizer. I had been at the club two years and one week with a drawer full of memoranda from my superior, James E. Bulger, praising my work, and thanking me for my new programs, when one sultry August afternoon, two well dressed men strode by Bulger's secretary, and went into his office and closed the door.

His secretary who was a close friend, turned to me and said, 'I wonder what that's all about?

'I never saw them before.' I replied.

The men stayed with Bulger for about an hour, and I could hear them arguing with him, but their voices were kept low. Finally, he buzzed for his secretary. She went in, and came back out immediately, and handed me a folded note. I opened it and read, 'You are allowed five minutes to get your things and get out of the office.'

'What's going on?' the secretary asked me.

I saw the tears were streaming down her face. I showed her the note.

'I know what's in it,' she said, 'but what's going on? Mr. Bulger is sick, we've got to help him—those men—'. She turned and ran to the restroom.

I put some personal memoranda into an envelope and left the office.

That evening, Bulger's secretary called me at home. She told me that the two men were FBI agents and that when they demanded I be fired, Bulger flatly refused. This was understakable as I was doing the work of four people. They then threatened him for nearly an hour. He had had five heart attacks in the past several years, and he began to writhe with pain. He begged them to let him call his doctor.

'Certainly,' one of the men replied, 'as soon as you fire Mullins.'

Bulger was then forced to write the note.

After I left the office, the FBI agents accompanied Bulger to the doctor, and then took him to his home, after warning him not to tell me what had happened or to give me my job back.

Being fired from the Chicago Motor Club was the greatest shock of my life. Certainly this was the goal of the FBI harassment. At the age of thirty-five, I had been one of the most active public relations counselors in Chicago, lunching at the best restaurants with the city's leading executives. Now I was on the street with no prospects.

Even so, I supposed that with my contacts, I would be able to get another public relations job. In the next few weeks, I was surprised that after each interview, I heard nothing more about a job. Friends at the Motor Club then told me that because of pressure from the Club's Jewish members, Bulger was telling everyone who inquired about references that I was a notorious criminal who was wanted in several states. He never put this into writing, giving out the slander on the phone, after instructions from the Jew who was the Club's legal counsel. Since I was fired from the Chicago Motor Club in August, 1958, I have never again been able to get a professional job.

After several weeks, I realized it as unlikely that I would get any work in Chicago. I began work on a book about Friedrich Nietzsche, and while doing research at the Newberry Library, I found a great deal of material on Ezra Pound's career. I wrote him suggesting that I do his biography. He immediately replied that he had been waiting for me to do this, and that I was to be his only authorized biographer.

I then asked Henry Regnery if he could give me an advance on this book. He replied that he could not — though he owned the largest window shade factory in the world, a bank, and other holdings, worth eighty million dollars.

He suggested, however, that H. L. Hunt needed someone to edit a book. I called Hunt and he agreed to pay me a hundred dollars a week. I said that I couldn't live on that. In fact, I was living on thirty-five dollars a week. Hunt now offered to let me live in his home. At that time, Hunt's income was ten million dollars a week, and he had accumulated a fortune of three billion dollars.

H.L. HUNT,
GAMBLER AND OIL TYCOON.

IN 1957 HE WAS THE EIGHTH RICHEST MAN IN AMERICA.

I arrived at Hunt's home in Dallas with one battered suitcase and an old Plymouth, purchased a year before for one hundred dollars, with the entire front end smashed in.

Hunt and I immediately established complete rapport, as he had lived for years out of a suitcase, traveling in the back-country picking up the oil leases which were the basis of his fortune. I resided in his best guest room, one which had always been occupied previously by Senator Joseph McCarthy when he came to Dallas. Hunt and I settled down to work on the book 'Alpaca.'

After several months of intensive work, the book was completed and I became restless. By this time, Hunt had installed me in an office next to his own, and whenever someone called him, he would say, 'Why don't you check with Mullins on that?' I realized he was only using me for a buffer, but it was a flattering situation for a penniless writer to be referred to as the confidential assistant of the world's richest man. However, I remained a penniless writer, and he remained the world's richest man.

I began to realize I should be getting back to work on the Pound biography, and one afternoon, I told him I had to return to Chicago. He was completely surprised, and I saw that he was hurt and disappointed by my decision. Nevertheless, I have always thought of him with affection and admiration, and he seemed well disposed toward me on later occasions when I talked to him in Dallas and in New York.

Although I knew nothing of it at the time, my association with H. L. Hunt had driven the Jews into a furious campaign of 'harassment' against my parents. The conspirators were terrified that Hunt might finance my publications or a political organization, although at the time I had no organization to which he might donate money.

I knew that my father had had a serious coronary attack in 1956, but I was not told until years later that the attack had been brought on by a series of vicious interrogations by Army Counter Intelligence Corps agents. My mother later told me they were determined to make my father reveal the names of persons financially supporting my travels and writings. Since no one had ever given me a cent, there was nothing he could tell them, but they refused to believe him.

Knowing he had Wednesday afternoons off from the store in which he worked, two agents waited for him in his car. They forced him into the car, drove him to the top of a nearby mountain, and interrogated him for several hours, telling him they were going to throw him off the mountain. At one point, he tried to escape from the car. They knocked him unconscious, drove him back to the store, and left him in the parked car. He finally came to, and drove home. The next day, he had a severe coronary attack, from which he never completely recovered.

My parents did not dare tell me these details, out of a desire to protect me, as they knew I would kill someone for these atrocities. Nevertheless, I knew they had been interrogated and I wrote to the Secretary of Defense. I received an answer, admitting that my father had been interrogated, and giving the names of the two men who had interrogated him. Some weeks later, I tried to contact these men in Washington. I was told they had been sent on a mission to Guam, and that the plane had crashed with all aboard being killed. The letter with the men's names has since disappeared from my files.

While I was with H. L. Hunt in Dallas, the FBI began to visit my parents. Their telephone was tapped, and they received harassing telephone calls during the night. The harassment and brutality of this campaign was intended solely to provoke me into some drastic action. I come from mountain people, and we never forget an injury, even if it takes fifty years to wreak our revenge. My temper remained under control only because my parents refused to let me know what was happening to them, and the ADL-FBI provocation failed.

Their campaign was intensified, however, and one evening in 1961, my father, whose heart conditions had steadily gotten worse during this harassment, received a telephone call from a known FBI provocateur, 'We've just sent out a national alert to pick your son up.'

My father dropped the phone. "They've finally got him' he said to my mother, as he collapsed.

He was taken to the hospital where he died of massive heart failure.

More than three years went by before my mother told me what had happened.

Of course, there had never been an alert, as I have never been arrested by anyone.

In *'My Life in Christ,'*[2] I openly accused Lyndon Johnson, who was then President of America, of murdering my father, although he had only been acting for Herbert Lehman, the Jew who had been supporting his bid for the Presidency.

---

[2] Published by Omnia Veritas Ltd, www.omnia-veritas.com

The only outcome of all this was that during Johnson's Presidency, every copy of my book that I mailed out was destroyed by the Post Office — until I began insuring each copy.

As I knew nothing of what my parents had been subjected to, I could not understand why my mother remained in a state of collapse after my father's funeral. As there was no one else to stay with her and my handicapped sister, I remained at home instead of returning to New York. I had no idea that seventeen years later, I would still be there.

In 1964, my mother told me what had happened before my father's death. Because the harassment had begun with the Army, I again wrote to the Secretary of Defense. The reply from Joseph A. Califano briefly stated that an investigation revealed "your father was interviewed briefly on December 3, 1957, but was not mistreated in any way." It was Mr. Califano's job to cover up for the Secretary of the Army. As a reward for this (and heaven knows what else) he kept advancing politically and now has become head of HEW.

We continued to receive harassing telephone calls. On Sunday mornings, after I took my mother and sister to church, I would return home to find the back door unlocked and standing open. My papers regularly disappeared from my desk, but I could never catch anyone in the house. Obviously the place was being observed by agents with walkies-talkies, who would notify the agents in the house whenever I came into view. (This is called "advanced paranoia" in the best Jewish circles).

On the night of June 1, 1969, I was awakened at about 1:15 a.m. by the ringing of the front door bell. I went downstairs, and opened the door, but no one was there. The bell continued to ring, and I supposed that someone had put in a pin to annoy us. However the bell had not been tampered with. I went into the kitchen and smelled smoke. When I opened the basement door, a storm of fire and smoke lashed out at me. I slammed the door, and ran to the telephone. It was dead. I got my mother and sister out of the house, and aroused a neighbor, who called the firemen. In a few minutes, they had chopped their way into the basement and put out the fire. One of the firemen said to me, "you had the Lord with you tonight. If the bell hadn't rung, you'd have died in your beds. I've seen too many of these old houses. The people don't have a chance to get out once it gets started."

We had been saved by Divine intervention. We supposed that the fire had been caused by an electrical malfunction, as the wires in the basement had burned. The next morning, when I cleared out the debris, I found an antique school master's desk, which had been given to my mother years ago. Strangely enough, it had only one drawer burned out. The rest of it was charred but intact. I wondered how it could have been so charred without actually burning, but, still in a state of shock from the night's events, I had it hauled away with the rest of our ruined belongings. That afternoon, the electrician came to rewire the basement. "What caused this fire?" he asked.

"It looks as though the wiring was bad" I replied.

"There is nothing wrong with this wiring", he said. "The wires have been burned in the fire, but I can tell you, this fire did not start in any wiring. You had better find out what happened."

I remembered the charred desk drawer. Some type of incendiary must have been placed in it, set to go off late at night. By this time, all the evidence had gone to the dump. There was nothing I could do. Had it not been for the Miracle of the bell, we would have been burned to death in our beds. Now, I had nothing to prove what had happened.

After this night in 1969, my mother never slept at night again. I was working in the next county, fifty miles away, and I left home early, often getting back at eight or nine in the evening. During this time, my mother was attacked and beaten on three occasions. The police refused to investigate, claiming that they believed she had only fallen down. Our windows were smashed, my car was vandalized, and the house was burglarized. Not once did the police make any effort to investigate. One of them confided to me that they had orders "to stay away from there". We were vulnerable because I had never been able to obtain any employment in the Staunton area. In 1961, the local newspaper had printed a column by Israel Sokol, a Zionist propagandist writing under the name of George Sokolsky. A virulent diatribe against me, the column called me "subversive". Despite his fanatical Zionist propaganda, Sokol was considered a "conservative" writer. He even founded a group which he imaginatively called "American Council of Jews Against Communism". The sole function of this group, apart from fundraising from gullible Jews, was to hold an elaborate annual dinner party in honor of George Sokolsky.

I hired a Staunton lawyer, to file suit for libel against the local newspaper. Almost a year went by, but each time I contacted him, he still had not filed the suit. On the day before a year had elapsed, when my suit would no longer be allowed, I fired him by telegram, and filed the suit as attorney pro se. This lawyer has since been disbarred. The Staunton courts now began a game of tag with me. Whenever they knew I was out of town, the suit would suddenly be tiled for that day, I would rush back. Finally, I filed a motion for summary judgement, which the court has ignored to this day.

One afternoon, I arrived home to find my mother lying on the front room floor. She could not remember what had happened, but her face was badly bruised. The next day, she died from a heart attack. I now faced the problem caring for my sister, who had been crippled by a drunken driver when she was four years old. The home had been left to her as long as someone would look after her. I supposed this would be no problem, but in the next few months, I found no one who was willing to keep house for her. Just a year after my mother's death, on a Saturday afternoon in June, 1972, a neighbor knocked on our back door, screaming, "Dorothy has been hit by a truck." I rushed out to find two policemen holding a man. My sister had already been taken to the hospital. The policemen, instead of coming to our door, had called my brother, who lived two miles away. They claimed they thought my sister lived alone.

I drove to the hospital, and found my sister in the emergency room. Her face was turning blue, "Doctor", I said "can't you do something? She's going into shock."

"Oh, I don't think there's anything wrong", he said. "She probably just fell down, I see a few bruises."

I stared at him. He was a young Jewish intern, who had come over from the University of Virginia that day. He has never been seen in the local hospital again. My sister was X-rayed and found to have two crushed vertebrae in her back. A neighbor said that Dorothy had walked to the grocery store two blocks away. She had an ice cream cone and was walking back, going through the yard of the house behind us, when the truck drove up into the yard and knocked her down from behind. I later learned tha the man whom the police held and charged with "drunk driving" was not drunk and was not driving the truck. He had agreed to take the blame for someone else. I realized that because the home belonged to Dorothy, an attempt had been made to murder her in order to close down my base of operations. After this "accident", she gradually developed arthritis throughout her body. She became completely helpless and depressed, requiring my constant attention. As a result, it became almost impossible for me to continue my writing. Many people wrote to me saying that my articles no longer had the "polish" of the Mullins they were accustomed to. No one was more aware of this than I, but the craft of writing demands the steady, methodical building of the sentence, the paragraph, and the completed structure of the prose. Being deprived of the time required to do this, I could only put the material together as well as possible under the circumstances. I have not written a book for ten years.

Like Pound, Viereck and many other patriots, I had now been immobilized by the Jews. Despite these drawbacks, I will continue to do as much as possible; always aware of how much others have helped me in this work in bringing to the attention of fellow patriots the sinister influences behind the Federal Reserve System, the Council on Foreign Relations, and other agencies of the Jews. I now begin to understand what I have learned in thirty-six years of struggle. The first precept is **The Jew is always in a state of war with all civilized nations.** There can be no peace between the biological parasite an the host people. The moment the Jew relaxes his control, the host tries to throw him off. The second precept is **All Jews are agents of the State of Israel.** A Jew holding any position any government holds that position solely as an agent of the State of Israel. Even if he wished to do so, no Jew could escape the total mobilization of the Jewish people in their war against the gentiles. Had I know these things thirty years ago, I would have been greatly strenghthened in my struggle by the knowledge of the enemy.

This brings us to the third precept… **The Jew always knows who he is.** Most frequently, his opponent does not understand who he is or what is going on in the war between the biological parasite and the host people. Finally, **whatever ambitions you may have, you cannot realize these goals because of the presence of the Jew.** It is the function of the Jew to systematically destroy the habitat and the lifestyle of the host people, to render them unable to resist his parasitic presence. In the beginning of their relationship, it is the Jew who is the displaced person, seeking a place for himself, while the host is secure in his home. To establish his biological presence among the host people, the Jew gradually replaces their life style with a totally synthetic environment, tailored to his needs. This maneuvers the host people into a position at the mercy of the Jew. This is where we are today. Where will we be tomorrow?

I believe in the Benevolent presence of Our Lord and Saviour Jesus Christ. I believe that our sufferings are for a purpose. I believe that the American Republic will be restore to its people. I believe that these criminals will pay the final price in retribution for all their crimes, not merely the murder of my parents and the attempted murder of my sister, but an absolute penalty for the sixty-six million gentile victims in Russia, and the massacre of the innocents which has taken place in other "civilized" countries under the auspices of the Jew. Every martyr will be with us in Paradise, but we will not be allowed into that rest until we have extracted the last retribution for every crime committed by the Jews.

THE WAR AGAINST CHRISTIANITY

The most devastating blows against the Christian religion are now being struck from within by Jewish moles, who have infiltrated Christian groups, often at the highest levels, for the sole purpose of continuing their destructive work. They intend nothing less than the ultimate annihilation of the Christian faith and the eternal enslavement of their victims, whom they always refer to with the utmost contempt as "goyim", or cattle.

When a "converted Jew" was recently named Archbishop of Paris, thus delivering one of Christendom's oldest and most faithful communities into the hands of the Jews, few of the victims had any concept of what a "converted Jew" was. They also had no understanding of the concept of the biological Jew, a scientific theory formulated from centuries of biological evidence that the Jew is a parasite whose entire life cycle is entirely dependent upon feeding upon a suitable host. The Jew can maintain his parasitic cycle and perpetuate himself only if he remains aware that he is different from the host and that he must always observe his differences. Consequently, the Jew continually fans the flames of hatred among his king against the host people in whatever country he has infested himself. The war against the host peoples is often concentrated in a relentless onslaught against the Christian religion, because Our Lord and Saviour Jesus Christ warned civilized people against the dangers of the Jewish presence.

In its extreme phases, the war conducted by the Jews against the Christians and any other non-Jewish peoples results in the most horrible massacres and atrocities of history, epitomized by the present relentless daily slaughter of women and children in Beirut, while the rest of the world watches in horror, but because of the all-pervasive power of the Jews, can do nothing to stop these horrors.

During intervals of "peace", the Jew continues towage his war of attrition against the host peoples on all fronts, using every wile which he has developed over centuries of his continuous war against civilization. Jewish humor consists wholly of vile and salacious attacks against the goyim, veiled in "jokes" about their bestiality and their stupidity. Jewish leaders constantly herd the captive leaders of the goyim, known as the shabez goi, the traditional gentile moron who is hired to light the candle in the synagogue, into public organizations where they denounce their own people and swear eternal fealty to the Jews. Two of the most disgraceful shabez goi leaders in the war against Christianity are President Ronald Reagan and the Reverend Jerry Falwell, both of whom daily pledge eternal allegiance to the State of Israel, and who arm and finance the Jews in their war against civilization.

The attack on Christianity is carried on all levels. Canadian Jewish News Jan. 7, 1982, stated, "Germans today have a personal responsibility to support Jews and Israel and denounce racism throughout the world, Rabbi Erwin Schild of Adath Israel Synagogue said here recently at a lecture sponsored by the Christian-Jewish Dialogue of Toronto, B'Nai B'rith League for Human Rights and the synagogue." It is noteworthy that no "Christian" was allowed to speak at the "Christian-Jewish Dialogue", and that only Jewish purposes were discussed. Schild also said, "After Auschwitz, you can't deny the evil of humanity and even Christian nature."

Schild reveals one of the basic tenets of the Jewish parasite, which is that anyone who opposes the depredations of the parasite is "evil", and must be punished as cruelly as possible. To this end, the Jew constantly fabricates myths of "persecution" and "extermination", while at the same time carrying out the most brutal massacres of Christian victims, who in past centuries have numbered into the hundreds of millions, most of them women and children who were butchered on the pretext that they were "evil".

To emphasize that this campaign against the Christians is waged constantly and relentlessly, on a worldwide basis, we cite the Newark Sunday Star Ledger, March 21, 1982, which quotes Newark Archbishop Peter L. Gerety as having issued a 24-page major pastoral letter directing Catholics to "root out anti-Semitism" in their lives, and "to engage in dialogue and collaboration with Jews based on their common Biblical heritage." Note the emphasis on the verb "root out", or to purge themselves by the most violent methods of their "hatred". For centuries, Catholic leaders warned their flocks against the Jews and ordered that no Jew should ever pollute a Christian place of worship by his presence, but now these leaders have abandoned their religious traditions and have wholly embraced the disgraceful practices of the lowest forms of shabez goi existence. The Archbishop does not merely suggest, he "directs" that Catholics must "collaborate" with the Jews. The traditional definition of a collaborator is one who cooperates with an enemy occupying force. Those Catholics who collaborate with the Jews are acknowledging that the Jewish enemy has now won major battles in his war against civilization, that he now occupies the land, and that those who wish to survive must collaborate with him or be exterminated.

This same issue of the Star Ledger quotes Bishop Joseph A. Francis, "one of only five black Catholic bishops in the United States" as "having challenged Catholics throughout the Diocese of Newark to exorcise racism". Neither he nor Archbishop Gerety demand that the Jews abandon their fanatical racism and hatred of all civilized peoples. They are simply instructing the intended victims that they should not resist their attackers. Can this be "religious doctrine" or the faith engendered by the true Church?

In the onslaught against the host peoples, the Jews indulge in the most arrogant and obscene attacks against Christian leaders. The Miami Herald, Feb. 26, 1982, Prime Minister Begin of Israel, was quoted as having demanded that West German Chancellor

Helmut Schmidt "Go down on his knees and ask the forgiveness of the Jewish people." This is the only time in history that the leader of one nation has ordered the leader of another nation to go down on his knees in an abject gesture of submission and slavery, yet Begin, who has boasted on the program "60 Minutes" that he "invented terrorism in our time", found nothing out of the ordinary in his demand as the terrorist leader of the worldwide parasitic community that one of the principal leaders of a host nation go down on his knees before the Jews. Ironically, Schmidt is the leader of a nation which, second only to the United States, has funded the parasitic bandit nation of Israel with more than thirty billion dollars extorted from German workers and given to Israel. The Germans paid the extortion demands only because the United States maintained a large military force in Germany with the threat to imprison anyone who refused to pay the extortion to the State of Israel.

Throughout many centuries, the Jews were weak and unable to publicly flaunt their goals of enslaving the Christians and destroying any Christian leaders who dared to oppose them. During these centuries, the Jews developed many cunning practices in order to carry on their evil work. One of the most vicious techniques was their masquerade as "converts to Christianity",' known in Spain and Portugal as "conversos", the converts, or "marranos", or "Jews who mark (amarran) the faith). (Encyclopaedia Britannica.) Colliers Encyclopaedia, v. 15. p. 436, describes the marranos as "Those Jews of Spain and Portugal who under duress became Christians. Some Marranos actively actively accepted Christianity, but many of them practiced Judaism in secret, while others waited only for an opportunity to throw off their Christian disguise. Many Marranos rose to positions of great prominence and subsequently married into noble and wealthy Spanish families."

In areas which remained predominantly Christian, the Jews had to wait for hundreds of years before they were strong enough to throw off "their Christian disguise". When the State of Israel was established in 1948, after a series of atrocities which shocked the entire civilized world, Jews in many nations came forward to announce that they had been "marranos" or "pseudo-Christians" and had maintained this disguise in their families for as long as five hundred years. Now they delighted in abandoning their masquerade and announcing to the world that at no time had they ever believed in the principles of Christianity. They had been Jews, and nothing but Jews, throughout the centuries.

One can only wonder whether Archbishop Gerety and other shabez goi wretches know or care anything about the true history of the Satanic forces to whom they direct the souls entrusted to their care to surrender themselves. Certainly no one with any knowledge of theological history can believe that any Jew who "converts" to Christianity has any purpose except the most diabolical program to enslave Christians and to destroy the principles of Christianity.

The Encyclopaedia Britannica states that "Conversos remained within the Jewish communities in the cities because their occupations (merchants, doctors, tailors) were monopolized by the Jewish people." In 1499, laws prohibited conversos from holding public or ecclesiastical offices. In the 16th century, laws called "limpieza de sangre", or laws of blood purity, were passed to halt the rapid intermarriage of marranos with noble Spanish families.

In his *History of the Jews*, Josef Kastein, p. 231, writes, "As early as the 6th century the Merovingian rulers of the Frankish empire decreed that at Easter no Jews were to be seen in the streets for four days." In 1982, a book appeared which claimed that the Merovingian rulers were actually descended from the family of Christ. They were driven from power a few years after promulgating anti-Jewish laws. On p. 233, Kastein writes, "Some of the Jews, who were wedded to their estates, pretended to go over to Christianity."

Note that this is not a description of impoverished Jewish tailors in the ghettoes, but of Jews with large estates.

Throughout the Middle Ages, when Christianity everywhere was in full retreat before the rapid infiltration of the Jews, the Christian Church valiantly attempted to stem the tide. Kastein states, p. 325, "The monks called on the people to exterminate the Jews. At Easter, 1506, when certain Marranos in Lisbon were discovered making preparations for the celebration of the Passover, the monks organized the "Blood-Marriage of Lisbon and over two thousand Jews were killed in two days." These stories of pseudo-holocausts abound in all Jewish propaganda. A street riot in which one or two Jews were killed by an outraged populace went into the history books as a "pogrom" in which many thousands of Jews were killed. This often ludicrous propaganda reached the height of nonsense in the twentieth century when the entire budget of the State of Israel was based on "reparations" from Germans who has supposedly killed six million Jews during a time when the world population of Jews actually increased, and while fifty million Christians were dying in the holocaust of World War II. No one ever suggested that any reparations be paid for the fifty million Christian dead because, as defined in the Jewish Book of Laws, the Talmud, non-Jews were not human, but were regarded merely as beasts of the field. Jewish law also states that goyim, or beasts, are not to be buried. As a result, during World War II, a Jewish war of extermination against the Christians, millions of Christian victims were never buried, but were left to rot in the open.

On p. 326, Kastein writes, "Very few of them (the Marranos) became resigned and abandoned the secret practice of Judaism." Christians, who believe and practice their religious faith, are unable to believe that members of other religions can infiltrate Christianity for their own purposes and masquerade as Christians while perverting the Christian religion into Satanic forms of worship. The Jews not only pretended to be Christians, but also infiltrated other religious groups as part of their worldwide plan to enslave all non-Jewish peoples or beasts. On p. 340, Kastein describes Jews in Turkey. "This movement created a new generation of Marranos, known as Donmehs, who in public behaved as Turks, but had their own private conventicles, in which they observed Jewish customs. They exist to this day."

Kastein goes on to describe how the Jews, masquerading as Christians, infiltrated every country in Europe. He writes that Marranos entered England and France in great numbers, and rapidly became wealthy and powerful. On p. 352, he writes, "Like the Marranos in Spain, the neophytes (pseudo Christian Jews) who had now become Polish aristocrats made the utmost possible use of their freedom, and managed to secure high social positions."

To the Jews, every such advance meant another breakthrough in their unceasing war against the Christians and their plans to overthrow all civilized governments. On p. 376, Kastein writes that they went into other countries "armed with considerable wealth and extensive international commercial relations." On p. 394, he describes the turmoil which these Jews created in Germany during the nine-teenth century. "A whole host of polemical writings for and against the Jews came into existence, which eventually became so outspoken that the censorship forbade the public discussion of the Jewish question." This censorship exists in "free Germany" today. No one is allowed to protest the exorbitant billions of dollars which German workers are forced to pay to Israel, no can anyone enter into any public discussion of whether the mythical Holocaust, also known as the "hoaxocaust" actually took place. Like all governments controlled by the Jews, the present-day German government denies to its goyim slaves any rights of free speech or free assembly. Germans cannot assemble in public or engage in public discussion of the Jewish problem, just as Kastein describes German censorship of the nineteenth century.

Today, because of Satanic Jewish power, every government in the world stands on the brink of complete economic and political collapse. Christian leaders in every field, particularly in religion and government, frantically assure the Jews of their fanatical devotion to the cause of Israel. Little do they realize that while the Jews may have temporary need of them at the present as collaborators to ensure the permanent enslavement of the goyim masses or beast of the field, the Jews have even less respect for them than for the most ignorant of the gentiles. They will be the first to be disposed of when the Jews openly establish their world dictatorship. It was the liberal government officials and educators in Russia who were the first to be massacred when Jewish Bolshevism openly seized power, and so it has been in every nation in which the Jews embarked on their bloodthirsty purges of all potential opponents. As we approach the beginning of the twenty-first century, God offers us one last opportunity to save civilization before our lives are swallowed up forever in Satanic Jewish world dictatorship. We can do no less than follow the example of Our Lord and Saviour Jesus Christ, who was martyred by the Jews only because His followers failed to take up the battle against this unholy empire. Once again, God extends this chance to us, our last opportunity to save ourselves and our civilization. A short time remains before the world descends forever into the darkness of Jewish barbarism.

F.D.R.

One of Franklin Delano Roosevelt's ancestors was Isaac Roosevelt, first director of the New York Trust after the Revolutionary War, when Alexander Hamilton betrayed our young Republic by funding the national debt and placing us in the hands of Jewish financiers in France and Holland.

As a young Harvard lawyer, FDR found himself one of the poorer Roosevelts. Old ex-President Theodore Roosevelt was living in comfort in Oyster Bay, after having made thirty-five million dollars profit in gold from the United States Treasury in one operation for J.P. Morgan Co. (Rothschild) & J. & W. Seligman Co., New York, when he purchased the Panama Canal. When he sued the *New York World* for libel for printing some of the more interesting particulars of this case, the United States Supreme Court unanimously threw out Roosevelt's suit.

His son, Theodore Roosevelt, Jr., was to do his bit for the family honor by acting as finger man in the hundred million dollar swindle, the Teapot Dome oil scandals of 1924. Despite the fact that he was publicized as the man who got Harding to sign the oil-land release to Sinclair, Theodore Roosevelt, Jr., then Assisstant Secretary of the Navy, formerly director of Sinclair Oil Co., was not even called to testify at the Congressional Hearings. In Some unexplained manner, this distinguished American became a General in the United States Army, and, venturing too near the front lines in France during the Second World War, heard a gun go off nearby and fell dead of a heart attack, thus vindicating the fighting tradition of his family.

F.D. Roosevelt was appointed Assistant Secretary of the Navy in 1915 by the Christian Jew Woodrow Wilson (Wolfsohn), who was determined to fill Washington with his own tribe. In this position, Roosevelt endeared himself to Jewish munitions makers by spending four times the allotted amount for naval armaments, when he and his Zionist friends knew two years before anyone else that we were going into the First World War. Roosevelt's reward came in 1923, when Baruch made him the head of United European Investors, Ltd., which made millions of dollars profit from the mark inflation in Germany. Thus Roosevelt had his first taste of Profiting from the misery of the poor, a sensation dear to the heart of every Hebrew usurer.

Roosevelt then set up his Wall Street law firm of Roosevelt and O'Connor, which did remarkably well, but he was intended by the Sanhedrin for higher things. He was made Governor of New York in 1928, when he helped sabotage the campaign of Al Smith for President in favor of the Rothschild candidate Herbert Hoover, who has an interesting history of suits against him in the law courts of London. Hoover's talent for keeping out of jail is one of the marvels of the twentieth century, and is documented by no less than five biographies, complete with photostats of court records, in the Library of Congress. This writer is fortunate enough to own two of these rare and fascinating volumes, which he prizes highly in his collection of obscure Americana.

As Governor of New York Roosevelt displayed his passion for justice in the famous case of John Broderick. Broderick, State Superintendent of Banks of New York, was tried for criminal neglect of duty in the infamous Bank of the United States case, when depositors lost many thousands of dollars after the bank failed due to its Jewish officers overspeculating in Central Park West real estate. It was brought out at the trial that Broderick was aware of the serious difficulties of the Bank and did nothing about it. He seemed certain to go to prison, when the White Knight of World Jewry, F.D. Roosevelt, came in person to plead clemency for Broderick. The Judge was forced to bow to a superior political figure, and Broderick went free. Roosevelt flaunted his defiance of the depositors by immediately reinstating Broderick as State Superintendent of Banks. Not satisfied with this, Roosevelt again proved which side of the law he was on by appointing Broderick a Governor of the Federal Reserve Board of the United States, on that unhappy occasion when a misguided people elected this Zionist traitor President. Broderick has retired to a comfortable old age as President of the venerable East River savings Bank of New York City, after a career of public service in the democratic tradition.

The interests which forced Roosevelt's candidacy on the Democratic Party in 1932 have never been made public, but it is significant that they were such a dangerous group of revolutionists that at first even Baruch refused to be associated with the Roosevelt movement. My history of the Council on Foreign Relations proves by extensive documentation that international Jewish bankers elected Roosevelt President for one reason only, the recognition of Soviet Russia by the United States, for which Felix Warburg and Otto Kahn of Kuhn, Loeb Co., had struggled so hard throughout the 1920s. Roosevelt's predecessor, Herbert Hoover, had steadily refused to aid the Soviet Union. One of his London promotion schemes before the First World War had been interrupted by the Jewish Communists, and he never forgot it. Roosevelt, on the other hand, was only too happy to recognize and prove his loyalty to the Jewish Communist Government of Russia. He was always willing to do anything to please his friends. In return, of course, it was understood that they should do anything to please him, such as contribute large sums to his multi-million dollar infantile charity racket. The *March of Dimes* which his law partner Basil O'Connor inherited upon Roosevelt's sudden death at its headquarters at Warm Springs, Georgia. It is not beyond the realm of possibility that Roosevelt's mysterious death had nothing to do with world revolution at all, but was merely a gangster's quarrel over the division of the spoils, it being in the spring, when the *Miles of Dimes* were converted into stacks of dollars, after an unusually successful attack upon the purses of our generous people.

Roosevelt fulfilled his debt of gratitude to Jewish Communism by assigning important Government posts in Washington to leading Communist agitators and spies, such as his famous protege Alger Hiss.

One of Roosevelt's first great feats as President was the gigantic gold swindle which he and Secretary of the Treasury Morgenthau put through, the Gold Trading Act of 1934, which officially committed our government to support Jewish bankers in their manipulation of the price of gold. After a stiff fight with the Supreme Court, Roosevelt jammed through this bit of treachery, because, as Morgenthau said, "If the Supreme Court had decided against us, we had legislation ready to push through Congress which would have given us the same result." This Morgenthau is the son of the Henry Morgenthau who paid Woodrow Wilson's way into the White House in 1912 so that Wilson could send him as U.S. Ambassador to Turkey, where World Zionists were completing the details of the Communist Revolution in Russia.

Morgenthau was also the author of the infamous Morgenthau Plan to wipe out the German people in 1944, which was broadcast to the German armies and caused the lives of thousands of American boys to be sacrificed because the Germans were warned what would happen after they surrendered. This Plan, so determined in its ruthlessness that it aroused the horror of the civilized world, is typical of Jewish Communist efforts to slaughter whole peoples.

DOUGLAS MACARTHUR

He Wanted To Win ... His Government Did Not

Thousands of American boys died on barren Pacific sandpits during World War II, never knowing they had been condemned to die because of the hatred the Communists felt for their commander, General Douglas MacArthur. Let us go back to Washington, D.C., for the birthpangs of this hatred; the time, July 28, 1932. The nation is in the depths of an economic depression brought on by classic gold movements of the international bankers. Some gold bricks had been moved from one section of the Federal Reserve Bank vaults in New York City to another section a few feet away; this seemingly insignificant act brought on a contraction of credit and the puncturing of the Wall Street boom. **Eighty-five billion dollars in inflated stock values vanished into the vaults of the bankers, leaving the American Middle Class a robbed and beaten people.** Since this middle-class created the jobs, the workers were now without employment and were in an ugly mood. This was the background of the dispatching of a special Communist task force to Washington to take over the Bonus March of the American veterans, provoke a massacre by local police or troops, and begin a conflagration which would quickly sweep the country and deliver us into the waiting hands of the Communists.

It was a simple technique, which had worked marvelously well in Czarist Russia. Some people were idling around in front of a bakery, a few Communists in the crowd threw stones at the Imperial Guard, shots were fired, and a few people were killed. Within weeks, the Imperial Government was no more; and the Czar and his wife and children were locked in a cellar, waiting to be executed by their captors.

There was no reason to suppose that this technique would not work in America, where the Communists were a well-organized, militant group. They had survived the "Palmer Raids" of the nineteen twenties with their revolutionary organization intact; despite the moans of the bleeding hearts that civil liberties had been violated, the Party had been strengthened by the arrests of a few hangers on and would-be Communist sympathizers, who were an embarrassment to the genuinely dedicated conspirators.

A detachment of American troops, neatly dressed and marching in perfect order, came through the streets of Washington, led by Major George Patton and General Douglas MacArthur, then Chief of Staff of the United States Army. The soldiers ignored the taunts and threats of the Communists sprinkled in the crowd. Suddenly a fat man dashed into the well disciplined ranks. "Shoot, damn you, shoot!" he screamed. The soldiers shoved him aside, not even bothering to poke a rifle butt into his protruding stomach. Disappointed, the man shook his fist. "We'll get you for this, MacArthur!" he shouted. The General, erect on his charge, stared straight ahead. He could hardly know that the man's threat would cloud the last two decades of his brilliant career and cost the lives of many thousands of his men.

The man was David Neyhus, who had accompanied the large detachment of Communists from New York. Although the revolutionaries were under the command of a well-known Communist leader, Emmanuel Levin, Neyhus was the Moscow contact, who dictated the strategy of the operation. Levin disappeared from history, **but Neyhus, using the name of David Niles, became an influential White House advisor and the principal architect of national policies during the Truman Administration.**

The Bonus Marchers were unemployed veterans from World War I, who had been ruined by the Crash of 1929. Some sixty thousand of them had come to Washington for an orderly protest against Congressional reluctance to grant them a bonus for military service.

Superintendent of Police Pelham Glass had only six hundred policemen to contain this huge force, but he gave them $733 from his own pocket, raised $2500 more to feed them by staging boxing matches for them, and enlisted the aid of Evelyn Walsh McLean in helping them.

The leader of the marchers, Walter W. Waters, was dedicated to maintaining an orderly protest, but on June 1, 1932, the Communist detachment arrived from New York with instructions to provoke a riot. Waters had his men arrest them; they were court-martialled, sentenced to fifteen lashes each, and their literature was burned. Nevertheless, they hung around, hoping that things would turn their way, as the men grew more disillusioned. The Communists chose John T. Pace, as the leader of their group, hoping to make a better impression than the lisping aliens. Pace testified in 1949 before the House UnAmerican Activities Committee, "I led the Communist section of the Bonus March. I was ordered by my Red superiors to provoke riots. I was told to use every trick in the book to bring about bloodshed ... General MacArthur put down a Moscow-directed revolution without bloodshed and that's why the Communists hate him."

One can only shudder to think that a Dwight Eisenhower, had he been in command of the troops in Washington, might have panicked and ordered the men to fire, and provoked a revolution. General MacArthur maintained perfect discipline, and not a shot was fired. Some of the Communists occupied an armory building, in a classic technique of revolution; and when the police tried to evict them, Glassford was attacked and his clothes torn off. The

Communists gleefully exhibited his gold badge, which they had ripped from him; it was then that the Commissioners of the District of Columbia asked President Hoover for troops. Hoover conveyed the order to the Secretary of War, Patrick Hurley, who passed on the request to General MacArthur as Chief of Staff. Although it was unheard of for the Chief of Staff of the United States Army to lead a riot patrol, MacArthur was determined that none of the marchers should be hurt, for many of them were men he had commanded in the Rainbow Division in France. He knew that his prestige would be placed on the line; for if a disaster should occur, he would be held personally responsible. Nevertheless, he did not hesitate to risk his career. Leading about one thousand soldiers, he marched them through the crowds of marchers, and on to the Anacostia flats, where the marchers had made their encampment. The camp was methodically torn down and the Bonus March was over.

The Communists, seeing their plans for revolution going up in the smoke of the burning Ana costia camp, went into paroxysms of fury. They immediately unleashed a terrible campaign of vilification against President Hoover, branding him as the "mass murderer" of the Bonus Marchers and a tyrant who had used armed force against peaceful demonstrators. This was the first really vicious propaganda campaign in the history of American politics. Based entirely on lies and personal attacks on Hoover, it swept him out of office and inaugurated as President, Franklin D. Roosevelt.

Roosevelt never forgot that it was the Communist support which turned his campaign from a lackluster effort against a wellentrenched incumbent into a national sweep to victory. Forty of the Communist members who had infiltrated the Bonus Marchers were appointed to government posts during Roosevelt's first year in office, while the national policies of Roosevelt's Administration were largely formulated and executed by members of the top secret Harold Ware cell of Communists, which comprised the Underground Cabinet of the Roosevelt White

House. One of the Harold Ware cell's first goals was to reduce the size of America's already small Army. The Communists considered the Regular Army as Cossacks, or an Imperial Guard, which was a counter-revolutionary force, and which, of course, had thwarted their plans during the Bonus March.

Soon after Roosevelt's entry into the White House, he summoned General MacArthur to inform him that the Army was to be cut by fifty per cent. MacArthur immediately contested the decision, arguing with Roosevelt while the cripple grew purple with rage in his wheelchair.

Finally, Roosevelt agreed to reconsider his decision, and Secretary of War, George Dern, complimented MacArthur, saying, "You have just saved the Army." However, MacArthur states in his memoirs that he was made physically ill by this encounter with the Great Cripple, and that he vomited on the steps of the White House, overcome by nausea and disgust at the thought of his native land being subverted by this man.

In 1941, Roosevelt maneuvered the Pacific Fleet into Pearl Harbor to await the Japanese attack, while MacArthur warned him of the Japanese buildup and was puzzled that he received no answer from the White House. When MacArthur assumed command of the defense of the Philippines, he anticipated little difficulty in halting the Japanese advance. The entire Japanese strategy had been detailed many years before by the brilliant American strategist Homer Lea. Knowing the Japanese plans, MacArthur was ready to thwart them. However, he was never informed of a high-level decision in Washington, soon after Pearl Harbor, that American military power would be concentrated on the defeat of Germany, in order to save Soviet Russia and the Jews from the German armies. General MacArthur was left holding the bag in the Philippines, while Churchill, Marshall and Roosevelt sent America's military aid to Russia. As a result, many thousands of MacArthur's men were doomed to die in the infamous Bataan Death March, after their capture by the Japanese, because their own President had abandoned them to the enemy.

Meanwhile, the Communists, firmly in command of the American press establishment, carried on a furious campaign of hate against MacArthur. Roosevelt ordered MacArthur to leave the Philippines and go to Australia, and the White House immediately leaked to the press that MacArthur was running away! Reporters printed wild stories that the departing general had planes carrying his grand piano and other possessions. In fact, MacArthur left with nothing but the clothes on his back, and lost most of his personal possessions in the Philippines. It was at this time that the Communist press coined the most cruel epithet of all, "Dugout Doug", implying that MacArthur was a coward, when in fact the General risked his life many times before enemy fire. MacArthur himself was unable to understand the press' vicious hatred of him. He had forgotten the encounter with David Niles and the other Communists in 1932, and in any case he was incapable of understanding such subhuman feelings.

Although MacArthur had by 1930 been considered America's most brilliant military mind, throughout World War Two he was never invited to participate in a single high-level conference! The war was run strictly by Roosevelt's Communist advisers, principally Lauchlin Currie and Harry Dexter White, a Lithuanian man whose real name was Weiss. It was "White" who thought up the infamous "island hopping" plan of fighting the Pacific War. The Japanese had occupied and fortified a number of Pacific islands between Hawaii and Japan. MacArthur devised a plan for mounting massive strike forces against the Philippines and against Japan herself, forcing an early end to the war. Roosevelt was upset by the plan, foreseeing that such a brilliant victory would make MacArthur a powerful political rival. Weiss immediately devised a counter plan, which delighted Roosevelt. Instead of leaving the little Japanese Maginot

Lines to wither on the vine, it would play into the Japanese hands by mounting huge assaults on each little island. The MacArthur Plan was never acknowledged by the White House, and instead, the Pacific forces were committed to a series of operations later called "Feeding the Fishes", whereby many thousands of American boys were shot down in the water while trying to storm almost impregnable Japanese island redoubts. The names of Iwo Jima and Tarawa recall the incredible heroism of American youths who gave their lives attacking these fortresses, but they also recall the incredible infamy of a sinister Lithuanian man whose only purpose was to bleed this country to death and weaken it for a Communist victory at some later date. The island hopping campaign ensured that MacArthur would have no great victory and that the losses in these battles would cause Americans to think he was a poor strategist. Nevertheless, Roosevelt, always a coward, continued to fear MacArthur as a political rival; and in 1944 he wrung from an astounded MacArthur a pledge that he would not be a candidate that year!

Despite his limited resources, MacArthur performed brilliantly throughout World War Two. He was able to make good his prophetic statement, "I shall return", when he left the Philippines at Roosevelt's order. His successful campaign to retake the Philippine Islands is regarded as a classic of military strategy.

Despite the Communist press vilification of MacArthur, he was repeatedly decorated during World War Two for his victories and for his bravery in combat. For instance, he won the Congressional Medal of Honor for his defense of the Philippines, he was awarded the Air Medal for personally leading the attack on Nadzab airstrip on Sept. 9, 1943, and he received the Distinguished Service Medal three times. Of course, the American public, like MacArthur himself, never realized the background of the press attacks on him, which continued unabated throughout the war.

With the conclusion of the war, the Communists feared more than ever the return to America of a victorious MacArthur. Once again "White" conceived the brilliant plan of ordering MacArthur to become Commander of the occupied nation of Japan, effectively removing him from the American political scene. Accepting this order without question, as he always did, MacArthur devoted himself to rebuilding a shattered Japan while his own nation, which solely needed him at home to counter the growing power of the Communists, was denied his services.

Beginning in June, 1949, MacArthur began to submit reports to Washington that the Communists in North Korea were building up forces for an assault on the non-Communist nation of South Korea. All of these warnings were ignored. When the Communists swept through South Korea, MacArthur was asked to stop them, but, as in 1941, was given insufficient forces. Making up for his lack of strength, MacArthur broke the Communist attack by a magnificent stroke, the Inchon landing. Admiral Halsey wrote to him. "Congratulations. Characteristic and magnificent. The Inchon landing is the most masterly and audacious strategic stroke in all history." President Truman wired him, "I know I speak for the entire American people when I send you my warmest congratulations in the victory which has been achieved under your leadership in Korea." A few weeks later, Truman fired him. What had happened? MacArthur was doing the unforgivable; he was beating the Communists.

Truman summoned MacArthur to a conference at Wake Island. Truman later told a number of lies about this meeting, boasting that he had circled for an hour making MacArthur wait for him, and in another version said MacArthur had made him wait by circling above his plane. Others present said they had arrived at the same time. Nothing was discussed at the conference, and MacArthur surmised Truman had summoned him merely to bolster a faltering Congressional campaign at home.

A series of directives now came from Washington forbidding MacArthur from "hot pursuit" of enemy attackers, or from bombing their marshalling yards, or bombing the hydroelectric plants in North Korea. The entire conduct of the war became a dress rehearsal for the Vietnam War, in which American commanders were forbidden to inflict any real damage on the Communist enemy. MacArthur asked to be relieved from command, as he could not fight under these restrictions, but Marshall begged him to stay on. Meanwhile, General Walker complained to MacArthur that his operations were known to the enemy in advance through their sources in Washington. MacArthur began to attack the Communist forces without revealing his plans to Washington. He won a series of stunning victories, whereupon the Communists insisted that MacArthur be removed.

Now David Niles would have his revenge for 1932. It was he who ordered Truman to relieve MacArthur from command. On April 11, 1957, Truman, with deliberate malice, held a press conference in Washington announcing that he was recalling MacArthur and relieving him from command. MacArthur heard the decision on Radio Japan! MacArthur noted in his Memoirs a significant comment, "Moscow and Peiping rejoiced. The bells were rung and a holiday atmosphere prevailed."

Certainly the Communists had reason to rejoice. The greatest anti-Communist soldier in the world had been fired. Now they were safe. Thus we come to the great final act of this hero's life. A military plane roars in from the Pacific, sighting the California coast. Aboard it is the world's most famous soldier, General Douglas MacArthur, with a trusted staff of aides. The plane continues high over the nation, bound for Washington. MacArthur believes that when he lands, a delegation of loyal Congressman will meet him with a request that he form a Provisional Military Government, and that he must arrest the pitiful Communist traitors who demanded his removal. In Washington, among the subhuman filth which has infested the offices of the nation's capital like some medieval plague of diseased rats, each bearing fearful contamination in its mangy hide, the treasonous garbage cowers in helpless fear, awaiting the inevitable landing of the exterminator. The fat alcoholic, David Niles, the Moscow Communist who had ordered MacArthur's dismissal, is now collapsed in a drunken stupor in his White House room. The members of the Harold Ware cell of Communists, who have directed America's national policies since 1933, have, according to prearranged plans, gone into hiding. Harry Truman impassively awaits the end, playing poker with a few cronies on the second floor of the White House. Described by the poet Ezra Pound in the Cantos as "always loyal to his kind, the underworld", Truman has little fear of arrest; it is part of a criminal career. He began his life as a bagman for the Kansas City brothels; his mentor, Boss Prendergast, has been in prison for years, having been convicted of stealing forty million dollars. However, some of the Communists had not given up. Desperate promises were made -- threats, deals, blackmail. When MacArthur landed, the expected Congressional delegation was not there. Supposing that he had already been named Provisional Governor, MacArthur proceeded to Capitol Hill. He was amazed to find that nothing had been done! There was no proclamation; his strongest supporters in Congress were strangely evasive. MacArthur, the greatest military strategist, found that he had no strategy for forming a government. After wavering for several hours, he was dissuaded by none other than Senator Robert Taft. Taft boldly declared that America must solve her problems at the ballot box, and that MacArthur could run for President and cure the nation's ills. Had MacArthur known that Taft was echoing the advice of Rabbi Hillel Silver, his mentor, he might have countered with the statement that Washington did not use a ballot box at Trenton or at Valley Forge. But MacArthur had been away from his country for many years. He still did not know what was going on behind the scenes. He supposed that there were only a few principal Communists behind Truman. He had never heard of the Harold Ware cell; he knew nothing of the Communists placed strategically in every major government office.

The moment passed. MacArthur made a stirring address to the Congress, and retreated to New York to await the still expected call to national office. It would never come. Instead, the communists double-crossed Taft, who had been promised the Presidency for diverting MacArthur from the takeover, and instead brought in the servile Eisenhower, who had already proven his willingness to serve his Communist masters, or anyone who was willing to accept his professional acts of self-prostitution. While MacArthur was making his address to Congress, the Communists were already coming out of their hiding-places and resuming their offices in Washington. Nothing had changed. In retrospect, we see that we Americans must now inaugurate a national campaign to honor MacArthur's memory by expelling the Communist rats from their holes. How much blood should we shed to avenge the dead of Iwo Jima and Tarawa, murdered by the Communist plotter Harry Weiss? We have only to recall that when a MacArthur Memorial Museum was proposed for Washington, the Communists boasted that it would be bombed within a week of its opening. The fearful government officials then moved the MacArthur Museum to Norfolk, where it remains today. Even in death, MacArthur could not win over the Communist traitors. In respect to his memory, and in order to save ourselves, we must unite in a massive national effort to defeat the traitors in our midst. Today it is not MacArthur who is in peril, but each of us, daily assaulted by vicious Communist officials from Washington who seek to strip from us the last of our personal property and our self respect.

England's leading military writer, Lord Alanbrooke, wrote of World War Two, *"MacArthur was the greatest general and the best strategist that the war produced. He certainly outshowed Marshall, Eisenhower, and the other Amencan generals, as well as Montgomery. In all of these operations I never felt he had the full support of the*

American Chiefs of Staff. I am convinced that, as the war can be viewed in better perspective, it will be agreed that the strategic ability shown by MacArthur was in a class of its own."

WHY GENERAL PATTON WAS MURDERED

In 2009 it will be sixty four years since one of America's greatest heroes, General George S. Patton, was executed by his Communist foes. General Patton was struck down the day before he was scheduled to make a triumphant return to the United States. He had just been removed from his command of the Third Army, which was in charge of governing the American sector of Germany, because he not only opposed the dismemberment of Germany, but also because he favoured military action against the Communists. As the most popular hero of the Second World War, Patton would have been unbeatable in a Presidential race. This was the reason his skulking enemies ordered his execution before he could leave Germany.

The Patton Papers, 1940-1945 published by Houghton Mifflin Company in Boston, gave ample reasons for the murder of General Patton. A few months before he was killed, his driver for five years, Master Sergeant John L. Mims, was replaced. Patton was asked by Major General Gay to accompany him on an excursion for a few hours the day before he was to return to America. At 11:45 a.m., in clear weather and on a straight stretch of road, the driver of a GMC military truck turned his vehicle directly into the side of the 1938 Cadillac 75 Special limousine in which Patton was being driven. Patton was the only person injured. He suffered some internal injuries but did not seem to be seriously hurt. On December 21, 1945, it was announced that he had died of an "embolism", that is, a bubble of the blood which is fatal when it reaches a vital organ. It can be introduced into the bloodstream with a syringe by anyone with brief medical training.

Patton was a vigorous sixty years old with enormous reserves of energy, who seldom needed more than a couple of hours of sleep a night. Not only did the U.S. Army make no investigation into the "accident" which had put him into the hospital, but no questions were raised about his "embolism". On previous occasions when attempts were made to kill him, no investigations were made, despite the fact that he was one of the most popular and most powerful figures in America's history. He recorded in his diary that on April 20, 1945, while observing the front in his personal plane, which was clearly marked, an RAF Spitfire made three passes at his plane, attempting to shoot it down, then went out of control and crashed. The story was later put out that a Polish flyer had been piloting the Spitfire, Patton was not injured.

Patton's military exploits were such that he was the only American general whom the Germans feared. They transferred entire divisions as soon as rumours were spread that he was on a given front. The Germans' contempt for Patton's fellow generals was shared by himself, as he proves on many pages of his diary. During much of World War H, Patton survived repeated efforts of his fellow generals, as well as the British leaders, to get rid of him. In 1943, when he had turned the tide in Africa with his brilliant victories at Gafsa and Gela, Patton was removed from command after Drew Pearson printed a story that Patton had slapped a malingerer at a field hospital and called him a "yellow-bellied Jew". Eisenhower used this incident as an excuse to refuse Patton command of American ground troops in England, giving the command instead to Omar Bradley, whom Patton exposed as a cowardly dullard. We will never know how many casualties Bradley's cowardice and incompetence cost us, but it must have been many thousands.

Patton wrote in his Diary Jan. 18, 1944, "Bradley is a man of great mediocrity. At Benning in command, he failed to get discipline. At Gafsa, when it looked as though the Germans might turn our right flank, he suggested we withdraw corps headquarters to Feriana. I refused to move."

Patton cited numerous other examples of Bradley's cowardice. As for Eisenhower, his references to him are always contemptuous, Patton refers to Ike as "Divine Destiny" but more customarily as "fool". On March 1, 1944 Patton noted in his Diary, "Ike and I dined alone and had a very pleasant time. He is drinking too much."

Patton was extremely disgusted with Eisenhower's infatuation with his "chauffeur", Kay Summersby, and he persuaded Ike not to divorce Mamie in order to marry her. Kay Summersby was a British intelligence officer who had been ordered to prostitute herself to Ike so that he would send American troops into the line instead of the British. England had experienced such a terrible bloodletting at the hands of the German armies in World War I. that Churchill and the other British leaders determined to sacrifice Americans wherever possible on the Western front. Although Kay Summersby secretly despised Eisenhower, she was a loyal British subject, and she successfully carried off the affair. It is estimated that she cost the United States 100,000 casualties which otherwise would have been borne by the British.

Patton had noted in his Diary, July 5, 1943 before his successful African campaign, "At no time did Ike wish us luck and say he was back of us - fool."

On July 12, 1944, Patton wrote in his Diary, "Neither Ike nor Bradley has the stuff. Ike is bound hand and foot by the British and doesn't know it. Poor fool."

As a result of Patton's bold advances in France, Field Marshal Montgomery persuaded Eisenhower to issue one of the most amazing military orders in history. All of the Allied Armies must advance exactly abreast, so that no one (meaning Patton) would receive "undue credit". Throughout the war, Patton achieved his amazing victories by being in the field, whereas the other generals remained far behind the front in their dugout "headquarters" or in luxurious villas far from the sound of gunfire.

During a press conference on May 8, 1945, Patton was asked, "Would you explain why we [the Americans] didn't go into Prague." "I can tell you exactly," Patton replied. "We were ordered not to." Patton wrote to his wife on July 21, 1945, "I could have taken it [referring to Berlin] had 1 been allowed."

Eisenhower's refusal to allow Patton to take Prague and Berlin, holding him back while the Russians occupied these critical capitals, remains one of the greatest performances of treason since Benedict Arnold, like Eisenhower, sold out to the British.

Patton apparently was writing his own death warrant when he entered his frequently voiced opinion in his Diary on May 18, 1945, concerning the advisability of fighting the Russians. "In my opinion, the American Army as it now exists could beat the Russians with the greatest ease, because while the Russians have good infantry, they are lacking in artillery, air, tanks, and in the knowledge of the use of these combined arms; whereas we excel in all three of these. If it should be necessary to fight the Russians, the sooner we do it the better."

The danger which Patton presented to his enemies was not merely that he was a great American patriot; he also was impervious to any sort of undue influence. He had married Beatrice Ayer, one of the wealthiest women in America. This made him financially invulnerable, and he was happily married, which made it impossible for him to succumb to the blandishments of foreign agents such as Kay Summersby. He opposed the Jews because he believed they were a lower order of human beings.

Shortly before he was killed, he wrote in his Diary, Oct. 1, 1945, "THE JEWISH TYPE OF DISPLACED PERSON IS, IN THE MAJORITY OF CASES, A SUBHUMAN SPECIES WITHOUT ANY OF THE CULTURAL OR SOCIAL REFINEMENTS OF OUR TIME."

Patton was removed from command in Germany because he actively opposed the swarm of Jewish locusts, such as the recently recruited Soviet agent, Henry Kissinger, who fought Patton to win control of the Military Government in Germany.

In his Diary, August 29, 1945, Patton wrote, "Today we received a letter in which we were told to give the Jews special accommodations. If for Jews, why not Catholics, Mormons, etc."

On August 31, 1945, Patton wrote to his wife, "THE STUFF IN THE PAPERS ABOUT FRATERNIZATION IS ALL WET. ALL THAT SORT OF WRITING IS DONE BY JEWS TO GET REVENGE. ACTUALLY, THE GERMANS ARE THE ONLY DECENT PEOPLE LEFT IN EUROPE."

Patton noted in his Diary on August 31, 1945, "I also wrote a letter to the Secretary of War, Mr. Stimson, on the question of the pro-Jewish influence in the Military Government of Germany."

As a result of Patton's opposition to the Kissingers, who believed they had won the war and should rule Europe, a furious press campaign again was launched against him. A pro-Patton observer named Mason wrote, "The Daniel-Bevin-Morgan plot to destroy Patton was successful because Bernstein of PM was the most powerful force in Germany in 1945 because he had the support of Harry Dexter White, and Henry Morgenthau, Laughlin Curry, David K. Nile and Alger Hiss."

On Sept. 29, 1945. Patton wrote to his wife, "The noise against me is only the means by which the Jews and Communists are attempting and with good success to implement a further dismemberment of Germany."

Removed from command by the Jewish plot against him, General George S. Patton would have returned to the United States to work for the good of his country. It was to prevent this that a truck smashed in the side of his car in one of the strangest and most-ignored events in America's military history. Those who fight for America are always in danger, always thwarted by the plotting and the treachery of the sub-humans whom Patton recognized and battled to the end of his life. His story is one which enlightens and inspires us all, and this is why we must, after sixty four years. remind the American people of the cowards who murdered him.

BEHIND THE FALKLAND ISLANDS STORY

Excepting the readers of CDL Report, few Americans will ever learn the facts behind the Falkland Islands crisis. The Jewish-controlled press propaganda line. All other information is verboten by the fanatical Zionist terrorists and Mossad agents who control the American press.

Adolf Hitler said, "All that is not race is dross." The Falklands Islands crisis is one of conflict between Argentina, one of the few white nations in South America, and the Jewish-poisoned dregs of the once mighty British Empire, a former bastion of the white race now consisting of a few whites inundated by a sea of coloured, and ruled by the Jewish banker family of Battenberg, who anglicized their name to Mountbatten in World War I, because even then they had already attained complete control of the formerly white nation of the British Isles. Lord Mountbatten reigned as First Lord of the Admiralty, and his son married Edwina Cassel, daughter of the fabulously wealthy Sir Edward Cassel, a German Jewish emigrant who formed one of the notorious "Jewish Seven" who comprised the Prince of Wales; and later Edward VII; inner circle, led by "Lord" Nathaniel Rothschild. These Jews saw to it that the Prince of Wales had everything he wanted in way of wine, women and song, and in exchange he allowed them to seize control of the British Empire.

Soon afterwards, the Jews collected their pound of flesh by forcing the half-witted son of King Edward, George V, to engage the British Empire in World War I, a war in which they had nothing to gain and everything to lose. Although World War I did not destroy the British Empire *per se*, it was such a massive blood letting that Great Britain almost ceased to exist as an entity of the white race. Deprived of the young men who could have maintained her empire, Great Britain easily let the remainder of her world wide holding slip from her grasp as a result of World War II. Hitler warned the British that if they declared war on Germany, they would lose the rest of their empire, a prediction which soon came true, despite Winston Churchill's bombastic boast that "I did not become Prime Minister to preside over the liquidation of the British Empire."

Deep in the bowels of London is the once secret War Room, disguised by a door which reads "Toilet", an example of Churchill's well known "water closet" style of humor. Here tourists are shown a bedroom, where the besotted Churchill "rested" every afternoon from two until six, safe from bombing and the effects of the war, while millions of young men whom he had sent out to their doom struggled and died in mud and filth.

It is the heirs of Winston Churchill who now propose to destroy the main anti-Communist nation in South America by driving it into the arms of the Soviets. The notorious pro-Jewish propagandist, Robert S. John, wrote in 1970 in "South America More or Less", p. 202, "The Argentines frankly admit that their antecedents, the early Spaniards, virtually exterminated the indigenous population. Today 98 per cent of the population is white."

Very few Americans realize that Argentina is the main white nation in South America. To the north is the mestizo culture of Brazil, a nation of mulattoes which is a cross between Puerto Rico and the present day United States, and Bolivia, whose population consists mostly of the Indians who fled from the early settlers in Argentina. Because it is 98 per cent white, Argentina is extremely anti-Communist, as a nation's opposition to Communism is in inverse ratio to the extent to which it remains a bastion of the white race. As the United States has become more negroid each year, so its opposition to Communism has steadily declined.

As a white nation, Argentina reached the apogee of its opposition to Communism under Peron. Along with is opposition to Communism, Argentina also reached the peak of its wealth and power during those years. St. John reports with typical Jewish horror of the "middle-aged people who were well aware that Peron had favored Nazi Germany and Fascist Italy during the last world war" and that "They would add: 'however, those were happy days for most of us here in Argentina.' "

On p. 213, St. John writes, "On political development while we were in Buenos Aires reminded us of the McCarthy era in the United States. A law was promulgated which would have delighted the late Senator from Wisconsin. It defined a Communist as 'one who carries out activities that are proved to be undoubtedly motivated by who carries out activities that are proved to be undoubtedly motivated by Communist ideology' and the law was made retroactive."

Unlike the farcical "anti-Communist" campaign in the United States, where the only offense of a Communist was his possession of a Communist Party card, the Argentine law went to the heart of the matter, and charged anyone who was "motivated by Communist ideology", a charge which would have resulted in the arrest of Roosevelt and Truman's staffs, as well as the active Jewish community in the United States. By making the law retroactive, it punished Communists whose activities stretched back far before the law was passed. In contrast, the "anti-Communist" campaign in the United States was dominated by "former Communists" persons who claimed to have seen the error of their ways. Sincere anti-Communists like the present writer found that they were frozen out of the anti-Communist campaign, as the "former Communists" maintained a phalanx restricted to their own ranks. Of course they were Jews, or Jewish stooges, such as Ben Gitlow and other founders of the Communist Party of America, including Jay Liebstein, who anglicized his name to Jay Lovestone, and reached the pinnacle of the "anti-Communist" movement in America by ghostwriting for J. Edgar Hoover a book on Communism titled "Masters of Deceit". Hoover took the money from the book and ran to the bank without telling anyone that "his" book had been written by a founder of the Communist Party of America.

As a white nation, Argentina naturally sympathized with those who fought for the white race against the Communists in World War II. After the pro-white countries had lost the war to the vengeful Jews, a swarm of hateful Jewish refugees like Henry Kissinger rushed into Germany to loot the nation and harass the defeated white men. Some of these whites emigrated to Argentina, which was at that time the only prosperous white nation in the world. To punish the Argentine people for offering a place to the refugees from Communism and Jewish terrorism, international Jewish bankers began a fullscale war of economic sabotage against the Argentines, with such success that for years Argentina has been beset by high rates of inflation and economic insecurity. High inflation is the hallmark of the presence of the biological parasite, the international Jew, because the Jew, in infecting the nation, raises the rate of inflation to allow him to parlay his small amount of cash into a giant fortune, just as the presence of fever in the patient is a warning of infection in the human body. Inflation did not become a problem in the American economy until the Jew achieved mastery of our economic system, and through the Jewish agency, the Federal Reserve System, was able to drive down the purchasing power of the dollar, erode savings and impoverish the American workers.

As the Jews gained wealth and power in Argentina, Peron was driven out and a succession of Jewish stooges accelerated Argentina's fall from prosperity and power. Terrorism is always a basis of Jewish drive for power, as we have seen in America with the murders committed by Mossad, and the atrocities committed on American soil by the Jewish Defense League. In Argentina, the nation was paralyzed by the atrocities committed throughout the country by the Montaneros, a group of Jewish Communist assassins, who amassed hundreds of millions of dollars in ransom and extortion from their victims. The laundering and banking of these huge sums was handled by a Jew named David Graiver. As a front for Gravier's operations, a Jew named Jacobo Timerman operated a newspaper and other economic fronts for the Montaneros. As government officials began to win their war on the Montaneros, Graiver fled the country. It was claimed he was "killed" in an airplane which crashed, by most officials believe this was a coverup story. Timerman was arrested, and immediately the worldwide Jewish claque began a clamor for his release.

Threatened with economic sanctions which would have finished off their weak economy, the Argentine officials gave in to threats from Jimmy Carter and released Timerman. He was flown to Washington, where he was introduced to the United States Congress amid huzzahs of praise as a "freedom fighter". He then published a book of his fantasies which has become a worldwide best seller, "*Prisoner Without a Name, Cell Without a Number.*" It compares with most "memoirs" of the alleged Holocaust, in which the victims were murdered every day but in some form of reincarnation now own apartment buildings in Chicago, vacation in Miami Beach, and buy millions of dollars worth of Israeli bonds.

The veracity of Timerman's meanderings may be summed up in a single sentence. On p. 70, he writes, "Between 1974 and 1978, the violation of girls in clandestine prisons had a peculiar characteristic: Jewish girls were violated twice as often as non-Jewish girls." Let us analyze this declaration from a link with terrorists who has been honored by the Congress of the United States. With no documentation of any kind, he asks us to believe (1) that he "knew" all of the girls who were held in clandestine prisons between 1974 and 1978; (2) that he knew everything that went on in these "clandestine" prisons during those years, including every "violation" of every girl. The word clandestine means secret and not known to the public or to any but a select few. Even an Argentine official in charge of these "clandestine" prisons would not have had access to the information which the Jewish propagandist inflicts on the American saps gullible enough to buy anything written by a Jew.

Argentines were so incensed by the foul fantasies of Timerman's book, and the worldwide circulation of them by his American publishers, that the Jewish community of Argentina hastily denounced him as a complete faker and liar. He admits in his book, p. 71, "The Argentine government steadfastly insisted that I was not arrested for being a Jew, nor for being a journalist." As the apologist for the Jews William Buckley pointed out, Timerman does not mention Graiver anywhere in his book, for to do so would be to admit his terrorist connection and the reason for his arrest. The arrest of Timerman signified that the Montaneros were now in significant retreat throughout Argentina, and this indicated that the Communists must take a new tack in their drive to subdue and conquer the only white nation in South America.

The Falkland Islands crisis is the new program of the Soviets to seize Argentina like a ripe plum. It was orchestrated by the pathetic Jew-ridden and bankrupt government of England, aided and abetted by the Jewish regime of Ronnie Reagan in Washington, and sparkplugged by the notorious Alexander Haig, former goy stooge of Henry Kissinger, who grovelled at the feet of this emigrant Jew for years in order to obtain his present position in Washington. To look at the face of Alexander Haig is to see the complete surrender of integrity by a shabez goi wretch who has embraced the possibility of exercising influence and power in the United States only by becoming the faceless tool of the biological parasitic Jew. Haig performed brilliantly in his adoption of the Kissinger "shuttle diplomacy" technique, as he travelled back and fourth between Argentina and England. His mission was simply to buy time for the British fleet to come within striking distance of the Falkland Islands, while stalling the Argentine government and holding out the false claim that "negotiations" would solve the issue. In fact, no negotiations were being carried on by either England or the United States. They sought only to give time for the British strike force to come into position for an assault on the Argentine garrison, while they hoped that the Argentine officials would then accept the offer of "assistance" from the Soviets. This "military aid" would, quite simply follow the tried and accepted technique by which the Soviets took over in succession the nations of Eastern Europe -- the installation of a Soviet "advisory group," public outrage by the people at the betrayal of their nation, and fullscale military dictatorship to "maintain order".

This plot was exposed, not by any journalist, but by a paid advertisement in the *Washington Post*, which had steadfastly refused to write the truth about the Falkland Islands "crisis". The advertisement, which appeared in the *Post* on April 30, 1982, was paid for by a pro-Argentine group, and was headlined "Russian Influence in the Falkland Crisis".

The advertisement stated that "The obvious intent of Russia is to sooner or later set up a puppet government in our country. "It pointed out that for months large numbers of Soviet submarines had been cruising in Argentine waters, well aware that the minuscule Argentine Navy had no means of discouraging them, and that the Russians had now contracted for 80% of Argentine wheat. Most ominous of all, the advertisement exposed the Soviet offers of "military assistance" which were made on the basis of the present artificial "emergency" in the hopes that the Argentine government would panic at the array of English military might, backed up by the influence of the American government, and that in desperation Argentina would accept the offer of the Soviets. This offer was first exposed in El Dia, Montevideo, April 7, 1982. The Argentine patriots who paid for the advertisement in the *Post* also demanded that "Argentina renounce numerous economic treaties signed with Communist countries".

The Jews cannot bear that any country in the world should exist as a "98%" white nation. Consequently the Jewish attack on Argentina has mounted each year since 1945, reaching a crescendo of hatred in the foul slanders against Peron and his wife Evita, a pious Christian whose life was devoted to charitable works. The Jews usually referred to her as "puta", the whore, just as they had referred to the Holy Mother of Christ in their sacred book of writings, the Talmud.

The arrogance of the Jews reached its height when a terrorist strike force flew to Argentina from Israel, seized a German refugee, Adolf Eichmann, and flew him back to Israel to be murdered. The purpose of the Eichmann case was to give some legitimacy to the Jewish fantasy that six million Jews had been killed in Germany during World War II. The Holocaust myth was a necessity for the continued existence of the bandit nation of Israel, because it was the vehicle by which they continued to extort many billions of dollars from the defeated German people. The United States continued to maintain a large force in Germany, solely to enforce the collection of the Holocaust funds from the captive German nation. At the same time, East Germany sneered at the ridiculous demands of the Jews and refused to pay Israel one cent. The American people were told that their soldiers were stationed in Germany to hold back the Soviets, although they admitted that the American forces could stop a Soviet advance for only one or two hours! The only purpose for the Americans in Germany was to ensure that any German official or citizen who objected to further Holocaust payments to the Jews could promptly be arrested and punished. This remains true to the present day.

When Argentina protested against the blatant violation of her sovereignty as a nation by the Israeli terrorists who invaded her soil to kidnap and murder Adolf Eichmann, the United States immediately threatened economic and military sanctions against Argentina and every possible step short of declaring war. The government of Argentina, aghast that the United States should aid and abet such a crime against international law, withdrew the protest against Israel, thus encouraging other transgressions by the Israeli terrorists, such as the bombing of the Iraq reactor, the daily slaughters of Arab women and children in refugee camps in Lebanon, and other crimes against humanity committed by the Jews. Few Americans care to admit that their nation is today the most despised country in the world, often finding itself standing alone in its defense of Jewish atrocities, because it has encouraged the Israeli bandits to commit every type of atrocity known to mankind against helpless civilians in every nation unfortunate enough to come into contact with these outlaws.

Once again, the United States, through such pathetic stooges as Reagan and Haig, incites against itself the hatred of the civilized world through its encouragement of the Jewish war against white nations. The announcement of American official support for the British plan of attack against Argentina means that once again the American people will be billed for the terrible costs of rousing the anger of all the Latin American nations against her, because she is once again committed to the most horrible plans of the Jews in their assault against civilized peoples. These bills are coming due each day in the declining world prestige of the United States, its collapsing economy, its culture of degenerate drug-crazed mulattoes, and its political actions on behalf of Jewish terrorism which have become a stench in the nostrils of decent people everywhere.

THE $5 TRILLION COLD WAR HOAX

INTRODUCTION

P T Barnum said it for all time, "There's a sucker born every minute." For more than four decades, the American people have been terrorized, not by a foreign threat, but by their own government. In order for the Federal Reserve System central bankers to continue to loot the nation after the successful conclusion of the I Second World War, they had to invent a new threat. The only candidate was our erstwhile gallant ally, the Soviet Union. The central bank conspirators faced the task of continuing to mobilize the people against a terrible threat, taxing them heavily in order to save them from destruction.

Today, we are burdened by a $5 trillion national debt. Coincidentally, that is the sum we have spent on "national defense" since 1945. The World Order billionaires launched a complex, long-term plan to demonize Soviet Russia. Overnight, they would undergo a sea change, from the darlings of the American political Establishment to a dangerous and possibly overwhelming enemy. la my researches of more than fifty years, I finally located the smoking gun which exposed this conspiracy, a little known article in the August 1977 issue of American Heritage magazine, "Who Started the Cold War?" by historian Charles L. Mee Jr., editor of Horizon magazine, and author of one of the first cold war books, Meeting at Potsdam.

"SCARE THE HELL OUT OF THE COUNTRY"

In this article, Mee writes that on Feb. 27, 1947, "President Truman met with Congressional leaders in the White House.

Undersecretary of State Dean Acheson was present at the meeting, and Truman had him tell the Congressmen what was at stake. Acheson spoke for ten minutes, informing the legislators that nothing less than the survival of the whole of Western civilization was in the balance at that moment; he worked in references to ancient Athens, Rome, and the course of

Western civilization and freedom since those times. The Congressmen were silent for a few moments, and then, at last. Senator Arthur Vandenberg of Michigan, a prominent Republican who had come to support an active foreign policy, spoke up. All this might be true, Vandenberg said, but, if the President wishes to sell his program to the American people, he would have to 'scare hell out of the country'. It was at that moment that the Cold War began in earnest for the United States."

This is one of the most revealing statements in American history. This is the smoking gun which proves that the federal government used a terror campaign to frighten the American people into supporting four decades of Cold War spending on armaments. The initial campaign was the "atom bomb scare", which raged for some years; it finally lost its effectiveness, and was replaced by the ogre, based solely on falsified and invented CIA statistics, that Soviet Russia was the most terrifying military power, with the fastest growing economy, in the world. These two CIA claims were mutually exclusive; no nation could have the world's greatest military machine and at the same time support the world's fastest growing economy, but the statisticians successfully sold this scare story for years.

CHURCHILL LAUNCHES COLD WAR

The Cold War, the Hegelian invention of Soviet Russia and the United States at each other's throats, the "free world" vs. the "slave empire", Capitalism vs. Communism, was the final triumph of dialectical materialism, also invented by the German philosopher, Hegel. He laid down the dictum that to rule the world, you create a problem; you find an antidote to that problem; and you throw the two conflicting theses against each other, to result in a consensus or resolution. This diabolical and cynical formula reached its apogee in the Cold War. Hopefully, we will not see another such travesty of history.

Hard on the conclusion of the Second World War, the Colossus of the United States stood astride the entire world. With the world's largest economy, never touched by a single bomb or artillery shell throughout the war, the largest army, and a proud and victorious people, it was incredible that the United States could for a moment seriously regard the war-devastated Soviet Union as a threat. Stalin lost forty million people during the war; his nation was in rains. He desperately needed a breathing space in which to recover. Miraculously, the World Order invention of the Cold War came to his rescue. None other than Stalin's co-conspirator, Winston Churchill, was chosen to launch this new "problem".. Now unemployed, Churchill was desperate to get back into the limelight. At the invitation of President Truman, Churchill was brought to the United States to deliver a speech at little Fulton College, in Truman's home state of Missouri.

On March 5, 1946, at Fulton, Churchill made his famous "Iron Curtain" speech. He warned that an "Iron Curtain" had descended upon Europe, the Communist enslavement of the Eastern European countries. He failed to mention that he and Franklin Delano Roosevelt had joined at Yalta to deliver Eastern Europe to Stalin, with Alger Hiss, the originator of the plan, beaming in the background. Not a single journalist, anywhere in the world, mentioned Churchill's overwhelming personal complicity in creating and maintaining the dire situation which he now publicly deplored.

The Conversion of Senator Arthur Vandenberg

One of Washington's leading political strategists, Senator Arthur Vandenberg had warned his co-conspirators at the Feb. 27, 1947 White House meeting that to sell the prospective Cold War program, they would have to "scare hell out of the country". He had an interesting background. A millionaire newspaper publisher in Grand Rapids, Michigan (later to become famous as the home of President Gerald Ford),

Vandenberg had been elected to the Senate in 1925. A rock-ribbed Republican, he voted against New Deal measures such as the Social Security Act. He was Republican minority leader, and Capitol Hill's leading isolationist. When the United Nations proposal came to Congress, no one in Washington doubted that Vandenberg would shoot it down.

All of Washington was amazed when Senator Vandenberg rose on the Senate floor, on January 10, 1945, and called for the establishment of the United Nations. As George Stimpson, founder of the National Press Club, later explained to me, America's leading isolationist had become a rabid internationalist in a single night. A beautiful blonde agent from British Secret Intelligence Service had been sent to his room. After an all night political discussion, Senator Vandenberg awakened to become the new champion of the United Nations. Although a little known story, it epitomizes how things are accomplished in Washington, today as yesterday.

This is the Senator who is described in the Dictionary of National Biography as "a jingoist and chauvinist who supported the aggressive foreign policies of Theodore Roosevelt and Taft." Franklin D. Roosevelt rewarded Vandenberg for his treachery by sending him as a special delegate to San Francisco with Alger Hiss to draft the United Nations Charter. The White House continued to shower gifts on Vandenberg, even going so far as to make his favorite nephew, General Hoyt Vandenberg, Commanding General of the United States Air Force.

THE FLOOZIES OF WASHINGTON

During our discussions at the National Press Club in 1948, the subject of Senator Arthur Vandenberg's overnight conversion to the congressional champion of the United Nations was examined in detail. We recalled a fellow agent of the blonde British Secret Service agent who accomplished this mission, one Kaye Summersby, who had been chosen to mollify General Eisenhower, Commanding General of the entire European Theater during the Second World War. Summersby's intelligence training included the arts of the ancient Byzantine hetaerae, who were skilled in the arts of "unendurable pleasure, indefinitely prolonged". With Summersby as his chauffeur, Eisenhower was delivered to small country hotels in England, while his adviser, the political commissar Capt. Edward M. M. Warburg, of the banking family, ran the war from London. The enraptured general notified his superior, George Marshall, that he was divorcing Mamie Eisenhower to marry the princess of endless delights, which of course was never in the cards. Marshall promptly reported this development to President Truman, who was furious, notifying Ike that it was out of the question (Plain Speaking, by Merle Miller). Kaye ended her days as a permanent house guest on a Rothschild estate on Long Island.

Another British agent, Pamela Digby Churchill, married to Winston Churchill's son, later married Averill Harriman, the unofficial foreign minister of the United States. Harriman's exploits in travelling the world, instructing the heads of nations in how to conduct their affairs, was legendary. He became the subject of a series of novels by Upton Sinclair, chronicling the feats of one Lanny Budd (Harriman) throughout the world. Harriman spent the last two years of World War II at Stalin's Kremlin headquarters, dictating to Stalin how he should conduct the war. After his death, Pamela Churchill Harriman took over the Democratic National Committee. She is now our Ambassador to Paris, the most desired appointment in our foreign service, presiding over 1100 employees.

HARRIMAN'S REPLY

When Charles T. Mee Jr.'s historic article appeared in American Heritage magazine in August of 1977, the editors notified Averill Harriman and gave him the chance to reply in the same issue. Harriman's response was headlined "We Can't Do Business with Stalin". The Communist dictator who had been Harriman's lackey throughout the war was now dismissed as uncooperative! Harriman recounts in great detail the repressive policies of Stalin towards the captive nations in Eastern Europe (policies which Harriman himself had initiated), and goes on to denounce Mee's astounding report as "revisionist". "Mr. Mee has made his own sketchy revision of standard revisionist doctrine," quoting Mee's statement that "the Cold War served everybody's purpose." Truman needed an excuse for deficit spending, because without it he could not have kept the American economy busy and productive. Thus he waged a Cold War, after the hot war was won, to justify continued deficit spending. With the Truman Doctrine and the Marshall Plan, the encouragement of American multinational companies, and a set of defense treaties that came finally to encompass the world, he institutionalized it."

As Charles T. Mee Jr. points out in his article, Stalin was a principal beneficiary of the Cold War. " Stalin needed the Cold War, not to venture out into the world again after an exhausting war, but to discipline his restless people at home. He had need of that ancient stratagem of monarchs the threat of an implacable external enemy to be used to unite his own people in Russia." Mee also names Winston Churchill as a prime suspect in the Cold War conspiracy. He states that Churchill "emerged from World War II with a ruined empire, irretrievably in debt, an empire losing its colonies and headed inevitably toward bankruptcy. Churchill's scheme for saving Great Britain was to arrange to have America and Russia quarrel, while America and Russia quarreled, England would as American diplomats delicately put it 'lead' Europe". As had been the case for some three hundred years, "leading" Europe and the United States meant that Great Britain would make frequent use of its secret weapon, the Secret Intelligence Service. Its powers included, as we have seen, reversing the entire foreign policy of the United States overnight, from isolationism to an abject embracing of the United Nations; making the most prominent American general and future President a "love slave" of a ruthless intelligence agent, and much, much more, most of which we shall never know.

THE FIRST VICTIMS OF THE COLD WAR

The first victims of the Cold War were not soldiers; they were American politicians who were reluctant to embrace the new campaign. The first casualty was elder statesman Henry Stimson, who wrote a memo to President Truman in the autumn of 1945, cited by Mee as the cause of Stimson's disappearance from Washington. Stimson's memo denounced the projected Cold War as a serious error, and called for "satisfactory relations" with Russia. Henry Wallace, Secretary of Commerce, also protested against the Cold War, he was allowed to resign. Mee identifies the "comers" in Washington as those who were quick to latch onto the Cold War as "the wave of the future". Those who tended to believe in an aggressive attitude toward Russia, were spotted, and promoted young men such as John Foster Dulles and Dean Rusk. George Kennan, then in the American Embassy in Moscow, was discovered after he sent a perfervid 8,000 word telegram back to Washington. "We have here a political force committed fanatically to the belief that with U.S. there can be no permanent Modus Vivendi, that it is desirable and necessary that the internal harmony of our society be disrupted, our traditional way of life be destroyed, the international authority of our state be broken." Mee mentions that, in his memoirs, Kennan says that he now looks back on his cable 'with horrified amusement'. "At the time, however, he was ideal for Truman's use, and he was recalled from Moscow and made chairman of the State Department's Policy Planning Committee, or as the New York Times called him, 'America's global planner'."

THE EGGHEADS

Critics of the new Cold War foreign policy quickly found a nickname for its architects, "the eggheads". Like George Kennan, they were liberal intellectuals, often prematurely bald, and unanimous in their dislike of the American people, whom they hated and feared, and their Constitution. Their goal, which they now seem to have achieved, was to liberate the federal government, which Thomas Jefferson and the other Founding Fathers had written to "bind down the government with the chains of the Constitution". While ostensibly following an "anti-Communist" policy, the eggheads never forswore their dedication to Marxism, and its monolithic state.

During the four decades of the Cold War, Hollywood, which never failed to bolster the goals of the Cold War architects, reserved its bitter scorn for "red-blooded Americans" who stood for flag and country. While forbearing from ever presenting lifelong Communists in a deprecating way, Hollywood made films deriding "anti-Communists" as flag-waving American Legion boobs, a stance which it continues to this day. If any one of the eggheads and their Hollywood lackeys were to be called a "patriot", they would be overcome with shame.

A PHONY WAR

During most of its history, the Cold War was a propaganda war, in which the opponents hurled invectives at each other. However, the military-industrial complex cannot make billions of dollars from propaganda; there had to be occasions of real shooting. We endured the Korean War and the Vietnam War, with hundreds of thousands of casualties, while Soviet Russia did not lose a man in either war. Both Russia and the United States were careful to have the scenes of battle take place thousands of miles from their own lands, in poverty-stricken countries such as Korea and Vietnam. We had the Cuban missile crisis, a soap opera in which the media convinced Americans that they had been on the brink of atomic destruction, being saved just before the bombs were launched by the "incredible diplomatic skills" of John F. Kennedy and Khrushchev, neither of whom before or after this crisis had ever shown the slightest skill at diplomacy. The Berlin Wall was built, to prevent all of its population from fleeing the desolation of Communist East Germany. The eggheads greeted the Berlin Wall with praise. President John F. Kennedy made a special trip to Germany to put his seal of approval on the Berlin Wall, and to reassure the Communists that the United States would not remove it. And we never did. It was the Germans themselves, driven beyond endurance, who ripped it down, much to the consternation of our eggheads in Washington.

A METEORIC CAREER

Although few Americans recognize the name of **George Kennan**, he not only was the source of the nickname "egghead", he also was the bureaucrat entrusted with the maintenance of the Gold War in Washington for many years. He was named after his uncle, George Kennan, who spent many years travelling in Czarist Russia on "missionary work" for the world Communist movement. He was entrusted with many millions of dollars by **Jacob Schiff**, known as "A Prince in Israel", who was born in the Rothschild house in Frankfurt, and who, according to his grandson, John Schiff, had spent twenty-two-million dollars of his, personal funds to bring about the Bolshevik Revolution in Russia. Most of this money was spent on revolutionary propaganda, which Kennan, with journalistic credentials, distributed throughout Russia. Some historians credit George Kennan as the pivotal force in the Bolshevik Revolution, pointing out that it was his distributing of thousands of revolutionary leaflets to officers in the Czar's Army which turned them against the regime and led to the downfall of the Czar.

George Kennan also worked with Jacob Schiff in financing Japan in the Russo-Japanese War of 1905. The Japanese government decorated Kennan with the Gold War Medal, and the Order of the Sacred Treasure. (The World Order, by Eustace Mullins, p. 64). Schiff instigated this war to strike a blow against the alleged oppression of Jews in Russia, and to create a governmental crisis by which the Communists could seize power. The "1905 Revolution" failed miserably; the Communists had to wait twelve more years, with Schiff's continued support, before they could seize power.

REMARKABLE HERITAGE

To those who have studied the history of the twentieth century, it is not at all paradoxical that the American government should have entrusted its foreign policy towards Russia to someone named after the man who is credited with bringing about the Bolshevik Revolution. When Franklin D. Roosevelt, repaying Communist support which gave him victory in his presidential race against Herbert Hoover, promptly extended diplomatic recognition to Stalin, it was George Kennan who was chosen to accompany Ambassador William Bullitt to Moscow to reopen the American

Embassy. It was George Kennan who wrote the notorious 8,000-word "long telegram" sent from Moscow to Washington on Dec. 22, 1946, where, as he points out, it caused a sensation, and led to his being summoned back to Washington to head the newly created post of head of Policy Planning.

Kennan states in his memoirs that he had the only office directly adjoining the office of Secretary of State General George Marshall, and that it was lie, Kennan, who actually drafted the text of the Marshall Plan.

THE POLICY OF "CONTAINMENT"

However, it is as "X", the anonymous author of an article which appeared in the July, 1947 issue of Foreign Affairs, the official publication of the Council on Foreign Relations, titled "The Sources of Soviet Conduct", that George Kennan continues to be remembered in Washington. This article laid down the principle of "containment" which was to be official U.S. policy towards Russia for the remainder of the Cold War. No wonder the New York Times called Kennan "America's global planner". Henry Kissinger, who inherited the Kennan policy of the Cold War, wrote in White House Years, p. 135, that "George Kennan came as close to authoring the diplomatic doctrine of his era as any diplomat in our history."

Paul Kennedy, in The Rise and Fall of the Great Powers, defined the "policy of containment" as follows: "The view from Washington was that a master plan for world Communist domination was unfolding and needed to be 'contained'." Walter Lippmann, who was a one-man think tank in Washington for fifty years, and an adviser to many Presidents, adopted Kennan's policy in his influential The Cold War; a Study in United States Foreign Policy, as America's senior elder statesman.

Kennan's "containment" policy was just that; that the Soviet Union and world Communism would be contained, but never openly challenged or fought against. It was a permanent guarantee that the captive nations of Eastern Europe, which had been delivered to Stalin by Roosevelt, Churchill and Alger Hiss at Yalta, would never be liberated from Communism. An organization championing the captive nations was for many years the most hated and derided group in Washington, Composed of a few Congressmen from Chicago and Cleveland who had strong ethnic backing from Poles, Czechs and other Eastern Europe countries, it was a political embarrassment for many years to the oligarchs of the Cold War.

THE MEN BEHIND CONTAINMENT

In his memoirs, Kennan mentions that one of the principal sponsors of his containment policy was then Secretary of the Navy James Forrestal, who later, as Secretary of Defense, became one of a long list of "Washington suicides", a special category a la Vince Foster. Although published in Foreign Affairs, a magazine read only by the Elite, it was quickly taken up by Arthur Krock of the New York Times, the most influential journalist in Washington. He reprinted the article in the New York Times, describing it as the "most important foreign relations document of the century". A shorter version of the containment article was then published in Life magazine. It had now inundated the country.

Kennan states in his memoirs, "I emphatically deny the paternity of any efforts to invoke the doctrine of containment today." He downplays both the "long telegram" and the article by "X", claiming that they have been "misunderstood". He modestly ignores the fact that he laid down the policy which our government has followed for forty years. His reward was a post as professor at the elite think tank in Princeton, the Institute for Advanced Study, where he has worked since 1950, with interim appointments as

Ambassador to Russia and to Yugoslavia. He also was awarded the Albert Einstein Peace Prize, presumably for avoiding a Third World War by his policy of containment (my studies have shown that a Third World War between Russia and the United States was never seriously considered by anyone in authority). It was only a "War Game".

TECHNIQUES OF THE COLD WAR

The government propaganda techniques by which the American people were terrorized for some forty years began with the dire threat of nuclear annihilation. School children went through daily drills of falling to the floor in terror of the atomic bomb which would destroy their school. Their parents built backyard "bomb shelters" stocked with food and water. Because "scientific studies" showed that the radiation peril would last for at least five hundred years, the survivors apparently expected to spend that much time in their shelters. Nationwide philosophical debates ensued as to whether the survivors, huddled in their shelters after the blast, should open the door to neighbors or to "minorities" who had neglected to build bomb shelters, or whether they should shoot those who battered down the doors to get food. Hollywood loyally produced many movies about the coming atomic debacle, such as Dr. Strangelove, in which insane fascists were determined to use the bomb to destroy the civilized world; War Games, in which a mad computer tried to trick the United States and Russia into destroying each other; and a steady stream of films depicting "Bette Davises" as little old librarians who were determined that students should be allowed to read the works of Karl Marx.

THE CIA RIDES TO THE RESCUE

After years of exposure to the imminent threat of being vaporized in an atomic blast, Americans began to ignore the threat;

many of them bulldozed their bomb shelters into swimming pools. It was obvious to our masters that new techniques of terror had to be developed. The Central Intelligence Agency now became the vehicle of mass terrorism. It became known as "the Company" under the leadership of stock promoter Bill Casey. He became highly skilled at peddling alarming statistics about the threat of Communism to Congress, who hastily voted vast increases in the "defense" budget. The oligarchs abandoned the now worn out doctrine of nuclear annihilation. There would be no need to spend two-hundred-and-fifty-billion dollars a year on tanks, guns and airplanes if they were all to be vaporized by a single bomb. The defense budget had been brought from a low of $13 billion in 1947 to a continuous budget in the hundreds of billions. With its top secret budget of hundreds of millions of dollars a year, never to be examined by anyone, the CIA sent its own James Bonds all over the world usually to attack and overthrow "anti-Communist" governments and "dictators" such as Ferdinand Marcos, who had been indiscreet in their denunciations of Communism. The CIA hired hundreds of journalists to write books and articles promoting its version of the Cold War, always at the highest prevailing rates.

EFFECTS OF THE COLD WAR

The effect on both Russia and the United States of the Cold War conspirators has been devastating. Russia's economy is in a state of collapse, with no improvement in sight. The United States has been looted; its infrastructure, its roads, bridges and other assets need many billions in immediate repair. We have the $5 trillion Cold War debt; but the most destructive effect on our nation is the Cold War's effect on our morality.

The years of being terrorized by the atomic threat had a very destructive effect on morality. If we were to be vaporized at any time, it seemed worthwhile to seize the moment, to take pleasure, money and any other rewards while they were available, without (bought for the consequences, since there would be no consequences. We have now endured the effects of this poisonous doctrine for several generations.

The effect of the CIA propaganda lies about the "great Soviet Union" which might take over the world at any moment has been equally destructive. When conservative economist Paul Craig Roberts landed in Moscow during the height of the CIA propaganda campaign, he was stunned to find that Soviet Russia had "a Third World economy". I had proved in my writings that the United States taxpayer had been subsidizing the Soviet Union since 1917. In fact, Americans have been living a lie for four decades, the lie that we were in dire peril from "the Communist threat". This lie has been demoralizing; it has placed us on the brink of bankruptcy; and it poses the challenge to us: When are we going to get rid of our Cold War conspirators? They must pay the price for the destruction they have wrought on our nation. We must drive them out of every office; bring them to trial for their high treason; and restore the Republic which our Founding Fathers bequeathed to us. It is this task not sad jokes about "balancing the budget" which will determine whether this nation will survive to the twenty-first century.

There's a Gulag in Your Future

America in the Bicentennial year showed many of the characteristics of Russia in 1910. The white middle class is working hard, saving money, educating their children, and buying real estate and insurance from their earnings. On the surface, it seems a comfortable, predictable world, but terrible forces are at work. Like Russia in 1910, America in 1976 has well organized revolutionary groups infiltrating every part of society, and especially into the religious, educational, and governmental institutions. As for the press, one need hardly mention that journalism has always been one of the most sordid types of prostitution, and American journalists have eagerly allied themselves with what they believe to be the great power of the immediate future, the Satanic powers of international Communism.

Despite the billions of dollars which Americans are spending on insurance, they are not spending one cent on any insurance against the only real threat on the horizon, that is, the certainty that all of their property will be confiscated and that they will be placed in forced labor camps to work and to die.

The following quote stands for itself: "Many camp points were known for executions and mass graves; Orotukan, and Polyarny Spring, and Svistoplyas, and Annushka, and even the agricultural camp Dukcha, but the most famous of all on this account were the Zolotisy Goldfields. At Zolotisty they used to summon a brigade from the mine face in broad daylight and shoot the members down one after another. (And this was not a substitute for night executions, they took place too.) When the chief of Yuglag, Nikolai Andreyevich Aglanov, arrived, he liked, at lineup, to pick out some brigade or other which had been at fault for something or other and order it to be taken aside. And then he used to empty his pistol into the frightened, crowded mass of people, accompanying his shots with happy shouts. The corpses were left unburied."

Of course, we have read this sort of stuff many times, from the Nuremberg Trials, about the Germans mistreating the Jews, but wait, Aglanov, Zolotisty, these are not German names. This must be a quote from Alexsandr Solzhenitsyn's book, THE GULAG ARCHIPELAGO. And on page 389, Volume Two of this work, we find a very significant passage:

"But some transports of condemned zeks arrived too late, and they continued to arrive with five to ten people at a time. A detachment of killers would receive them at the Old Brickyard station and lead them to the old bathhouse to a booth lined with three or four layers of blankets inside. There the condemned prisoners were ordered to undress in the snow and enter the bath naked. Inside, they were shot with pistols. In the course of one and a half months about two hundred persons were destroyed in this way. The corpses were burned in the tundra."

In this passage, Solzhenitsyn is describing the execution of Trotskyite prisoners at a Moscow train station in April 1938. It sounds all too familiar, because hundreds of pages of sworn testimony describing these incidents were taken down at the Nuremberg Trials and used to condemn the legally elected officials of the German nation to be executed for "war crimes"! How did this come about? When the German Army made its lightning dash into Russia in June of 1941, the Soviet leaders realized that Jews in the captured border cities would be the first to collaborate with their conquerors. Stalin ordered all the Jews in the path of the German advance to be rounded up and hauled to the interior on cattle trains. Many of them were sealed, and most of them had no food or water. As a result, many thousands of Jews died in horrible circumstances. Also in the path of the German advance were a number of huge

Soviet slave labor camps. There was no possibility of evacuating them, and the Russian guards herded prisoners into large groups and massacred them with machine gun fire. When the Germans captured these areas, they were stunned to find large mounds of unburied corpses.

In order to have proof of the savage mentality of the Communist commissars, the Germans methodically photographed the scenes of these massacres, and took statements from some survivors who had fled into the woods. At Nuremberg, in order to have a legal excuse for killing the captured Germans, the victors changed the statements and photos to read "German guards" where they had formerly read "Russian guards" and changed the locale of the massacres to read "Auschwitz", "Dachau" and other German camp areas instead of the true Russian ones.

The Henry Kissinger' s, German refugee Jews who swarmed into Germany with the American Army, and who became the new commissars of the defeated people, had embarked on this venture with the modest proposal of using these forged accusations as their excuse for exterminating the entire German people, a la Morgenthau. However, as usual, the Jewish duplicity paid unexpected dividends when it was decided to extort ten billion dollars in "reparations" from the vanquished Germans to pay for the Jews whom the Soviets had killed. Today, the defeated Germans are still paying vast sums of money to the State of Israel for the Jews who died in Stalin's death trains.

Solzhenitsyn does not touch upon this aspect of history, apparently because he does not know of it. However, he does expose the fact that the entire Soviet slave labor camp system was built up by Jews. On page 79, vol. II *GULAG ARCHIPELAGO*, he reproduces the faces of the six Jews who were responsible for designing the entire system and bringing it into being. They are Aaron Solts, Naftaly Frenkel, Yakov Rappaport, Matvei Berman,

Lazar Kogan and Genrikh Yagoda. So little has been known to the West of the Soviet slave camps that the first four names are unknown to students of the Communist atrocities. Luzar Kogan (Cohen), of course, became the Commissar of Industry, and Yagoda became head of the secret police. In fact, most of the Soviet hierarchy under Stalin worked their way up from managing the slave labor camps, because this was the only part of the entire Soviet economy which was functioning! Even today, the slave labor camps are the only portion of the Soviet system which meet production norms, and the Soviet system depends on them and on aid from the Western democracies. Without these two factors, the Russian economy would collapse within a few months.

The faces of the six Jews whom Solzhenitsyn exposes as the founders of the slave labor system give a more than adequate explanation why the German Zionist, Henry Kissinger, refused to allow President Ford to meet with Solzhenitsyn. Recruited as the Soviet agent Bor while serving with the U.S. Army in Germany, Kissinger had carried out many high-level operations for the Soviet Union, but few were more crucial than preventing Solzhenitsyn from coming to the White House. Our Washington officials have always denied any knowledge of the existence of the slave camps even though hundreds of American citizens have been imprisoned and died in them. Solzhenitsyn quotes a figure by Professor of Statistics Kurganov that from 1917 to 1959, sixty-six million people have died in Russia's slave labor camps! At the end of World War II, the Jews at Nuremberg, in casting about for a figure which they could claim as the number of Jews killed in the war, at first seized upon the then total of the victims of the Russian camps, sixty million, and seriously proposed this as the basis for negotiating their extortion of money from the defeated German people! cooler heads among them prevailed, and they decided upon the more reasonable figure of six million Jews, which they claimed had been "exterminated" by the Germans. The actual figure, of course, was about two thousand Jews who had died from typhus in the German camps after American air strikes had cut off German supplies.

Since the Communist system could not function without slave labor, concentration camps appeared only a few months after Lenin and the Bolsheviks seized power in Russia. Solzhenitsyn reports that in August 1918, Lenin sent a telegram to the Penza Provisional Executive Committee, where the peasants were already revolting against the Bolsheviks, "Lock up all the gulag doubtful ones in a concentration camp outside the city". Ten days later, a decree was sent out ordering mass executions. It also stated, "Secure the Soviet Republic against its class enemies by isolating them in concentration camps".

In prior usage, concentration camps had referred to prisoners of war, but no nation had ever considered using such camps to imprison its own citizens. Furthermore, the "class enemies" of the new Soviet Republic were no longer the "aristocrats" and "oppressors", but the peasants and workers who were to be enslaved to support the new regime. Thus began the vast network of camps which came to be known as the Glavnoye Upravlenye Lagerei, or Office of Penal Labor Camps, whose initials were read as Gulag, and which became known as the principal part of the Soviet Empire, the Gulag Archipelago, the many millions of faceless slaves who toiled for their Soviet masters.

Maps detailing the location of these camps have been circulated in the United States since 1947, but the State Department has always denied their existence. Furthermore, the United States has persistently refused to bring up the question of these camps before the United Nations, thus sparing the largest slave holding state in the world, the Soviet Union, the public embarrassment of discussing its slave policies. No wonder Kissinger was told by Moscow that Solzhenitsyn must not be allowed to come to the

White House. Suppose Ford, with one of his usual gaffes, would later refer to the slave camps in talking with reporters!

Solzhenitsyn describes the most important single official who devised the scheme of operations of the Gulag Archipelago as Naftaly Frenkel, a Turkish Jew. Frenkel had become a multi-millionaire timber king in Turkey, and after the Bolshevik Revolution, he became a resident Soviet intelligence agent in Constantinople. In his role, he created a large black market exchanging Soviet paper rubies for gold. Although he obtained millions for the Soviets through these transactions, there were large scale frauds, and in 1927, while in Russian, he was arrested and sent to prison. After a few months at Solovki prison, he arranged a personal meeting with Stalin, with whom he talked for three hours. The entire time was spent by Frenkel describing the methods he had devised for getting the most work out of the slave labor. Stalin was so impressed that he adopted the entire package. Basically it consisted of making sure that every prisoner worked every day of his entire sentence, and that a system of food rationing be adopted which he had copied from the Eskimos, a fish on a pole held out in front of the running dog team.

With Stalin's blessing, Frenkel was freed and placed in charge of the construction of the White Sea Baltic Canal, also known as the Belomor Canal. One hundred thousand prisoners died during the first winter of working under the Jew Frenkel's command.

Nevertheless, foreign visitors were brought to such projects to be convinced of the greatness of the Soviet Union. Supreme Court Judge Leigowitz of New York State visited one of these slave labor camps and rapturously wrote of it in Life Magazine, "What an intelligent, farsighted humane administration from top to bottom. In serving out his term of punishment, the prisoner retains a feeling of dignity". Thus we come to a basic emotion of the biological parasite, which sees the gentile slave toiling for the enrichment of the parasite, and is overcome at the justice and the humaneness of it all.

Solzhenitsyn gives us many descriptions of mass killings at these camps, which were usually carried out because of a failure to meet a production norm, or because some of the prisoners balked at the terrible conditions. On page 390, he writes:

"A. B._v has told how executions were carried out at Adak----, a camp on the Pechora River. They would take the opposition members with their things out of the camp compound on a prisoner transport at night. And outside the compound stood the small house of the Third Section. The condemned men were taken into a room one at a time, and there the camp guards sprang on them. Their mouths were stuffed with something soft and their arms were bound with cords behind their backs. Then they were led out into the courtyard, where harnessed carts were waiting.

The bound prisoners were piled on the carts, from five to seven at a time, and driven off to the Gorka----, the camp cemetery.

On arrival they were tipped into big pits that had already been prepared and buried alive. Not out of brutality, no. It has been ascertained that when dragging and lifting them, it was much easier to cope with living people than with corpses. The work went on for many nights at Adak."

Despite many fictional accounts of the imaginary atrocities which were claimed to have occurred at German concentration camps, none of the Jewish faked stories equals the raw horror of Solzhenitsyn's true accounts of the Russian slave labor camps. The Jews must be green with envy. They had tried, to the limits of their imaginations, to invert terrible things which they could use to accuse the vanquished Germans, and Solzhenitsyn has surpassed them in horror a thousand times.

Americans may wonder why no story of the Russian concentration camps ever makes it into the movies or television. The reason is quite simple, there is no room. All of American television and movies are taken up with horror stories of the Nazis and their camps. Despite the fact that the Nazi camps have been empty since 1945, for forty years thousands of American movies and television shows have depicted fictional happenings at these camps, while not one movie has been made about the Russian camps, despite the fact that millions of slave laborers continue to die in these camps. The notorious Zionist propagandist, Billy Graham, is currently raking in millions of dollars to finance his propaganda work for Israel by distributing a movie "The Upper Room", about the supposed terrors of Nazism, yet he has ignored many letters asking why he doesn't film stories from The Gulag Archipelago.

However, we write today of the horrors of the Soviet slave camps, not merely from pity for their victims, but because these camps are the blueprint for the America of tomorrow, the America which our educators and our preachers and our government Officials are planning for us. The locations of the camps are already known, and the ingenuity of our nation is adding a new dimension in horror for our complacent white American middle class. Not only do we have thousands of clever Jewish Naftaly Frenkels to plan the operation of the American slave labor camps, but they will be staffed with the most brutal types of black guards, who can be relied upon to surpass the brutalities of the Soviet terrorists. All over America, thousands of Negroes are being recruited into "correctional" work (The legislation making the concentration camps official in Russia was called the Corrective Labor Act of 1924). These Negroes are being trained in the most advanced techniques of brutalizing and dehumanizing the white Americans who will become their vlctuns. And perhaps our American leaders, with their genius for exceeding numerical accomplishments reached in other countries, will be able to surpass the world record of sixty-six million victims murdered in the Soviet slave labor camps. Perhaps we can murder one hundred million white Americans in the camps which are expected to be put in operation here in the next several years.

Meanwhile, the white American middle class spends not one penny to avoid its certain fate, but continues to pile up savings and real estate for those who are ruthless enough and determined enough to take it away from them by force. We refer, of course, to the biological Jew and his willing ally, the Negro terrorists. It is no accident that Henry Kissinger, at this very moment in time, is in Africa hysterically preaching the destruction of the white race, for he and his colleagues intend to wipe us out, not merely in Africa, but throughout the world. It was not an idle observation when his close friend, the Jewess and writer Suzanne Langer, wrote in the New York Times, "The white race is the cancer of history".

THE HOLOCAUST EXPLAINED

Holocaust -- from the meaning wholly burnt. 1) a sacrifice wholly consumed by fire. 2) complete consumption by fire. Oxford English Dictionary.

If the Jewish claim that they were the victims of a holocaust in Germany is true, then they were consumed entirely by fire. This Jewish claim is unacceptable because there were so many survivors. Not only were the Jews not consumed wholly by fire, as they claim, but, forty years after this non-event, there are more Jews claiming to be survivors of the Holocaust than there were Jews living at the time of the Holocaust. In one small American suburb, Skokie, are now residing many thousands of healthy Jews who claim to be "survivors" of the Holocaust.

For more than thirty years, American voters have mutely accepted the fact that anyone seeking public office in the United States must make a routine pledge of undying allegiance to the State of Israel. Few of these voters realize that these office-seekers must also make a ritual obeisance to the Myth of the Holocaust and swear eternal belief in the doctrine that six million Jews were killed by the Germans during World War II. As was noted on the editorial page of the *Washington Post*, the regnant world journal of international Zionism, on October 29, 1981. "Anyone who refuses to support the State of Israel admits his sympathy for the murderers of six million Jews."

Webster's dictionary defines treason as "the offense of betraying the state or subverting the government of the state to which the subverter belongs." Officeholders of the United States who are sworn to uphold the Constitution of the United States and who then pledge allegiance to a foreign government and act in allegiance to that foreign government are guilty of high treason and are subject to the death penalty. The situation is more flagrant in the case of the State of Israel because, from its inception in 1948, the State of Israel has maintained a state of war against the citizens of the United States. If the objective of making war is to subdue another people and to seize their goods and enslave them, then Israel's activities towards the United States can only be described as engaging in constant warfare. Thus the Zionist collaborators all over the United States are giving aid and comfort to the enemies of the United States during a time of war. These acts of treason can only be punished by the death penalty.

The Zionist collaborators have as their sole excuse that they are aiding the Jews because they were the victims of the Holocaust. Unfortunately, this excuse has now been demolished by the revelations that there were no gas chambers and that the Germans had no plan to "exterminate" the Jews. In 1952, I wrote in "Blood and Gold", "The claim that Hitler killed 6,000,000 Jews is belied by their own figures in the *World Almanac*. Immediately after Germany's surrender, a plane load of American editors and correspondents were flown to the concentration camps, where they were shown huge piles of bones. These were the remains of Russian prisoners of war, but they were filmed and shown all over the United States as 'Jewish bones'. In one of the most revolting attempts to influence public opinion ever known, Jewish owned movie houses showed these gruesome photos over and over again."

Once again, we are inundated by the Jewish propaganda, as the ludicrous bone pictures, some of which have been established as having been taken during World War I, become our daily fare. The Public Broadcasting System, financed with taxpayers funds, recently showed a series of "holocaust" films, each more incredible than the last. In one, an elderly Jewess returns to Auschwitz, where she claims to have been incarcerated forty years age. "It voss a death camp?" she exclaims. She then stated that she remained there for four years, although the Germans "killed everybody every day." She was then asked how she has survived. "I hid in the camp," she explained, "but I had nothing to eat for three years."

After this astounding statement, she pointed to the rows of peaceful barracks and shrieked, "But just look! You can see for yourself it actually happened!" The bemused viewer, seeing only a pleasant rural scene, apparently was expected to conjure up visions of six million Jews being marched to the gas chambers.

Nearly all of the Jewish "survivors" claim that they lived in the "death camps" from three to four years, while "everybody was being killed". It seems obvious that no one could survive in a "labor camp", which is what these camps actually were. Over the entrance to each camp was placed a sign, "Arbeit Machs du Frei," or, "Work Makes You Free".

In the "Nation", Sept. 26, 1981, Albert Speer, the German Minister for Armaments, was quoted as having answered, in response to a demand from the leaders of the Jewish community in South Africa that he verify that Jews were killed during World War II by the Germans, so that they could prosecute the distributors of the pamphlet, "Did Six Million Really Die?", "I couldn't." Although Speer refused to submit to pressure from the Jews that he lie and "confess" that the Jews had been killed, he did admit some sort of "collective guilt" in the matter, but denied that he had any direct knowledge of any Holocaust activities. His admission of "guilt" brought praise from the Jewish agitator, Simon Weisenthal, who then proceeded to endorse Speer's new book, "Infiltration". However, this book defined the camps as labor camps. On p. 9, Speer writes, "During factory inspections, I saw concentration camp prisoners working in our plants among German workers."

Note that Speer does not even identify these laborers as Jews. On p. 41, he writes, "During my inspection (at Mauthausen, March, 1943,) I was surprised to see expensive granite retaining walls, on which barracks, likewise of native stone, had been erected. Everything was clean and orderly. The level, say, of an average anti aircraft barrack. The camp made an almost romantic impression with its stone portal and mediaeval castle yards, its pseudohistorical walls and towers."

The German soldier in the field never enjoyed such pleasant quarters as did the labor camp workers. Otto Friedrich, a senior editor of Time Magazine, wrote an article in *Atlantic Monthly*, Sept. 1981, which he stated was based entirely on the writings of survivors of the camps, and which could hardly be accused of painting a rosy picture of their existence. In "The Kingdom of Auschwitz", Friedrich writes, "Auschwitz was a society of extraordinary complexity. It had its own soccer stadium, its own library, its own soccer stadium, its own library, its own photo lab, and its own symphony orchestra ... There was no reason that a death camp should have a hospital at all, yet the one at Auschwitz grew to considerable size, with about twenty doctors and more than three hundred nurses."

Friedrich ignores the implications of his own writing, that a "death camp" with a large modern hospital is not a death camp at all, but a health camp. All of the camps had their own symphony orchestras, an amenity which was not provided by any of the twenty-two military stations at which this writer served in the United States Air Force throughout World War II. Friedrich also writes that Auschwitz had its own brothel for the workers. And a photo lab, in which the inmates could develop their snapshots of the millions of Jews being herded into the gas chambers? No such photos have ever been exhibited. Later in his article, Friedrich writes that Auschwitz actually was developed throughout the war into a vast industrial complex, with a network of thirty-four outlaying camps, which provided workers for cement plants, coal mines, and a steel factory. I.G. Farben operated a huge synthetic rubber plant there.

An intensely religious person, Adolf Hitler had written in *Mein Kampf* that "Hence today I believe that I am acting in accordance with the will of the Almighty Creator: by defending myself against the Jew, I am fighting for the work of the Lord ... The fight against Jewish world Bolshevization requires a clear attitude towards Soviet Russia. You cannot drive out the Devil with Beelzebub."

During the war, while fighting on two fronts, Hitler allowed himself to be swayed from these fervent sentiments by an extremely clever campaign on the part of the Jews. Having been warned that the Allies planned a campaign of terror bombing against German civilians, it was necessary that the Jews be evacuated from German cities. Through their close contacts with a number of Nazi bureaucrats, the leaders of the Jewish communities organized whereby the Jews would be evacuated in "the eastward migration". Even Speer approved the plan, but specified that "The ablebodied Jews destined for eastward migration must therefore interrupt their journey and do armaments labor." The result was that the labor camps were established in rural areas, far from the cities, and the Jews were spared the ordeal of the terrible bombings which engulfed German women and children in torrents of flame and phosphorus bombs. There was a Holocaust in Germany during World War II, but the victims were Germans, in a well-planned campaign of genocide, while the evacuated Jews survived en masse.

After the war, with their genius for perverting the truth, the Jews completely reversed the facts. Instead of the Holocaust engulfing German non-combatants in the cities, the victims were now the Jews, who had been "exterminated" in the "death camps". Since the evacuation of the Jews, the "eastward migration", had been organized at the behest of the Jewish leaders, many Jews now believed their own propaganda, and accused the Jewish leaders of having organized the "extermination" of European Jewry. Thus Hannah Arendt, a leading Jewish intellectual, writes bitterly, in "Eichmann in Jerusalem", "Wherever Jews lived, there were recognized Jewish leaders, and this leadership, almost without exception, cooperated in one way or another with the Nazis." Of course they cooperated, so successfully that while a million German women and children died in mass bombing raids on German cities, not a Jewish life was lost. The Allied bombing of Berlin killed so many German families that Eisenhower is remembered there today by the wry sobriquet, "the Mad Butcher of Berlin".

The firestorms created by bombing the cities of Cologne, Hamburg, Dresden and other German cities remain the greatest atrocities of World War II.

It was to obscure the real atrocities of World War II that the Myth of the Jewish Holocaust was invented. Its earliest application was intended to cover up the discovery that the Soviet Army had systematically murdered 14,000 Polish officers in the Katyn Forest. These Polish officers comprised the most highly educated and skilled segment of the Polish population. Stalin ordered them exterminated to facilitate Communist rule in Poland. It was the Katyn massacre which later became the inspiration for the stories of columns of Jews being marched into rural areas and executed. Indeed, the basic purpose of the invention of the Holocaust Myth was to prevent Soviet Russia from being embarrassed by any mention of the Katyn Forest massacre at the Nuremberg Trials. Roosevelt's pro-Communist regime battled valiantly to assist Russia in covering up the Katyn horror. Elmer Davis, who had been placed in the Office of War Information by James Paul Warburg, refused to mention this atrocity in his broadcasts, while W. Averell Harriman cooperated in keeping the story out of print until the Nuremberg Trials had been completed. "Jewish Comment", May 21, 1943, sneered at the German discovery of the massacre as follows; "After its sensational success with the story of the 10,000 Polish officers allegedly killed by the Soviets, the German Propaganda Ministry has evidently determined to explore further possibilities of splitting the Allies."

Because of the many atrocities committed by the Jewish-directed Allies, not only the firestorm incineration of German civilians in many German cities, but the incineration of hundreds' of thousands of Japanese civilians in the atomic bombing of Hiroshima and Nagasaki, Operation Keelhaul, the murder of one million anti-Communist Russians who were ordered handed over to the Soviet executioners by Eisenhower, and many other horrors, it was necessary to invent a German atrocity which would eclipse these horrors. The "extermination" of the Jews seemed made to order. Since there was no basis for any numerical figures, the earliest projections were that 12,000,000 Jews had been killed. Wiser heads among the Jews suggested that no figure higher than one million should be advanced, since a larger figure was likely to be discredited, thus invalidating the entire Holocaust claim. Some Jewish writers in New York began to publicize a figure of six million, and this soon gained such wide currency that the Jews had to settle for it, and it has remained the standard figure ever since. The self appointed "historian" of the Holocaust, Lucy S. Davidowicz, coyly presents a figure of 5,933,900 in her "Holocaust Reader". Certainly no one objects to rounding this off to the more practical figure of six million. Congressman George G. Sadowski, in opposing the Marshall Plan, stated, "That 10,000,000 Jews were killed, tortured, placed in slave labor camps ... that all means nothing." *Congressional Record*, Feb. 23, 1948.

While protecting the Jews from the horrors of the Allied bombing raids, the Germans were forced by the exigencies of the war to leave the Jews largely to their own devices. As a result, the Jews, in the midst of war and universal devastation, thrived with their talents for black marketeering and scavenging. As Werner

Sombart has written, "Wars are the Jews harvests." In "The War Against the Jews", Lucy Davodowicz writes of the Jewish profiteers, "This new class -- smugglers, underworld, nouveaux riches -- became the clientele for dozens of cafes, restaurants, and nightclubs that mushroomed in the ghetto. They passed their time dining, drinking, dancing."

In the camps, the Jewish inmates assumed complete charge of their administration. They converted the camps into training schools in which they subjected their students to the most intensive methods of Jewish survival and victory. Every morsel of food, clothing, every sexual pleasure and other aspect of life, became the vehicle of the most vicious bartering and maneuvering for advantage. Friedrich quotes one of them in "The Kingdom of Auschwitz".

Concentration camp existence ... taught us that the whole world is really like a concentration camp. The world is ruled by neither justice nor morality; crime is not punished nor virtue rewarded. The world is ruled by power. We are laying the foundation for some new, monstrous civilization."

In fact, the Jews used the camps as the opportunity to recreate the most intensive Talmudic training schools for themselves, a rigid education which they had lost since emerging from their mediaeval ghettoes. Now, raging in their genetic powerhouses which they recreated in the camps, they prepared themselves for the inevitable ending of the war, when they loosed themselves upon the wartorn nations of the earth like the most devastating plagues from Pandora's box. When they descended upon the helpless Christians, they immediately created a "new, monstrous civilization". As one Jew boasted, "When I left the concentration camp, I suddenly realized that I could take anybody."

The graduates of this school for power quickly became wealthy and influential residents of many countries. One and all, they were fanatical Zionists; they were united in their contempt for the "goyim", the gentile cattle whom they proposed to enslave and manipulate. With the establishment of the State of Israel in 1948, they quickly converted the government of the United States into a vassal of Tel Aviv, and used the wealth of the greatest country in the world to advance their goals in other nations. In every instance, they used the Myth of the Holocaust to advance their objectives. The goyim were inundated with stories and movies of "the extermination" of the Jews. Anne Roiphe wrote, in "Generation Without a Memory,", p. 62, "When gas became costly and ran short, they threw the infants and children directly into burning ovens." She fails to tell us what sort of fuel the Germans were using for their "burning ovens". The Jews continually wrote of the "modern technology" which had enabled the Germans to dispose of millions of Jews, and invariably, the sole illustration of this "technology" was a pair of small ovens which seemed a relic of the nineteenth century, and which could have disposed of only a few bodies a day. A crematorium requires a temperature of 2200 degrees Fahrenheit for the first ninety minutes, and then 1800 degrees for from sixty to one hundred fifty minutes, and even this does not burn bones. Lacking fuel supplies, the Germans could not even have provided the necessary fuel to embark on any program of burning victims.

The Jews then introduced lurid stories of chemical experiments on the victims. In fact, the *Washington Post* recently carried a series of horror stories in which helpless victims were given chemical substances which caused then intense agony, vomiting and convulsions, loss of hair and many other excruciating symptoms. However, the victims were not Jews in Nazi concentration camps. They were patients at the National Institute of Health in Washington, where government doctors experimented on them with various chemicals for cancer treatments. Most of the victims died in agony, without the slightest amelioration of their cancers. In American prisons, chemical testing of various substances on prisoners has been going on for many years. While our government continues to appropriate millions of dollars for the pursuit of "Nazi war criminals", these chemical experiments in our prisons and hospitals go on without interruption.

The "Nazi hunter", Simon Weisenthal, has become a cult figure in Washington, despite the revelations that throughout World War II he was a Gestapo agent. He has come under increasing criticism from many of his fellow Jews for his claim that he alone has kept the Holocaust Myth alive in recent years. Soon he may even claim that he invented the entire myth. Meanwhile, the American people, driven to the brink of bankruptcy by our support of the State of Israel, can find no prospect of relief.

Now the United States faces the possibility of a lawsuit projected by a group of German citizens, for the sum of $400 billion. This claim is based on the more than 100 billion marks which West Germany has been forced to pay the State of Israel as "reparations" for "the extermination of six million Jews." Not only was the claim false, but it was extorted from the German people solely because of the continued military occupation of West Germany by the United States. The Germans point out that in all the prosecutions of former camp guards, they have only been charged with "beating and kicking" the Jewish inmates. None of them has been charged with actually "gassing" anyone. Kurt Becker, of the Press Information Office in Bonn, Germany, stated in *Newsweek*, June 8, 1981, that as of Dec. 31, 1980, West Germany had paid to the State of Israel 63 billion DM, or $30 billion, and was still committed to pay a further $9.5 billion. In addition, German firms have been forced to pay Israel many more billions as reparations to Jewish "laborers", and to furnish many billions of dollars worth of electrical systems, telephone systems, and other technological gifts to Israel.

In contrast, after World War I, the Reparations Commission submitted to Germany a demand that $30 billion be paid, to be divided among *all* the nations which Germany had fought in that war. Of this demand, only a few million dollars was ever paid, yet the State of Israel has already exacted from West Germany more money than was asked by all the nations whom Germany fought in World War I. The East Democratic Republic of Germany has denied that Germany owes any reparations to the State of Israel, and has paid nothing, leaving the United States as the nation solely responsible for forcing West Germany to pay many billions to the State of Israel. The German government would never have paid this money without the force of the American occupying power, yet American taxpayers are told that we maintain a military presence in West Germany to oppose Russian aggression. The farcical nature of this explanation of our military collection agency is exposed when it is admitted that American forces in West Germany could only delay a Russian advance from two to four hours!

The payments which the American military has demanded that West Germany pay to Israel have contributed heavily to West Germany's economic problems, and are responsible for the growing anti-American feeling in Germany. Many Germans openly sneer at the "mongrel culture" of the United States and call us a "nation of mulattoes", due to the presence of many black troops occupying West Germany.

Because of the nature of the dictatorship maintained by the force of the American military occupying army, in which no German is allowed to question the Myth of the Holocaust, the German patriots believe the only way to expose this conspiracy on behalf of Israel is to sue the United States for the return of all the "Holocaust" payments to Israel, with interest. This demand will soon be brought before the World Court. Meanwhile, Americans must decide what action to take to salvage their collapsing economy from the demands made on it by the insatiable Israeli power. Only the complete exposure of the Holocaust hoax will free our government officials from their commitments to ever increasing payments to the State of Israel.

GENOCIDE IN AMERICA

Although the United Nations has adopted a strong measure against the crime of genocide, or the attempt to massacre entire groups of people, the United States Congress failed to adopt the genocide measure. The reason it was voted down is that under this measure, many United States officials could be tried and executed, as they have been actively pursuing a genocide policy against White American citizens for more than forty years. Dozens of laws have been enacted by the United States government which have as their sole purpose the elimination of the White race and the converting of our population into a mulatto mass which can easily be politically controlled. While enacting many laws which were expressly intended to aid in multiplying the Negro population, these same laws were intended to, and have, actively reduced the numbers of White American Citizens.

After achieving an astronomical increase in the non-white population of the United States, the government in its genocide policy began a national campaign to castrate the remaining Whites by denying them employment opportunities. Unable to earn a living, these Whites cannot afford to reproduce and to rear their young. At the same time, non-whites have been given preference in both government and private sectors of employment. They have also been given preference in educational opportunities, forcing colleges to admit them even when they were barely literate and could not carry college work. The result of this black invasion is that many private colleges are being forced out of business, unable to afford the millions of extra dollars needed to educate the uneducable Negro students. As a result, many fine schools which were established by White citizens have closed their doors.

The United States government campaign of genocide against the Whites encompasses every bureau of the federal bureaucracy. For many years, the Federal Bureau of Investigation has ignored the rapidly mounting crime rate while devoting its efforts to investigating the complaints made by Negroes against Whites. FBI agents never investigate atrocities committed by Negroes against Whites. In one incident in Mississippi, the kinky-haired, gray skinned, thick-lipped J. Edgar Hoover dispatched 722 FBI agents to search for a missing Negro agitator. Because it has abandoned its role in combating crime, the FBI has left American Whites naked and unprotected while Negro thugs roam the streets raping and killing Whites on purely racial grounds.

The war of genocide against American Whites has been relentless efforts by every Federal agency to attack the Whites in their schools, in their churches, in their neighborhoods, and in their homes. The Whites have been driven out of every major American city, while the Black Plague has converted formerly beautiful White areas in Washington D.C., New York City, and Philadelphia into hideous slums in which every type of vice and disease rages unchecked; Today the last bastions of White working class neighborhoods in Boston, Mass., scene of the Boston Tea Party and many other crucial acts of the American Revolution are being attacked by large forces of police, as the White children are taken from their homes and bussed many miles away to schools in the worst Negro slums. So far, American Whites have lost every battle in this genocide campaign. Every channel of communication is controlled by the pro-negro terrorists. The churches and schools have become primary agents in carrying out genocide againt the Whites.

Only a few Whites are defending their race against this terrorists campaign. The strange passivity in the face of disaster suggest that fluoridation of water supplies and other chemical means have been employed by the government forces to weaken the Whites' will to resist. Certainly no group in history has face destruction with so little effort to save themselves as the White citizens of America.

Phoney Wars for Phoney Peace and the Ministry of Fear

The Orwellian doctrine, Perpetual War for Perpetual Peace, has not been updated to the more practical version, "Phony Wars for Phony Peace." The established governments have long since abandoned their exhortations to be patriotic, loyal and sacrificing for the higher good. It has proven impossible to maintain their former shibboleths as the excuse for human sacrifice. Indeed, sacrifice has reverted to its original mode, that of religious ritual. The previous rituals which conditioned the brainwashed victims to lay down their lives to propitiate the gods have been replaced by more psychological "correct" methods of persuasion, in which the victims nudge each forward in their anxiety to take their places, laying themselves down on the stone altars and baring their breasts to sacrificial knives, which slash open their bodies to remove the still-beating hearts.

In 60 years of studying the causes of wars, and the mechanisms by which they have been achieved, I have employed one of the principal methods of great cooking, that of reduction. As the chef continues to mix and manipulate his ingredients, they are distilled into a more concentrated form, usually by heat, until the flavors "marry." (This is also a recipe for great painting - a certain period is required for the various colors painted onto the canvas to marry, to reconcile with one another, eventually subsiding into a beautiful jewel like overall tone, which we call "great art.") These are the works of the Old Masters, who used the formula known for many centuries. They were well-known in Pompeian Wall Painting and Roman art, and can be viewed in their pristine colors today. There are no shortcuts to achieving these effects, which is the sole reason why "modern art" became the travesty that it is today.

All wars since 1900 have been totally fakes. This will prove unsettling to many veterans, who were crippled or killed in these fake wars. I served throughout World War II in the United States Army Air Corps, which was the first to use weapons of mass destruction on civilian populations, a fact which our opponent Saddam Hussein has strangely neglected to mention, probably because Saddam Hussein is a "replacement" not the opponent which we wanted at all, but a last-minute choice because no more suitable replacement was available. He has no illusions about his desirability, and no doubt accepts his billing without resentment, relieved that he had made the cast after all. The first question asked of anyone in the world of the theater is, "Are you working?" which remains the principal goal of the profession. Everything is a charade, which may or may not be entertaining. In fact, for me the sole entertainment has been in the research. It is amazing how often the same characters have been trotted forth to go through the same clichés, "the war to end war" and "the war to save democracy," ad inifitum. In fact, most of these clichés sprang from the less than agile mind of Woodrow Wilson during the First World War. However else you might choose to characterize Woodrow Wilson, you must admit that he never failed to bore.

But to get to the business at hand, my statement that the great wars have been exercises in sheer fakery. We might begin with a seminal event in American history, our Civil War, which ostensibly began with the firing on a federal fort in Charleston Harbor at Ft. Sumter by "Southern hotheads." Ft. Sumter had little military or strategic importance, which would make it the seminal event in our greatest loss of life in our history. The "hotheads" were agent provocateurs of the Scottish rite, which had originated in Charleston. The rest of the South had no knowledge of participation in this event, which was the sole provocation of the Civil War. It worked so well that it has been used over and over again.

Organizations were set up to provide the necessary umbrella for these provocations. To start World War I, the conspirators set up three organizations - the Navy League, the Council on National Defense and the Carnegie League to Enforce Peace. It is our first encounter with the ubiquitous term "defense," but all three organizations were deeply committed to the steel industry, through the Carnegie connection, with J.P. Morgan's (Rothschild) banking interests, the required tax exempt status, and the absence of the very man whose name it more.

Carnegie had turned over his entire fortune to his foundations, virtuously announcing that he would sever all connections with their prospective operations. This handsomely suited less virtuous operators, principally John D. Rockefeller, who took over the Carnegie Foundations, manipulating them as satellites of his own Rockefeller Foundation so that his name was never connected to any of their achievements. World War I, with the passage of the Federal Reserve Act, was ready to begin.

Dress rehearsals had occurred in the 1890s, with the Spanish-American War, when the U.S. battleship Maine was blown up in Havana. And with the Boer War in South Africa, which occurred almost as an afterthought when some Boer farms in South Africa were found to be teeming with gold and diamonds. These riches were promptly acquired by the British Empire, with the aid of its ubiquitous military forces, and in the process invented the concentration camp and making war on women and children, which became standard operating procedure of subsequent twentieth century wars.

With these impressive examples, World War I set new records in casualties, and by design, unseating most of the crowned heads of Europe. The British royal family survived intact, which made it the real victor in the war and chaos in which it had occurred. British intelligence, known as the British Secret Service, now roamed unchallenged across the world. They perpetrated the Bolshevik Revolution in Russia, an event in which few if any Bolsheviks were active. In World War II, almost as an afterthought, they created their American counterpart, the Central Intelligence Agency, a group which has always been characterized by its singular lack of intelligence, as was defined by its supposed lack of knowledge of 9/11. The CIA enabled the British Secret Service to remain unseen as its work throughout the world was carried out by its CIA underlings.

THE ADL-FBI CONSPIRACY EXPOSED

A spectre is haunting the halls of government in Washington the spectre of J. Edgar Hoover. Should this man's crime against the citizens of our Republic become known to the American people, it could topple the conspirators from their throne of power. Why have government officials persistently but quietly proceeded with efforts to have the new headquarters of the Federal Bureau of Investigation, which was dedicated **without ceremony** as the J. Edgar Hoover Building, given a new name which does not recall the infamous director of the FBI? Why have government officials placed in dead storage some personal mementoes of J. Edgar Hoover which were willed to the new FBI building by Hoover's lifelong intimate, Clyde Tolson? These mementoes were to have been the prize exhibits in a special "J. Edgar Hoover Memorial Room", but officials have announced that there will be no J. Edgar Hoover Room in the building.

Those who still believe J. Edgar Hoover's propaganda that he was the great "anti-Communist", the "American Champion of Law and Order", and the "Great Gangbuster" fail to realize that he spent many millions of taxpayers' dollars to foist his personal myth on the American public, and spent more millions to conceal from the public his real history of scandal, blackmail, extortion and conspiracy.

J. Edgar Hoover came into prominence by riding the coattails of a minor government imbroglio which was built up as "the scandal of the century", the Teapot Dome scandal. He met his end as one more victim of a second imbroglio which was built up by the controlled press as the "crime of the century", the Watergate Break-in. Throughout his public life, J. Edgar Hoover was successful in maintaining two goals - to conceal his personal history from the

American people, and to use the FBI, not as a force against crime, but as a private police force dedicated to the service of the most vicious criminal conspirators in the world, the homocidal maniacs of the Zionist terrorist movement.

On June 8, 1978, the Washington Post reported the strange case of an American citizen, Sarni Esmail, who visited Israel to be at his dying father's bedside. As he stepped off the plane, he was arrested by Israeli security forces and taken to jail, where he endured extensive torture. He was kicked in the stomach, his hair pulled, and 'he was forced to stand naked for many hours while the tortures continued. The crime of which he was accused in Israel was that he had joined a Palestinian student group while he was attending Michigan State University. The FBI, which maintains paid informants in every Arab organization in the United States, has up-to-date files on every member of these organizations. Although these groups are very small and have no political influence in the United States, in 1976 the FBI spent **four million dollars** for surveillance of one hundred and eighteen members of these Arab student organizations, about twice as much as it spent in 1976 on surveillance of members of organized crime!

When the American student Sarni Esmail purchased a plane ticket to Israel to bewith his dying father, the FBI, through its militant surveillance of the Arab students, immediately informed the Israeli police, who were waiting for him when the plane landed. Although Sarni Esmail had never committed any crime in Israel, and as an American citizen was not subject to arrest there UNTIL he had committed some offense, American officials refused to intervene on his behalf. Hewas arrestedsolely asthe result of FBI surveillance in the United States where, also, he had never committed any crime and was not a proper subject for surveillance or intelligence information from the FBI! Sarni Esmail was now threatened with tenyears in prison, and further torture, unless he became a double agent for the Israeli intelligence service. His crime:

That he belonged to a "proscribed organization", not in Israel but in the United States, where supposedly the Israelis have no jurisdiction. In fact, the Israeli intelligence service has jurisdiction over every American citizen throughout the United States directly through the FBI. To convince him of the hopelessness of his position, two "American" Jewish lawyers visited Sarni Esmail in his Israeli prison. These lawyers, J. Momoe Freedman and Alan Dershowitz, then announced to the world press that Sarni Esmail had not been tortured, and that he was grateful for the kind treatment he had received from his Israeli torturers!

As the citizens of the United States cringe fear of their lives, not daring to go out after dark, as the criminals have taken command of the streets, we taxpayers well might ask: "What is the FBI, our famed gangbuster organization, doing to protect us from the ravages of the criminals?" The answer is NOTHING. Quite a few years ago, the FBI ceased to be a bureau of the government of the United States, because it was taken over by an alien organization, and became the umegistered agent of a foreign power, the Anti-Defamation League of B'nai B'rith. After this takeover, the FBI devoted most of its efforts to the ADL's subterranean terrorist activities against all American citizens, while the forces of organized crime and underground Communism were left to rage unchecked throughout the nation.

During the heyday of the excesses committed by various Jews in charge of the Watergateimbroglio, several members of Nixon's staff were charged with what seemed to be a new crime in the American history of jurisprudence, lying to an FBI agent. These officials could never have been convicted of this charge if they had made the obvious defense that it is not a crime to "lie" or to give inaccurate information toan umegistered agent of a foreign power. The crime was that anumegistered agentof a foreign power, posing as an agent of the American government, was seeking information for the purposes of that foreign government from an American citizen.

Further, it is a crime for any American citizen to give information to an FBI agent who is acting as an agent of the state of Israel and who is subverting the authority of the American government and committing crimes against the people of the United States. Any American who provides information to an FBI agent under these circumstances becomes an accessory after the fact to the operations of an illegal and subversive force acting on American soil to undermine the sovereignty of the American Republic.

Now we must ask, where was the famed Director of the FBI, J. Edgar Hoover, while this takeover was going on? The answer is that J. Edgar Hoover unofficially abdicated as the head of the FBI and let the ADL terrorists take over the organization which hehad built upfrom nothing, because the ADL gave him no other choice. He must submit to have his personal history opened to the American public, complete with photographs, affidavits and other documentation, or he could continue as the nominal head of the FBI (with a new Assistant Director of the FBI, a Jew, in charge of operations). J. Edgar Hoover chose to submit to the ADL blackmail, because he had used the instrument of blackmail against others too many times to be unaware of its devastating consequences should thevictim refuse. From this moment, the FBI no longer existed, except as an arm of the ADL, to be used for its sinister purposes of undermining the American Republic and the sovereignty of the American people.

In order to understand why J. Edgar Hoover (ostensibly the most powerful single official in the history of the United States, with a nation-wide private army at his beck and call, its agents answerable only tohim,a power which no president of the United States has ever enjoyed) should meekly surrender this vast power to the most sinister aliens operating in the United States on behalf of a foreign power, the state of Israel, we must reveal here for the first time some details of the private life of this man, details which will shock and dismay many Americans who had beenpersuaded by J.

Edgar Hoover's propaganda that he was a sincere patriot and a dedicated anti-Communist, but detailswhich have been known for manyyears to politicians and journalists in Washington, D.C.

Throughout his career, J. Edgar Hoover, while ruthlessly exposing weaknesses in the characters of those whom he wished to intimidate in order to maintain his burgeoning political power, successfully concealed cardinal facts about his personal background. (These facts have become part of the tragic history of the white race and are well known and completely documented.) One of thesewas his descent from Harriet Hemings, a mulatto slave. Elizabeth Hemings, a full-blooded African, had a child by Captain Hemings, the master of an English whaler which sailed from England to Williamsburg. Elizabeth became the slave of John Wales, a Welshman living in Williamsburg. John Wales' wife died, and Elizabeth became his concubine, bearing him six children, the fifth of which wasSally Hemings (the concubine kept the name of her former lover).

While he was a member of the legislature meeting in Williamsburg, Thomas Jefferson visited the home of John Wales, where he met and married Martha Skelton, Wales' widowed daughter by his deceased wife. Martha was the same age as Sally Hemings, her half-sister and personal maid. When John Wales died Martha Jefferson inherited the children along with her father's other property. Sally Hemings later became the mother of Harriet (who was rather light-skinned in color), a forebear of J. Edgar Hoover. Although this heritage was not particularly noticeable in his youth, as he advanced in age, his mulatto origins became more and more pronounced - the bulging eyes, the kinky hair, the thick lips, and the gray skin - all of which advertised his African ancestry.

John Edgar Hoover, who was born in Washington, D.C., onJan.1, 1895, was the son of DickersonN. Hoover, a life-long career bureaucrat who became head of the Coast and Geodetic

Survey. As a youth, John Edgar was known as the smallest boy in his class at Central High School. He weighed only 119 pounds, the smallest cadet in the school corps. In later years, his classmates, in recalling him, used such words as "demure" and "petite", adjectives not usually employed to describe a boy. They also mentioned that, although he was never known to date a girl throughout his high school career, he had formed a close friendship with the burly captain of the football team, who carried John Edgar's books home for him each afternoon. If this association caused any ribald comment among his peers, it remained subdued because of the physical strength and size of John Edgar's friend.

When John Edgar graduated from Central High School in 1909, he immediately went into government service, obtaining a position as an indexer at the Library of Congress, at a salary of $30 a month. At night he studied law at George Washington University, receiving his LLB in 1916, and his Master's degree in 1917. During these years, he resided at home with his parents, who lived well in upper-middle-class comfort. Despite his hours of work during the day and his classes in night school, he had developed an active social life, which remained secret even from his parents. He had already learned the method of making powerful friends in Washington. Although he still displayed no interest in the opposite sex, the demure, petite youth had attracted the interest of a number of prominent politicians who, while maintaining their reputations as well-established family men, enjoyed an occasional evening with a discreet youth...John Edgar found himself sought after by several men in Washington who would be very useful to his career in the coming years. The first of these strange alliances was with the prominent lawyer and political figure Harlan Fiske Stone. As soon as Hoover received his law degree, Stone secured a position for him in the then Bureau of Investigation. This bureau was only a few years old, and had but eight investigators. It was initially established in 1908 by Attorney General Josepb Bonaparte, a nephew of the late Emperor of France. Within a short time, he bad misgivings about the operations of government investigators in a free republic.

On April 2, 1908, testifying before the hearings of the Sundry Civil Appropriations Bill for 1909, Joseph Bonaparte testified that there was a strong possiblity of "agents provocateurs"

developing in the investigative branch of the Department of Justice. This was a remarkably prophetic statement, as within fifty years, the operations of the FBI consisted almost solely of the activities of agents provocateurs and paid informants. Despite Bonaparte's testimony, the appropriation for the investigators was approved. His successor as Attorney General, the Wall Street lawyer George Wickersham of Wickersham and Taft, named the new investigative branch the Bureau of investigation. In 1935, J. Edgar Hoover persuaded F.D. Roosevelt to give this bureau greater authority, and to rename it the Federal Bureau of Investigation, despite the fact that there were already federal investigators working in a number of departments, such as the Treasury Department, Post Office and others. Presumably, these investigators for other federal departments were no longer "federal" investigators.

Other concerned Americans in addition to Bonaparte saw in the new bureau a danger to the liberties of the people. At the 1908 Hearings of the House Appropriations Committee, Congressman Walter J. Smith, Iowa, 60th Congress, strongly opposed the authorization for this branch. He declared: "No general system of spying upon and espionage of the people, such as has prevailed in Russia, in France under the empire, and at one time in Ireland, should be allowed to grow up." Congressman Smith's opposition immediately aroused the ire of President Theodore Roosevelt, a former police commissioner of New York who had thrown his support behind the establishment of the Bureau of Investigation. Roosevelt claimed that detectives who were sworn to uphold the law could never violate it. In an effort to prevent the establishment of the Bureau of Investigation, Congress passed a bill on May 30, 1908, forbidding the Department of Justice from borrowing detectives from the Secret Service or any other agencies.

A month after Congress had adjourned, the Department of Justice quietly set up the very agency that Congress had refused to authorize, calling it the Bureau of Investigation. Thus the FBI from its very inception was set up in an atmosphere of deceit and trickery, destined from its beginnings as the tool of powerful and unscrupulous behind-the-scenes figures. a number of congressmen were infuriated by the deception which had been practiced on them by the Department of Justice. However, when they returned from their summer adjournment, they could find no practical way to force the Department of Justice to disband its investigators.

Congressman Shirley had also voiced his opposition to such a force at the Congressional hearings, stating: "In my reading of history I recall no instance where a government perished because of the absence of a secret service force, but many there are that perished as a result of the spy system. If Anglo-Saxon civilization stands for anything, it is for a government where the humblest citizen is safeguarded against the secret activities of the execution of government... Not in vain did our forefathers read the history of the Magna Carta and the Bill of Rights..." The Fourth Amendment declares: "The right of the people to be secure in their persons, houses, papers and effects, against unreasonable searches and seizures, should not be violated."

Americans today should honor the memory of these forgotten congressmen who sought in vain to protect future generations from the depredations of agents provocateurs. Today, no American citizen is secure in his home, because he is subject at any moment to search and seizure by federal agents from any one of half-a-dozen departments. In this writer's researches over the past thirty years, one fact has emerged - that those American leaders who sought to defend the liberties of the people have had their names erased from the records of public service, while those leaders who have betrayed the American people into the hands of sinister aliens, such as Woodrow Wilson, Franklin D. Roosevelt, and their many mis-shapen followers, are hailed as the champions of liberty and the saviors of the nation. One of J. Edgar Hoover's first assignments with the Bureau of Investigation was to accompany the team of federal agents which attacked the home of Congressman Charles Lindbergh. The team had instructions to destroy all copies of Lindbergh's books which revealed the origins of Woodrow Wilson's involvement of our country in World War I. They were told to use "all necessary force" to carry out this objective, which gave them carte blanche to kill if resistance was encountered. Although young Hoover was sent along merely as a departmental observer, a safeguard against complaints because of Congressman Lindbergh's political prominence, when the young Charles Lindbergh rushed out to defend his father's property, Hoover kicked him in the stomach, and he was dragged away by two of the agents. Young Lindbergh never got over this youthful tragedy, while J. Edgar Hoover in later years avoided meeting Lindbergh whenever he came to Washington. It is doubtful if Lindbergh ever connected Hoover with the team which attacked his home, but this may have been one reason why Hoover withdrew all cooperation of the FBI with the prosecution of Richard Bruno Hauptmann. The most important reason, of course, was that Hoover had been informed that the Jews were manufacturing a totally false and perjured chain of witnesses and testimony against Hauptmann, and he wished to protect his beloved Bureau from becoming involved in such a precipitously dangerous affair.

The Lindbergh attack by the fledgling Bureau of Investigation proves, that from its inception, its principal function has been the control of political dissidents by any means, book-burning, the manufacture of evidence, and the work of agents provocateurs. Because Congressman Lindbergh had made his greatest speeches on the floor of the House inopposition to the establishment of the Federal Reserve System by the Money Trust, he was performing a heroic role indefending the liberties which our forefathers had won for us. Like all revolutions since the beginnings of time, the high-water mark of the people's freedom was the exact conclusion of the American Revolution. The freedoms they had won at such cost had begun to be eroded away as soon as the fighters laid down their arms.

At the time J. Edgar Hoover began his career of public service, government employment, which even then was the city's largest industry, was regarded with polite contempt by Washington's older families. To the city's moneyed class, with interests in real estate, banking and other businesses, government employees were beyond the pale. Local businessmen strictly adhered to a long-standing principle that they would never hire anyone who had been in government employment. Their reasoning was beyond question. Because the government paid the lowest salaries in the area, no one of ability would take a job there ifhe could obtain employment in the higher-paying private sector. If a former government employee sought work in private business, he encountered the suspicion that he must be unemployable if he could not hold a government job. This was the local status of the class of government servants to which J. Edgar Hoover had been bred and born. Significantly, throughout his life he had never considered any job in private business, although, once his propaganda had built himself up as an important figure, he had a number of attractive offers. In fact, no private salary could have met the enormous expenses of his life as a public servant, with its many fringe benefits.

When young Hoover had completed his schooling, there was nothing in the area for him to do but go into government service. So greatly hasthe situation changed that today it isdifficult to reconstruct the atmosphere of the Washington in which Hoover grew up. Government servants are now an arrogant, well-paid bureaucracy, with higher salaries than the corrsponding private sector. Washington itself is one of the wealthiest communities in the United States, with a "depression-proof" economy and the highest average family incomes. Sixty years ago, Washington was almost a depressed area, with modest homes, very modest salaries, and very little social life. Crime was almost nonexistent. It was a sleepy southern town, rigidly segregated, with Negroes occupying the bottom of the scale in housing and income. Certainly those who had passed for white would make every effort to put as much social distance between themselves and their co-racialists as possible. Today the District of Columbia is the largest Negro city in the world, with a crime rate eighteen times higher than that of London. This is the change which the "Great Gangbuster" lived through in his home town.

In that day, it would have been unthinkable to cultivate a government employee for his influence, as he had none. The press corps consisted largely of a group of "stringers", journeyman reporters who filed stories whenever something occurred which was noteworthy (which was not often) and who were paid by the column-inch. Consequently, they lived very close to starvation. Washington generated very little news of national importance, and the government bureaus had no public relations officials. Statements about changes of policy would be delivered by the department heads themselves to two or three reporters, if any showed up at all. There was no mad dash to the telephone when these pronouncements were received. Instead, the reporters sauntered to the nearest dingy bars for several hours of serious drinking before they returned to their newsrooms. Although billions of dollars had swept through the city during the government's orgy of spending during World War I, very little of the money had remained there. It had all been seized and removed by various entrepreneurs in New York and otherstrongholds of the Zionists, for World War I had been the Jews' first great bid for power. The Washington government clerks continued at their usual low salaries.

Young J. Edgar Hoover's status began to emerge when he was appointed Special Assistant to the Attorney General of the United States in 1919. At this time, the handsome young man was twenty-four years old and still could be described as "petite" and "demure". One of his special friends was the leonine Senator Henry Cabot Lodge, who was leading the opposition in Congress to Woodrow Wilson's attempt to abandon American sovereignty by involving us in the League of Nations. Learning of Lodge's association with young Hoover, Woodrow Wilson sent an emissary to him suggesting that this involvement should persuade Lodge to reverse his stand against the League of Nations, with the clear threat that if not, much could be made of the situation. This identical ploy was to work some years later when Senator Vandenberg, leader of the congressional opposition to our involvement in the United Nations, was seduced by an attractive British Secret Service agent. Faced with exposure, Vandenberg astounded \Vashington politicians by suddenly announcing that he was abandoning all opposition to the United Nations and would henceforth support it. He then led the fight for confirmation of our joining the United Nations.

However, Henry Cabot Lodge was no Vandenberg. He informed the emissary that he should return to Woodrow Wilson and tell him that he was too deeply involved in preparing an edition on the Peck letters for publication to consider Wilson's proposal at the moment. The Peck letters, of course, consisted of Wilson's indiscreet outpourings to a lady friend. The Jews had already blackmailed Wilson with them by forcing him to appoint the radical Zionist leader Brandeis to the Supreme Court. Lodge's reply sent Wilson into deep depression and, shortly afterwards, he suffered a massive stroke.

In 1948, George Stimpson, founder of the National Press Club, introduced me to a florid, paunchy man in his early sixties. His name meant nothing to me, and I paid little attention to him. The next day, Stimpson, in his wry way, said to me, "Just what does it take to impress you, anyway?" "What do you mean?" I asked. "I introduced you to a former President of the United States yesterday, and you virtually ignored him." "That man was a former President of the United States?" "He was indeed," said Stimpson. "I remember it well, as I was fairly new in Washington at that time. When Wilson had a stroke, it was feared that if word of his true condition got out, it would paralyze the fight to secure approval of the League of Nations bill. So that no one could see his condition, he was spirited out of Washington, and his daughter-inlaw took him to the Pine Grove Inn in Asheville, North Carolina. They stayed there six weeks. During that time, the fellow to whom I introduced you was a White House aide. Word was given out that although Wilson could not see anyone, he would continue to fulfil his duties of office. Bills were signed and returned to Congress, statements of policy were issued by the White House, and it was all done by the fellow you met here. He and Mrs. Wilson were running the United States, while Wilson remained hidden in Asheville, N.C., unable to speak or move. That story has never been told."

I later searched through all the biographies of Woodrow Wilson, and was never able to find mention of this unofficial President, who remained with Mrs. Wilson during the remainder of Wilson's Presidency.

J. Edgar Hoover's reputation as a great anti-Communist originated with his service under William J. Burns, Chief of the Bureau of Investigation until 1924, when Hoover replaced him. Harry Daugherty, President Harding's right-hand man, and Burns had led the battle against the Communists and had thwarted the take-over of the United States government by a Communist revolution. During this battle, on June 2, 1919, Atty. Gen. A.

Mitchell Palmer's home at 2132 R. St. N.W., Washington, D.C. was blown up. Across the street, Assistant Secretary of the Navy Franklin D. Roosevelt opened his front door to find bits of the body of one of the bombers on his front porch. The bombing was in retaliation for the famed "Palmer raids", in which thousands of wild-eyed Jewish Communist revolutionaries had been rounded up and deported as undesirable aliens.

The Communists now counter-attacked on all fronts. The demand for "civil-rights" dates from this period, as well as the work of the American Civil Liberties Union. On June 1, 1920, a special House of representatives Committee summoned Atty. Gen. Palmer before them, demanding that the "rights" of the aliens be protected. It was the opening gun for the systematic destruction of the entire Harding administration team and for the replacement of William J. Burns by J. Edgar Hoover at the Bureau of lnvestigation. At this time, William]. Burns was renowned as the world's most famous detective. Bum's father had been Police Commissioner of Columbus, Ohio. At the age of twenty-four, young Burns exposed the election frauds of 1883. He joined the U.S. Secret Service, and soon uncovered a vast counterfeiting ring which had operated unmolested for twentyfive years. In New York, he solved the murder of gambler Herman Rosenthal and sent a police lieutenant and four gunmen to the electric chair. The drive against the Communists resulted in the labeling of the Harding administration as the "most corrupt administration in history" a falsehood which persists to this day. One of Daugherty's aides, Jess Smith, supposedly committed suicide, and the sum of $10,000 was found in his room. As it was promptly confiscated by the government, the ancient ploy of planting it there was probably used. The discrediting of the Harding administration proceeded in a step-by-step program which was remarkably duplicated in the indictment of the Nixon administration a few years later. The "scandals" of the Harding administration resulted in the jailing of Daugherty, who was replaced as Attorney General by John Edgar Hoover's longtime friend and ally, Harlan Fiske Stone. Stone, a notorious left-winger, irnrnediatelyfired Burns, replacing himwith John Edgar Hoover. Furious at having been ousted after having wiped out the Communist menace in the United States, Burns sought help on Capitol Hill, telling friendly congressmen that Hoover had gotten his job "by the back door". He received sympathy but no active support. Under Stone and Hoover, the Bureau oflnvestigation's anti-Communist work came to a halt. The voluminous files on Communist subversion were packed away, never to be seen again. Priceless documentation onsuch Communist agitators as Felix Frankfurter was quietly disposed of. However, this was but the opening gun in the campaign of the Communist apologists.

A nation-wide press campaign attacked the Harding administration as "the most corrupt in history". The keystone of the campaign was the "Teapot-Dome" scandal. Like the Watergate scandal of a later era, it was labeled "the crime of the century". For the first time, my researches have exposed the Teapot Dome as a "media event", which was never a scandal at all. Instead, it was a convenient coverup for a much greater scandal, perpetrated by the very interests which now accused the Harding administration of corruption! In the early 1920's, a few patriotic congressmen had begun investigations into the billions of dollars stolen from the government during the Wilson administration. The targets of this investigation were Bernard Baruch (Wilson's head of the War Industries Board), Eugene Meyer (head of the War Finance Corporation, who printed millions of dollars of Liberty Bonds and sold them in duplicate, keeping profits from the sale of the duplicates for himself) and the Rockefellers, who double-billed the military services for billions of dollars worth of oil and other supplies. One interesting result of this swindle was that Eugene Meyer used his profits to buy the Allied Chemical Corporation and the Washington Post. It was the Washington Post, purchased with money stolen from the U.S. Governrnent, which "broke" the Watergate "scandal". The details of the Rockefeller swindles had been worked out by their banker, Jacob Schiff of Kuhn-Loeb Co. and his Jewish cohort, Herbert Lehman of Lehman Brothers banking house, who had taken a job as procurement officer in Washington with the U.S. Army. At the same time, Senator James A. Reed was accusing Herbert Hoover of having squirreled away millions of dollars in graft while acting as the head of another Rothschild swindle, the Commission for Relief in Belgium. To forestall these investigations, Baruch, Meyer, and Schiff invented the Teapot-Dome story, selecting as their victims two oilmen, Harry Sinclair and Edward L. Doheny, whom the Rockefellers had been trying either to buy out or force out of business.

Teapot Dorne was a western oil field which held much of the Navy's oil reserves.

However, geologists found that because of the sandy formation, the oil was sinking into the ground and should be recovered soon or it would be lost forever. It could only be saved by pumping it out and storing it in tanks. Officials approached Harry Sinclair and Edward L. Doheny, proposing that they undertake the salvage operation. Sinclair, an astute oil operator, investigated, and found that he could make a profit from the operation. He and Doheny set up a company, the Mammoth Oil Co., which leased Teapot Dome from the government. The Secretary of the Interior, Albert Fall, knowing little or nothing about the mechanics of the operation, signed the lease as an ordinary part of his job. Little did he know that his name was to enter the American language as "fall guy", a "patsy who takes a fall" or serves a prison term for a crime inwhich he is taking the blame for someone else.

At this very time, Fall suddenly faced a financial crisis. New Mexico officials, without prior notification, doubled the taxes on his ranch in the Tularosa basin. Fall, operating as the Tres Rios Land and Cattle Co. (jointly with his son-in-law Mahlon Everhart) owned the largest ranch in New Mexico, controlling 750,000 acres in an area of fifty-five miles by twenty-four miles. Faced with the loss of his ranch, Fall mentioned to Harry Sinclair, who habitually dealt in million-dollar deals, that he needed a loan to pay his taxes. Sinclair promptly lent him $200,000 and Doheny lent him $100,000. The loans were fully secured by notes against the land. Unknowingly, these principals were about to be "exposed" as the "criminals of the century".

The Rockefellers approached New York papers with the story, but not one editor would touch it because of the obvious libels against the principals. They sent one of their hangers-on, an oilmannarnedJohnLeonStackwhoranerrands for them, to the most unsavory newspaper publisher in the United States, Harry Bonfils of the Denver Post. Bonfils had been run out of Kansas City after operating a fake lottery there. His swindleswere so notorious that he caused nearly all states in the United States to enact laws prohibiting lotteries, which laws remained in effect for many years. With his profits, Bonfils bought the Denver Post, not because he was interested in journalism, but because he could and did use the newspaper for extortion and blackmail. He would print up a front page detailing an escapade of a local "mark", and send the page over to the "mark", still wet from the press. Bonfils would demand from ten to twenty thousand dollars to refrain from printing the story, which the "mark" usually paid. If he refused, Bonfils had a lurid circulation-building story for his front page.

Without revealing that his backers were the Rockefellers, Stack promised Bonfils one hundred thousand dollars if he would print the Teapot Dome story. Bonfils, who immediately saw the hand of the Rockefellers in the deal, demanded two hundred thousand dollars. Stack agreed, paying Bonfils an advance of five thousand dollars. Bonfils immediately headlined that the greedy vultures, Sinclair and Doheny, had "stolen" the nation's oil reserves, leaving the Country helpless in the face of possible attack. This treasonable act had been made possible by their bribing of Secretary Fall. Once the story hit the front page, other editors across the United States took it up, and any possible denials were ignored. In fact, the records of the subsidence of the oil were not made public until 1944, after Fall had died!

Whatever fee Stack had been promised by the Rockefellers to publicize the story, he refused to pay Bonfils anything further, pocketing whatever was left after the initial five-thousand-dollar payment. Bonfils imperiled the entire Teapot-Dome story by threatening to sue him for "breach of contract", but in some way, he was persuaded to remain silent, and Teapot Dome became history. Like the Watergate break-in, the story remained front page news for many months, as the government dragged out proceedings against the principals. The advantages of this strategy were obvious. All of the proposed congressional investigations of Baruch, Meyer, and the Rockefellers (and the billions of dollars they had defrauded the United States government) were quietly dropped, never to be mentioned again, while each week government officials revealed new prosecutions planned against the "criminals" of the TeapotDome affair.

Like the Watergate-show trials, the Teapot Dome prosecutions were allowed to dragon for many years. It was not until 1931 that Secretary Fall was finally sent to prison, which conveniently revived the entire "scandal" just in timefor Roosevelt's successful campaign for the presidency. The congressional investigations of the affair, also like the Watergate burglary, were conducted along strict party lines, with the Democratic leaders howling for more action and the Republicans fighting a desperate and losing retreat. A Democratic congress, led by Sen. Thomas J. Walsh of Montana, achieved the complete annihilation of a Republican administration. Another Democratic prosecutor of the Teapot-Dome affair was Senator Burton K. Wheeler. He was extremely anxious togenerate as much storm about Teapot Dome as possible, to cover up his own indictment in 1924 for having accepted a $100,000 bribe from an oil promoter, Gordon Campbell. Unlike Fall's loan from Sinclair, Wheeler's acceptance of $100,000 from Campbell was an out-and-out payment for Wheeler's influence in obtaining oil rights in Wyoming. Nevertheless, Sen. Walsh, the prosecutor of Teapot-Dome, acted as Wheeler's counsel and successfully defended him on the charge of bribery.

The Wheeler scandal was to have a permanent effect on John Edgar Hoover. The Bureau of Investigation had sent agents to Wyoming to look into the Wheeler affair, possibly from political motives. Walsh, a fierce partisan, vowed revenge on both Burns and Hoover. He cheered when Burns was removed, but was no less resolved to have Hoover fired, publicly stating on Capitol Hill that he would not rest until he got that "little...." When Franklin D. Roosevelt was elected President, he announced that Sen. Walsh was to be his Attorney General. On his way to the capitol to be sworn in, Walsh boasted that his first official act would be to fire J. Edgar Hoover. Before he could be sworn in, Walsh died of a heart attack. Fate, or some more directly concerned agency, had intervened miraculously to save Hoover's career. Walsh's political friends, dismayed and perhaps suspicious of Walsh's sudden demise, pursued the campaign to have Hoover fired. Postmaster General Farley joined in the campaign to get Hoover not from any personal animus, but because he wanted the post for an old friend, Val O'Farrell, under the time honored spoils system in which Farley had been brought up. Not only was Farley's effort unsuccessful, but it later cost him the presidency of the United states. John Edgar Hoover, never one to forget an injury, persuaded Roosevelt to refuse Farley the vicepresidency which would have later given him the White House.

As the battle raged around Hoover, his oldest ally, Harlan Fiske Stone, who had ascended to the Supreme Court, wrote an impassioned letter to FDR on Jan.2, 1932, urging that he be retained as head of the Bureau of Investigation. FDR cannily postponed a decision, allowing both Hoover's friends and his enemies to do favors for him while they waited for his answer. The rash of kidnappings and bank robberies gave Roosevelt his out when he claimed that it was too dangerous a time to change the leadership of the Bureau. Not only was J. Edgar Hoover never allowed to forget that FDR had saved his job, ensuring his continued loyalty, but Hoover launched on a furious campaign to amass as much dirt on all possible political supporters in the future. The new Atty. Gen. Homer Cummings, had also urged Roosevelt to retain Hoover, simply because his closest friend, J. Bruce Kremer, national Democratic committee-man from Montana, was a long-time enemy of Burton Wheeler and wanted Hoover to remain and possibly do further damage to Wheeler.

Deeply shaken by his narrow escape, Hoover ever afterwards devoted at least a third of the Bureau's manpower and resources to doing favors for political friends and to researching and maintaining his famous Black Cabinet, the special files which he maintained in his personal office. These files contained details in the sexual and financial peccadilloes of every prominent politician in the United States. They became as feared for what they did not contain as for what they actually contained, because every politician had reason to fear that wiretaps and photographs of his most sordid moments reposed in the Black Cabinet. The result of this campaign was that J. Edgar Hoover became director of the Bureau for life, even though every President after FDR swore that he intended to get rid of J. Edgar Hoover.

For some years, a young man named Clyde Tolson had been a close friend of J. Edgar Hoover. Tolson's background was similar to Hoover's, an amiable young man who was taken up by important political figures. He had been confidential secretary to Newton D. Baker, Secretary of War, and later went to night school and obtained a law degree. In 1928, he joined the Bureau of Investigation as John Edgar's personal confidant. An associate,

William Sullivan, later said, "But, for reasons that were never entirely clear, Tolson rose quickly and was soon working at the Director's side."

If Sullivan had ever intended to make these reasons more clear, he was denied the opportunity when he was shot and killed during a mysterious hunting "accident".

On May 18, 1934, FDR signed six special crime bills which greatly increased Hoover's power. The Bureau was renamed the Federal Bureau ofinvestigation, and given mandates to investigate bank robberies, kidnappings and other felonies. Atty. Gen. Homer Cummings requested]. Edgar Hoover to publicize the work of the Bureau, in order to give his agents greater public authority and acceptance. Hoover, who had always managed to avoid the limelight, suddenly found he must make a complete reversal. He somewhat reluctantly embarked on a public relations effort, hiring a well-known Washington newsman, Henry Suydam. Suydam proved a brilliant success, and soon magazines, radio and newsreels were filled with glowing reports of the FBI achievements, even though (on closer inspection) they could have been seen to be less impressive than they were portrayed.

J. Edgar Hoover suddenly realized that to the press corps, Suydam was beginning to be the FBI. Suydam was let go, and his name was never again mentioned in the FBI building. He had become a non-person. Hoover now dealt directly with the press, making announcements of the arrest of crime figures, and personally editing all press releases to put himself in the most favorable light. An old friend of Sen. Walsh, Sen. McKellar, complained on the floor of the Senate that Hoover had never fired a gun or made an arrest. Hoover quickly set up the arrest of a prominent fugitive, whom the FBI had been following for several months, the gang leader Alvin Karpis. When Karpis left his room, FBI agents rushed up to him, seized him, and took his gun. J. Edgar

Hoover then stepped up and informed Karpis that he was under arrest. In a typical FBI rnixup, it was discovered that no one had any handcuffs. An agent gallantly whipped off his tie and secured Karpis' hands behind his back. The nation's press headlined Hoover's fearless deed, and silenced his critics on Capitol Hill.

After some years, J. Edgar Hoover allowed another protege, Louis Nichols, to take over much of the public relations chores. Not only did Nichols name his son after J. Edgar Hoover; he also set up the J. Edgar Hoover Foundation.

Nichols found a number of Jewish multimillionaires who were more than willing to put up money for the J. Edgar Hoover Foundation. The principal donors were the toy tycoon, Louis Marx, whose son-in-law, Daniel Ellsberg, stole the Pentagon Papers and gave them to the New York Times, and the two largest whiskey tycoons in America, the Bronfmans of Seagram Distilleries, and Lew Rosenstiehl of Schenley Distillers. These two Jews controlled seventyfive percent of retail liquor sales in America. They also were long-time mobsters who had survived the rum-running wars of the 1920's.

In his book, *Secret File,* Henry Messick wrote, p.197: "Reinfeld had headed the Reinfeld Syndicate during the great days of the Big Seven, in partnership with the Bronfman brothers in Canada and Longie Zwillman, "the Al Capone of New Jersey". Much of the liquor brought to Rum Row off the East Coast was transported there by the Reinfeld Syndicate." On page 277, Messick writes: "The Reinfeld Syndicate was divided into two parts; the Canadian end was headed by the four Bronfman brothers, Samuel, Abraham, Harry and Allen. Theybegan asowners of a small hotel and ended as the richest men in Canada and head of Distillers-Seagram. It was the Bronfmans' duty to buy Canadian booze and ship it around the East Coast to the Rum Rows of Boston and New York".

The ADL propagandist Drew Pearson, who was succeeded by Jack Anderson, entered many items in his diaries which he never saw fit to publish in his column. On July 18, 1949, he noted concerning Bill Helis, who had purchased the Tanforan race track from Joe Reinfeld: "Now I understand why Bill Helis contributed three thousand dollars to the J. Edgar Hoover Foundation. Heliswas a front for Joe Reinfeld." On April 10, 1950, in a speech before the United Jewish Appeal in Newark, N.J., Drew Pearson noted that Joe Reinfeld had contributed $110,000. Reinfeld's partner, the Jew Longie Zwillman, later was under investigation and conveniently "committed suicide" with a length of light cord when it was feared that he might talk.

The Bronfmans and Rosenstiehl were heavy contributors to the ADL, which had longstanding Mafia ties with the Jewish banker of the Mafia, Meyer Lansky, and other Jewish gangsters who directed the supposedly "Sicilian" crime syndicate. Their contributions to the J. Edgar Hoover Foundation became bread cast upon the waters, as they were richly rewarded when Louis Nichols used his FBI and Capitol Hill connections to lobby through bills which saved them many millions of dollars. In 1958, Nichols lobbied an excise tax bill through Congress which saved Schenley $50 million in taxes. He sponsored the Forand Bill which extended the storage period for whiskey from eight to twenty years. Schenley stock increased 67 percent in value as soon as this bill was passed. Nichols retired from the FBI and acquired large estates in Virginia and New Jersey.

J. Edgar Hoover and his consort Clyde Tolson for many years spent their winter vacations as the guests of the Roney Plaza Hotel in Miami Beach, Florida. The Roney Plaza, which was also the Miami base of the columnist Walter Winchell was the national headquarters of the crime syndicate. Here the dons of the Mafia families could gather in absolute safety. Hotel thieves knew better than to ever set foot in the Roney Plaza, as they would exit in a box.

This hotel was the show place of the Schine chain of hotels. Upstate farmers can still recall the days when J. Meyer Schine walked from farm to farm with a pack on his back, peddling household supplies to their wives. New York mobsters resolved that they needed a quiet place in the country in which they could torture and kill their victims without interference. They bought a hotel and asked J. Meyer Schine to run it for them. Soon Schine was the president of a nationwide chain of hotels and theaters. When Robert F. Kennedy was assassinated, it was in the Ambassador Hotel, a Schine Hotel, a fact which his biographer (Arthur Schlesinger) found more than curious.

The press showed no curiosity about Hoover's residence in the headquarters of the Mafia in Miami Beach, nor did they offer much comment on what became an annual ritual, Hoover's press conference in which he denounced the oft-repeated "myth" of a national crime syndicate. He dismissed all such reports as the inventions of a few sensation seekers and as complete nonsense. He continued to maintain this article of faith even after the Kefauver Hearings, which Kefauver had hoped would propel him into the presidency, but which had the opposite effect, because three-fourths of potential campaign funds could only be raised from the Mafia-ADL alliance. The Valachi revelations did little to convince J. Edgar Hoover of the existence of the Mafia, nor was he disturbed when Valachi insisted he would talk only if he would not be turned over to the FBI. Valachi knew that if the FBI got to him, the Mafia contract on him would promptly be carried out. He obtained residence on an Army base and survived for many years.

For a number of years two special agents of the FBI actually carried out many Mafia "hits" on contract from the leaders of organized crime. When Ian Fleming was stationed in Washington, he was told of the existence of these two "specialists" who were "licensed to kill". He was inspired to write his famous .007 series, even though the British never had such an agent as James Bond, who was based solely on the FBI models.

Not only did the leaders of organized crime lead a charmed existence during themany years that J. Edgar Hoover headed the FBI; his agents' actual ventures into gun battles with criminals were often ludicrous or disastrous. State and local police were dismayed when these "Keystone cops" stumbled into carefully planned forays against gangsters and completely wrecked the setups designed to entrap them. On Dec. 15, 1936, one of the wildest gun battles in the history of New York took place, when FBI agents attacked the hiding place of a notorious bank robber, Henry Brinetta. Local police had Brinetta staked out and were waiting for his partner, Merle Vandenbush, to appear, when the FBI (directed from a safe place in the rear by J. Edgar Hoover) launched a frontal attack on Brinetta's hiding place. The ensuing fusillade was described by one reporter as reminiscent of the Battle of the Marne. Buildings caught fire from the hail of bullets, and firemen tried to put out the flames while dodging bullets from both sides. New York Police Commissioner Lewis Valentine publicly denounced Hoover and the FBI agents for needlessly endangering the lives of hundreds of citizens. Undaunted, Hoover retired to his table at a night club toregale Walter Winchell and other hangers-on with his story of the battle. Local police later captured Merle Vandenbush in Armonk, N.Y., without a shot having been fired.

Because of such exploits, FBI agents had long encountered considerable hostility from state and local police officials. To counteract this hostility, J. Edgar Hoover set up a National Police School as an adjunct to his FBI Academy at Quantico Marine Base in Virginia. The ostensible purpose was to train police in the latest crime-fighting methods perfected by the FBI. In fact, the ADL took over the entire program of the police academy and used it to "politicize" the police departments throughout the United States. Crime problems were ignored as the academy curriculum, prepared by the ADL, focused on "minority rights" and the treatment of the "disadvantaged". Those police who adopted the ADL propaganda techniques were rapidly promoted, while those who resisted this Jewish indoctrination soon found all doors closed to them. The direct result of the FBI-ADL training has been the death of more than one thousand policemen at the hands of black thugs, the most recent case being a 16-year-old black youth who was brought to a station in a Washington, D.C. suburb for routine questioning. He seized a revolver from a policeman's holster and shot down two policemen in cold blood. He was convicted of manslaughter and is expected to serve about nine months in a "juvenile facility" where he will be a hero because he got two "hankies".

One of the techniques developed by the ADL and used at the police academy requires a white policeman to stand rigidly at attention while blacks shout every possible obscenity into his face and then spit directly on him. Policemen who resent this treatment are weeded out as being"racially biased". The ADL also instituted Civilian Review Boards to harass white policemen who arrested black criminals. The result of the ADL-FBI campaign has been a national breakdown of the enforcement of law and order. The American people are terrorized by thugs; elderly white people starve to death in their apartments because they dare not goout into the street to buy food. Some of them commit suicide because they can no longer face the horror of their daily existence, in which gangs of black thugs stalk the streets, maiming and killing for profit, or (equally often) for pure savage pleasure in beating an elderly white person to death. In the name of "minority rights", policemen follow the training they received at the FBI Academy, and look the other way.

The chief publicist for the Mafia-ADLFBI alliance was a ratty New York Jew named Walter Winchell. FBI agents learned that they should read Winchell's column every day, not only for the routine laudatory references to "The Director", but also to get the list of the day's enemies. During World War II, Winchell demanded a commission asan officer in the U.S. Navy. He held court each night at the Stork Club in his lieutenant-commander's uniform while American boys were dying in trenches fighting the enemies of the Jews. J. Edgar Hoover and Tolson were often guest at Winchell's table, along with Frank Costello and other leaders of organized crime. In answer to widespread public protest over Winchell's antics as a "combat hero", Cong. John Rankin was asked on the floor of Congress, "Just who is this \Valter Winchell, anyway?" "Oh, he's just a dirty little kike," responded Rankin. Congressman Dickstein of New York, who had wangled Winchell's naval commission at the personal request of the ADL, jumped up to protest Rankin's remark, but became so excited that he dropped dead. Dickstein was the Jew who set up the original House Committee on Un-American Activities to harass anti-Communists. It was then taken over by the Texan, Cong. Maury Maverick, to expose the Communists. The ADL at that time began a frantic campaign to abolish the House Committee on Un-American Activities, and succeeded after thirty-years' struggle.

During the years before Pearl Harbor, when the Jews were frantically maneuvering the American people into their war tosave Communism from the German armies, the ADL forced J. Edgar Hoover to place the entire FBI at their disposal to harass patriots and to end all resistance to our entering the war. They soon perfected their techniques of ADL-provocateurs which they have used ever since, and which follow an unvarying pattern. An extremely enthusiastic person joins a patriotic group, immediately begins to contribute money, organizes meetings and entertainments, and soon begins to criticize the members for not taking "more direct action". The provocateur proposes dynamiting buildings, killing prominent Jews and politicians, and other actions, and brings in supplies of guns and dynamite, which in every instance is provided by the FBI.

A typical operation concerned The Christian Front Sporting Club in Brooklyn. On Jan.15, 1940, the FBI arrested seventeen members of this group and charged them with plotting to overthrow the government. The New York World Telegram observed:

"Although the men were taken to court in handcuffs, guarded with care by deputy marshals and G-Men, they looked anything but dangerous. They were a shame-faced lot of lowpaid white-collar workers and laborers."

The trial soon brought out the fact that theonly plot was the oneset up by the FBI, which paid a professional informer, Denis Healey, and his wife $1,300 to infiltrate the sporting club. Healy obtained guns for the club from a National-Guard armory, with FBI assistance, and wined and dined the club members with FBI funds. When the members were drunk, Healy opened the doors of the club, and FBI agents with drawn guns rushed in and arrested the "conspirators". The outraged jury promptly acquitted the Christian Front members of all charges.

During the 1950's, the FBI became the chief financial backer of the Communist Party of America. At one point, it was estimated that 75 percent of all Communist Party donations came from informers, who comprised 18 percent of the active employees.

J. Edgar Hoover, who had been appointed Director to paralyze anti-Communist activity in the United States by his mentor, the left-wing Harlan Fiske Stone, systematically thwarted efforts to combat Communist subversion. He ignored dozens of reports that Alger Hiss, FDR's personal assistant, was a Communist courier. When Elizabeth Bentley tried to expose a ring of communist agents, she had to visit FBI offices in New York and Connecticut for more than three months before she could get anyone to listen to her. In almost every trial of a Communist agent, the FBI surveillance had been conducted in such a way that the judge was forced to throw out the indictment because of wiretaps or illegal searches.

J. Edgar Hoover made public appeals that anyone having knowledge of Communist subversion should do absolutely nothing except notify an FBI office. The result was that citizens who reported instances of Communist espionage were committed to insane asylums as "deluded overwrought paranoid cases with obsessions of persecution". Many patriots (myself included) were systematically hounded from their jobs and homes, their families were harassed over a period of years, their telephones were tapped, their mail was seized, and their neighbors were turned against them.

The nation now began to suffer an epidemic of bombings and killings which were the work of paid FBI provocateurs. In 1970, the FBI paid two informers $38,500 to set up an assassination in Meridian, Miss., in which a woman was killed. Thousands of hippies went on the FBI payrolls across the nation to set up other bombings, riots and killings. The famed Kent State massacre litigations which were blamed on the National Guard, were dismissed in court because the fatal shots had been fired by an FBI provocateur.

Although each president after FDR swore to get rid of J. Edgar Hoover, not one of them succeeded. Harry Truman had his friend Max Lowenthal write a book attacking Hoover and the FBI, the first such work ever printed in this country, but later he had to call on Hoover for assistance in protecting his homosexual assistant, David Niles, a drunken Jewish Communist who wandered the streets picking up truck drivers. When they threatened to beat him up, the FBI agents who crouched behind garbage cans while Niles was cruising, would rush forth and rescue him.

There were repeated charges of a "Homintern", an international homosexual and pro-Communist network of officials in

Washington and other countries. After swimming nude with President Lyndon Johnson in the White House pool, his intimate assistant, Walter Jenkins, would wander over to the basement restroom of the nearby YMCA in search of further entertainment. He was arrested there in January 1959, but a second arrest (on Oct.7, 1964) by vice-squad detectives exposed his White House connection. He was rushed to a hospital, suffering from "fatigue". J. Edgar Hoover sent him flowers and despatched a horde of FBI agents into the streets to counteract the publicity. They conducted more than five hundred interviews in a vain attempt to cover up the case. J. Edgar Hoover made it a nightly practice to call Lyndon Johnson and regale him with the latest information on the sexual peccadilloes of his enemies on Capitol Hill. Johnson's presidency was a welcome change from the abuse which J. Edgar Hoover had to take from Atty. Gen. Robert F. Kennedy, who liked to stroll into Hoover's private office, unannounced (in shirt sleeves and leading a huge vicious dog) while he announced to no one in particular, "I hate queers". Clyde Tolson was heard to exclaim, after one such visit, "I hope someone shoots and kills the son of a b...". Robert F. Kennedy had been the first Attorney General to summon]. Edgar Hoover to his office, instead of making the pilgrimage to the venerable Director's sanctum. He also demanded that Hoover immediately hire a large number of black agents. Hoover, like many who are passing as white, made no secret of his long-standing dislike of Negroes. One can envision the glee with which J. Edgar Hoover learned of the approaching affair in Dallas, plans which he carefully withheld from the hated brother of the victim. As soon as the good news was flashed from Dallas, J. Edgar Hoover picked up the phone and called Robert F. Kennedy at his McLean home."Your brother's been killed," he said, and hung up. A few minutes later, the phone which Robert F. Kennedy had demanded he install on his desk for personal communications began to ring.J. Edgar Hoover let it ring for a few minutes, and then turned to Clyde Tolson. "I think it's time we put this damned thing back out on Helen Gandy's desk where it belongs," he said. He later boasted that he never spoke to

Robert F. Kennedy again during the six months that Kennedy stayed on as Attorney General. Having obtained his job as a result of the Teapot-Dome scandal, he now found himself in a predicament as a result of the Watergate affair. He had learned that the money for the Watergate break-in, which had been laundered through Mexico, had come from Dwayne Andreas. The interesting thing about this discovery was that Andreas had been a principal financial backer of Hubert Humphrey's campaign for the presidency, and had contributed many thousands of dollars to Humphrey to pay for his children's education. It was unlikely that he would have paid for the Watergate break-in unless it was to provide a possible excuse for Nixon's impeachment if Humphrey should lose the election.

J. Edgar Hoover faced a dilemma. Should he let Nixon know about this discovery, which would save Nixon from impeachment; or should he let matters take their course? He now made the mistake of consulting his aides during his indecision. The conspirators were immediately informed of Hoover's findings. The entire plot to thwart the expressed will of the American electorate was imperiled. Hoover must be disposed of at once. That evening, as he entered his bullet-proof limousine, he was immediately strangled. He was driven to his home and the body was dumped by his bedside, where it was discovered at 8:30 a.m. on May 2, 1972, by his maid, Annie Fields. Another little item we will never be able to prove. An era had ended.

BOYCOTT: THE JEWISH WEAPON

IN 1950, Senator Pat McCarran said to me, "If the American people ever find out what the Jews are doing to them, they won't leave a Jew alive from coast to coast." An official of the American Jewish Congress said "We must never lose sight of the fact that the only thing preventing pogroms in the United States today is our watchful control over the channels of communication." And in 1977 a Jewish columnist wrote, "We have been overthrown by the television show Roots, as many whites have been inculcated with feelings of shame, fear and guilt by this revelation of black history. This should warn us that we are sitting on a powder keg, if unfriendly elements should be allowed the chance to present the Jews in an unfavourable light on television. The success of Roots must reinforce our determination to deny native fascist elements any and all opportunities to use the media to spread their poison to impressionable Americans."

This fear among the Jews is real because the crimes of the Jews are real. As Senator McCarran pointed out to me the rage of Americans, once aroused by a factual chronicling of the of the Jews, would be unleashed in one of the most terrible strokes of vengeance ever known.

We all know that the principal function of the United States Government today is to maintain Jewish dictatorship over the American workers. On every hand, American citizens groan under censorship, denial of civil rights and oppressive taxation which finances the genocide campaign of the Jews against the Arab people. We suffer the proliferation of government agents who force their way into every aspect of our private lives to enforce Jewish decrees against the people. How did the Jews attain this power? The record can be useful to us. A numerically small and physically weak group.

of parasites encysted itself in the main avenues of American life. By maintaining absolute discipline in their ranks, they seized control of the most powerful nation in the world. Always beginning in commerce, frequently by dealing in second-hand or stolen goods, they branched out into government, religion, education and communications. In every case, their gains were used to increase Jewish power over the people.

The fanatical self-discipline of the Jews is shown by their use of the boycott. In 1933, the German people democratically elected a non-Jewish government. During the 1920's, the Germans had suffered under a victorious Jewish government called the "Weimar Republic", which dominated every aspect of German life. The German people defeated this Jewish dictatorship in 1933 by voting against it. Immediately the Jews called a world conference in Amsterdam, the diamond capital of the world, forming the "Non-Sectarian Anti-Nazi League" with a multimillionaire Jewish lawyer from New York, Samuel Untermyer, as its president. Untermyer demanded a "sacred war" against Germany. The League was hardly non-sectarian, since it was one hundred per cent Jewish. Gentiles paid little attention to this declaration of war, not realizing it was the first shot of World War Two. They supposed that war meant armies marching against each other, and did not understand that for the Jew, life is war. He is born battling against the gentiles, and spends his entire lifetime in a state of war. Gentiles know little of the subterranean type of warfare waged internationally by the Jew, in which poison, arson and murder are the most typical weapons.

While Untermyer presided over the visible attack against Germany, a worldwide campaign of terrorism was launched against Germany by Vladimir Jabotinksy, founder of the Irgun Zvai Leumi, the terrorist wing of the Zionist movement. Jabotinsky's mastery of terrorism ensured the establishment of the State of Israel in 1948, and Jabotinsky became a respected member of the Israeli Parliament. In January 1934, Jabotinsky declared in his newspaper,

Natcha Retch, "The fight against Germany has been carried on for months by every Jewish community, conference, congress, trade organization, by every Jew in the world. Our Jewish interests demand the complete destruction of Germany."

This terrible outcry of hatred reveals the true nature of the Jew, whose motto of "Solidarity Forever" indicts their state of war against all civilized people. Jabotinsky is saying that no Jew can ever be a loyal citizen of any nation, because "our Jewish interests" take precedence over all other ties.

Despite this declaration of war by the Jews, Germany took no anti-Jewish measures for nearly five years, until provocateurs forced five to take steps to protect themselves. Max Warburg continued to reside unmolested, in Germany until 1939, when he packed his possessions and moved to New York. However, the worldwide boycott by the Jews against Germany, organized in 1933, had taken immediate effect. Such boycotts are illegal in the United States, because they comprise acts of "criminal syndicalism", the alliance of criminals to inflict damage upon others by criminal combinations. Nevertheless, the Jews, operating with complete freedom under Roosevelt's New Deal, or Jew Deal, as it was known to many Americans, conducted their illegal boycott openly, advertising the fact that they were in criminal restraint of trade. They carried on a national campaign of terrorism against anyone who dared to handle German goods. Since forty per cent of Americans were of German origin, one might suppose they would have little effect, but most of the German descendants joined in the boycott, hoping to prove that they were "good Americans". Operating on a multimillion dollar budget, the Non-Sectarian Anti-Nazi League poured forth a flood of publications from their headquarters in New York City. One such, The Idealist, in August 1937 carried a front page list of merchants who were still handling German goods. These were small shops, as the large firms had long since yielded to vicious Jewish pressure and had agreed to boycott

Germany. Another paper, the Anti-Nazi Bulletin, boasted in February 1939 that Germany would be brought to her knees by the worldwide Jewish boycott. It stated editorially, "The boycott is the solution, its effect as inexorable and inevitable as the march of time." A few months later, the German armies stood unchallenged as the masters of Europe, but the Jews could afford to wait.

Many Americans were horrified by the hate campaign of the Jews, realizing that the Jews were determined to use American youths in their war against Germany. One who dared to oppose them was America's greatest living hero, Charles Lindbergh. Lindbergh's father, a Congressman during WW I had his home broken into by federal agents and his books burned because he spoke out against the enactment of the Federal Reserve Act. In 1932 the Jews backing the Roosevelt campaign were terrified that Charles Lindbergh might decide to seek the office of President. Should this handsome blond hero, the most famous man in America; decide to run, the misshapen Roosevelt, crouching in his wheelchair, would not stand a chance. In March of 1932, Lindbergh's baby son was kidnapped and killed by ritual murder. The sorrowing Lindbergh withdrew from public life, and Roosevelt's campaign was secure. Years later, a German carpenter, Gerhart Hauptmann, was electrocuted for this murder. A recent book proves that the FBI fabricated the evidence which sent him to the electric chair, as a vital part of the Jews' Hate-Germany campaign. Another book proves that the Jews set fire to the Zeppelin Hindenburg in New Jersey, a few miles from the scene of the Lindbergh murder, which was touring here on a goodwill mission from Germany.

Knowing that the Jews intended to use American boys as cannon fodder to attack the non-Jewish government of Germany, Charles Lindbergh came forth as the leader of the American First movement. The Jews launched a national smear campaign against him, which continues to this day. During World II the Jews refused to allow him to serve as a commissioned officer in the armed forces, but he flew many missions as a "civilian observer" in the Pacific.

Few Americans today recall the unpleasant aspects of life during World War II. Black markets flourished as the Jews made billions of dollars in profits from illegal sales of sugar, gasoline and other commodities. At the same time, they instituted tight rationing controls on white Americans, and demanded that they inform on each other when an extra pound of butter appeared. Hordes of Jews and their Mafia allies counterfeited millions of rationing stamps, and ploughed their profits into urban real estate.

Successful in their boycott and war against Germany, the Jews confidently proceeded with their plans to exterminate the entire German people. In 1941, Theodore Kaufman wrote in "Germany Must Perish. To achieve the purpose of German extinction it would be necessary to only sterilize some 48 million." Henry Morgenthau whose father had made millions of dollars by turning the pleasant New York area of Harlem into a vast black slum, persuaded Roosevelt to adopt his Morgenthau Plan for exterminating the Germans. His assistant, the Lithuanian Jew and Soviet agent Harry Dexter White, succeeded in dismantling hundreds of Germany's factories and shipping them to Russia, where they rusted for years on railroad sidings, because the Russians did not know how to reassemble them. During this time, the Germans built new factories which forced the economies of the Jewish allies, England and France, towards. bankruptcy.

The British writer, George Orwell, horrified by the total control which Jewish society exercised over every aspect of members of the Jewish community, wrote a book warning that this Jewish society might someday extend its dictatorship over all peoples. He called his book "1984", and it became a best seller, but to this day no one has ever revealed that it is a case history study of Jewish dictatorship.

Many naive gentiles supported the establishment of the State of Israel, which was founded on the horrors of such terrorist acts as the bombing of the King David Hotel and the murder of the United Nations observer, Count Folke Bernadotte, because they supposed that all of the Jews would emigrate there to live. They knew nothing of the phenomenon of biological parasitism, or that Jews had no intention of voluntarily giving up their encysted positions in Western civilization. Anti-Jewish sentiment has always been a hallmark of Western culture, and has usually been found only in the most advanced centres of our society, such as Vienna, where Hitler first studied the Jewish problem, and in London and Paris. The greatest thinkers, such as Lothrop Stoddard and Houston Stewart Chamberlain, warned us of the Jewish peril, while the Jews hired the most craven and diseased politicians in the Western nations, such as Roosevelt and Churchill, to advance their cause.

During World War II, the brilliant Virginian, Lady Astor, was present at a wartime meeting of Churchill and Roosevelt and remarked to her companion, "Just look at those two great humanitarians! Franklin hates anyone who can walk, and Winston hates anyone who is sober."

While the Jewish dominated powers have lamely defended Israel's continued acts of aggression and genocide against the Arab people, other nations have demanded that she be brought to account. In response, the Jews intensified their worldwide propaganda campaign to defend their atrocities. They brought off a master stroke when they placed a Jew in New York as head of all Arab propaganda activities in the United States. Of course the American people remained uninformed about the Arab cause after this new treachery. Nevertheless, worldwide feeling against the Jews continued to mount. A new master stroke of propaganda was needed. The Jews achieved this by their ancient technique of claiming that their opponents were guilty of the very atrocities that the Jews were committing. Founded on terrorism, the State of Israel now became the secret organizer of an "anti-Israel" group, the Palestine Liberation Organization. One Yasser Arafat, whose mother was Jewish, became the head of the greatest Jewish hoax in history. Nevertheless, the PLO was responsible for the survival of Israel, as each attack by the PLO has resulted in renewed worldwide sympathy and support for Israel. Each PLO attack has come just at the moment when the demands that Israel return to its 1948 borders have reached a crescendo, and after the attack the demands against Israel have been hushed. Thousands of young Arabs were persuaded to join the PLO under the delusion that they would strike at the enemy. Instead, they were sent out to be slaughtered. For years, Jewish insiders have joked about the nightly "turkey shoots", as Israelis leisurely shot down the PLO infiltrators, whose exact route, number and armaments had been radioed to the Jews even before the "terrorists" had left their base. The "turkey shoots" became a popular Israeli sport, and high-ranking officials such as Moshe Dayan took part in picking off the "terrorists". On one occasion, a very high-ranking State Department official was allowed to pick off his "turkey", a seventeen-year-old Arab youth.

On necessary occasions, to stifle foreign critics, the Jews allowed a few of the infiltrators to proceed to some small Israeli village where they shot a few Jews before being killed. The Jews also ordered the murder of two State Department officials in the Sudan, to excite Americans against the Arabs. The greatest propaganda stroke of the Jewish-directed PLO was the "massacre" of Israeli athletes at the Olympic Games in Munich. Yasser Arafat was invited to speak to the United Nations, where he stood brandishing a gun. He was repeatedly interviewed on the Jewish program, Sixty Minutes, where his interviewer, Mike Wallace, showed no discomfort at being in the presence of "the most dangerous Jew-killer in the world". Col. Eugene Sanctuary told me in 1952, "To find out who the Jews have in their pocket, merely observe to which of their 'enemies' they give the most publicity. Their true enemies always get the silent treatment."

Meanwhile, the Arab leaders were kept busy denying any connection with the PLO, making them seem even more disunited than before. It was obvious to experienced political observers that the PLO was being directed by the Jews. None of its activities were of the slightest benefit to the Arabs, but every act of its "terrorists" reaped a vast new harvest of support for Israel. The "outrages" committed by the PLO were particularly useful to the craven politicians in the United States, because it gave the cover of "humanitarianism" to their acts of high treason in support of Israel and against the interests of the American people.

The next great hoax of the Jews was the creation of OPEC, the cartel of oil producing nations. OPEC was not an Arab creation at all, but the brainchild of two Jews from Venezuela, who conceived the idea of persuading the Arabs to triple the price of their oil. The Arabs were sceptical of Jews bearing gifts, and they had no real need of increased revenues. However, the Arab world was one of startling paradoxes, as the Arab nations which had outlawed the Communist Party were being supplied with arms by the Soviet Union. The Arabs finally agreed, and the Western democracies were thrown into economic chaos, while fifty, billion dollars of their capital funds flowed into Arab banks. It should surprise no one that most of this money wound up in Jewish hands. There was one important exception, the Arab banks in Beirut, Lebanon. It was imperative to the wellbeing of the Jewish financial empire that these Arab banks be destroyed. Southern Lebanon was the site of many Palestine refugee camps and the staging area for PLO "raids" into Israel. After each of these abortive raids, Israeli planes attacked the refugee camps and killed many women and children. The world remained silent in the face of these atrocities. King Hussein of Jordon, who was married to a British secret service agent, had already mounted a terrible attack against the refugees. On Feb. 18, 1977, Bob Woodward, of Watergate fame, revealed in the Washington Post that since 1957, the CIA had privately paid King Hussein one million dollars a year for his private life of sports cars and planes, while furnishing him with blond prostitutes from London and New York.

This was in addition to the $200,000,000 a year which the United States gave Jordan in "aid". In return, Hussein acted as an agent of the. Jews, furnishing intelligence information against the other Arab leaders. This twenty-year-old story was considered "a great scoop"!

King Faisal who opposed further OPEC increases, was assassinated. Suddenly a violent civil war broke out in Lebanon, between the dominant Christian "right-wing" party, which was controlled by the CIA and the Jews, and the Moslems, who were considered left-wing. The PLO apparently was in the middle, being attacked by both sides.

Their refugee camps were wiped out, with terrible atrocities being committed against the hapless inhabitants. The Arab banks in Beirut were blown up and burned. During the many months of this "civil war", none of the hundreds of correspondents in the area could offer an explanation of what the fighting was about, who was financing it, what the goals were, or any other details. Meanwhile, the State of Israel basked in peace and security as the Arabs massacred each other. In the United States, the Congressional investigation of the CIA came to a screeching halt when it was on the verge of exposing the CIA setting up of the "civil war" in Lebanon.

The Jews continued their boycotts in the United States, while howling about a non-existent "Arab boycott" of U.S. firms which supported Israel. Since all U.S. firms contributed to Israel, both directly and indirectly, such a boycott could not exist. When Mexico supported a U.N. resolution that "Zionism is Racism", the Jews launched a boycott of Mexican hotels which was later called off when they realized that most of the hotels and restaurants affected were owned by Jews.

As an astute student of the Roosevelt road to power, Jimmy Carter knew that from 1933 to 1941, all of Roosevelt's social programs were disastrous farces. Since he planned to remain in power for four terms, repealing the limitation on Presidential service, he has drew up war plans which he believed would take him down Roosevelt's successful power play in 1941 and into a foreign war. However, Carter did not have eight years to fumble with social programs, as ne was elected only by Ford's moronic decision to debate him and by Jack Anderson's smear of Howard Baker's wife as an alcoholic, panicking the Neanderthal Ford into choosing Dole and losing the Southern states Baker would have brought him. Carter's advisers told him that we would have TWENTY PER CENT inflation and a war plan should be instituted by that date. The Chiefs of Staff gave him two areas where Russia would allow him to go without precipitating World War III—South Africa and the Middle East. His black adviser Andrew Young insisted that we go into Southern Africa and destroy the white governments of Rhodesia and South Africa, but his Jewish advisers prevailed with their final solution to the Arab problem. The American Army will impose a Pax Judaica on the Middle East, controlling or deposing as many Arab governments as possible and taking over their oil fields as they now have done in Iraq, a move which has been very popular with the American public. Russia has been given a great deal of influence in Iran. as the price of keeping hands off and will likely has been and the United States will gain control over Afghanistan and Pakistan at a later date. They will cause as much strife in Iran as they can to keep that country from playing a major role in their plans.

Having wiped out the last vestiges of opposition in the Middle East, the Jews can then turn to their final task, eliminating their last opponents, the recalcitrant white minority in the United States. A successful campaign to swamp them with non-whites has resulted in more than thirty 30 million Mexicans and other non-whites being imported into the United States. The Jew, is, trying to destroy, the moral fibre of the remaining whites through drugs, pornography, and public lotteries. These vices have no effect on the non-whites as they comprise their normal way of life.

Many years of struggle lay ahead! The bones of our dead are crying out for, REVENGE!

Our ancient thirst for justice and for the triumph of our nation will be re-enacted in solemn rituals over the graves of our enemies. AMERICA VICTORIOUS!

SIGMUND FREUD – ANTICHRIST DEVIL

Few Americans realize that the principal tool of Communist penetration in the United States is the pseudoscience of psychotherapy. Not only have many patriots who opposed Communist subversion been imprisoned for life without trial, but many others have been rendered helpless, their fortunes seized, and their exposures of Communist treachery discredited by the accusation of 'mental illness'. In 1848, Karl Marx issued his Communist Manifesto, detailing the Jewish plans for subduing the gentile, but it was not until 1896 that the most workable system to achieve this goal, 'psychoanalysis', was unveiled by his fellow-Jew Sigmund Freud.

No one suspected at the time that Freud (pronounced Fraud) had invented the indispensable tool for the biological parasite in his quest to gain absolute control over the life of the gentile host.

Psychoanalysis became the instrument which the Jew used to probe the deepest recesses of the mind of the host, thereby learning his best secrets, as well as the hidden fears and doubts which could be exploited by a clever enemy in order to become his master.

Beginning his career as a medical student, Freud concentrated on the study of the nervous system, obtaining a degree in neuropathology. Up to this point, his education had been strictly scientific, conducted according to methodical Teutonic principles of study in the Vienna Medical School. He now abandoned these principles. For the rest of his life, he would be the typical Jewish adventurer, seeking one path after the other until he hit upon the one which would lead him to fame, riches and, more important than either of these to the Jew, power over the gentile host.

For several years, Freud experimented with "cocaine therapy" or, as a policeman might put it, drug peddling.

The only outcome of this was that he himself became a convert, and continued to use cocaine throughout his life. Even today, cocaine is the favored drug of the wealthy and influential Jews in New York and Hollywood who control the minds of the American people through television and the news media.

They are loyal to cocaine solely because it was the drug of their master, Sigmund Freud.

After Freud discovered that putting his patients on cocaine brought him no sudden wealth or prominence, he began to cast about for some quicker road to fortune. He seemed to have found it when he began to practice hypnosis on his patients. For more than a century, hypnosis had been the favorite practice of Europe's most notorious charlatans, Mesmer, Cagliostro, and Charcot. Freud now became the legitimate heir of these mountebanks. But how did he escape being branded by their well deserved reputations as necromancers and frauds? Early in his use of hypnosis, he made the fortunate discovery that it was no longer necessary to put his patients "under", or to subject them to hypnosis in order to get them to reveal their innermost secrets. He had only to establish a suitable atmosphere of confidence and trust, and they would begin to talk about themselves. As Thomas Szasz, the famed critic of this pseudo-science, revealed in his book, THE MYTH OF PSYCHOTHERAPY, "Psychotherapy is merely talking."

Freud's reputation as the great inventor of an entire new science rests solely on his discovery that he could get his patients to talk about themselves without the use of hypnosis. Nevertheless, much of the mumbojumbo of psychotherapy was invented in order to create a hypnotic atmosphere. Freud's discovery freed him from the stigma of the charlatans of hypnosis, and put a great distance between him and his discredited predecessors such as Mesmer, the father of Mesmerism. Nevertheless, the practice of psychoanalysis depends heavily on creating and maintaining a pseudo-hypnotic atmosphere in the psychiatrist's office.

The patient must be persuaded to relax, to place himself completely in the power of the psychiatrist, and to reveal his innermost self. Thus the pseudoscience of psychotherapy functions only because it is pseudohypnosis.

No wonder that Freud is pronounced Fraud!

Once he had broken away from the unsavory reputation of his predecessors, and had put the stigma of charlatanism behind him, Fraud began to build an elaborate facade of intellectual supports for his new "science" of psychotherapy. This proved to be a difficult task, for, as Szasz has pointed out, psychotherapy is merely talk. It would not be easy to erect a vast superstructure of scientific procedures around the basic principle of a patient lying on a couch and chatting about himself to a listening doctor. Nevertheless, Freud, exhibiting all of the talent of his race for bewildering and misleading the gentile host, proceeded to do just that. He devised a "system" based upon incorrect and often obscene theories, using these theories to attack the basis of all family life by such developments as the "Oedipus complex'.

Not only has an "Oedipus complex" never existed, but Freud either completely misunderstood or more likely, purposely misrepresented, the entire basis of this 'complex'. He based it upon an ancient Greek myth, the story of Oedipus. Although he first advanced the theory of the Oedipus complex in 1910, it was not until 1920 that he published three essays which purported to establish the foundations for this theory, the projection of "infantile sexuality'.

It has been said that the Oedipus complex is the nuclear complex of the neuroses and constitutes the most important part of their content, because this complex, appearing early in life, is the basis for all later neuroses. It represents the peak of infantile sexuality, which Freud claims appears in the first year of infancy, and forever after molds the nervous structure of the adult. In fact, there is not the slightest evidence that "infantile sexuality" reaches its peak in the first year of life, or that there is even such a phenomenon as infantile sexuality. Of course, this did not bother Freud. If there were no such thing as infantile sexuality, he would invent it. He built the Oedipus complex by tacking his pet sexual obsessions onto the myth of an ancient Greek King, Laius of Thebes. When Laius consulted the Delphic Oracle to divine his future, he was told that a child born to him and his wife Jocasta would become his murderer. A son, Oedipus, was born to him, and he had the child set out to die on Mt. Cithaeron. Years later, Oedipus, who had been rescued and brought up by a kindly shepherd who found him lying there, met Laius on a narrow path. After a quarrel as to who had the right of way, they fought, and Oedipus killed him. He continued on to the city of Thebes, where he met Laius' widow, Jocasta, who was also his mother, and married her.

The shepherd then appeared, and revealed the true origin of Oedipus, who was overcome by remorse. He blinded himself, while Jocasta hanged herself. This legend, typical of its overtones of traditional Greek tragedy, had deep implications that we must become aware of our identity if we are to lead satisfactory lives, but Freud showed no understanding of this. Instead, he completely distorted the legend by claiming that every male child, even in the first year of infancy, as it writhes in torments of infantile sexuality, is bedeviled by jealousy of the father, whom the child wants to kill so that he can have sex with his mother.

Only a Jew could bring to a traditional myth such perversion and such distortion. As Szasz points out, the Freudian elements, jealousy of the father and the desire to have intercourse with the mother, are completely lacking in the original myth. Donald Wormell, writing in the Encyclopedia Britannica, notes that the Freudian interpretation has no similarity to the classical Greek story, because Oedipus as an infant had no jealousy of his father, whom he did not know, or any desire to have intercourse with his mother, whom he did not know.

Despite these inconsistencies, Freud claimed that much of the neurosis of the twentieth century was caused by the Oedipus complex. The frustration of the infant, being unable either to kill the father or to have sex with the mother, became "repressed", and was thus mentally affected for the rest of his life. This tissue of distortions, falsities, and perversions became the cornerstone of Freud's entire "science" of psychotherapy.

Freud's reputation as "the father of psychoanalysis" rests upon the Oedipus complex.

The second foundation of the Freudian system is Freud's "theory of repressed homosexuality".

Early in the course of his hypnotic treatment of patients, Freud had encountered a number of wealthy and dissolute aristocrats who, wearying of the usual vices of drug addiction, gambling and alcoholism, had taken up the practice of sexual perversion. After "treating" a number of these perverts, whose real problem was not so much their "homosexuality" as their boredom and their ability to spend as much money as they wished to purchase partners for their perverted acts, Freud decided that "homosexual impulses" were universal among men. Why, then, did not most men engage in homosexual acts? Freud had a ready answer for this:

They "repressed" their homosexual impulses.

Now that he had created the problem, Freud had only to erect a "scientific" foundation for it.

This proved to be a simple task for one of his racial duplicity and lack of morals. He appropriated the greatest figure of Western culture, Leonardo da Vinci, to carry the banner of his new theory. Freud decided that Leonardo da Vinci must have been a homosexual. Da Vinci had once been brought before a court on a charge of homosexuality, and had been acquitted. No other evidence existed that he had been a homosexual, and it had been several centuries since anyone had been around who could testify about it one way or the other.

But Freud, the Jewish mountebank, found this important in order to denigrate da Vinci because he was a great non-Jewish artist.

After a notable lack of success in his efforts to find any basis for his theory that da Vinci had been a homosexual, Freud finally came upon a rather dubious recording of a faint childhood memory, in which Leonardo da Vinci wrote that a vulture came down to his cradle and struck him in the mouth with his tail.

Eureka! Freud had found what he had been looking for. He immediately interpreted this childhood memory, or dream, as an illustration of Leonardo's "passive homosexuality". Flimsy though this basis was, it became the cornerstone of Freud's theory of universal repressed homosexuality among men. Unfortunately, as Freud's disciples have desperately sought to conceal for many years, Thomas Szasz reveals that Freud's entire theory was wrong because of his defective scholarship. He had based his theory on a German text in which the translator had incorrectly translated Leonardo's word for "toy kite" as a "vulture".

The tail of a toy kite had dragged across Leonardo's cradle and brushed him. Freud, relying upon the wrong translation of the kite as a vulture, devised a complicated sexual theory by which Leonardo's memory of the bird's tail touching his mouth had been the conscious fulfillment of his subconscious homosexual desires!

From a wrong understanding, Freud now erected a vast superstructure of Leonardo's entire art and, subsequently, the art of the Western nations being created from his homosexual nature. In so doing, Freud unleashed a terrible weapon against Western civilization. Single-handedly, he created the enormous problem of the "gay" communities which plague America today. By identifying the greatest artist of Western culture as a homosexual, Freud gave an aura of respectability to a sexual deviation. By his claim that all men have "repressed" homosexual desires, he unleashed a torrent of sexual acts and a great blow against established family life. Young men who not only are searching for a career but who also have doubts about their sexual identity have only to abandon themselves to Freud's theories, and they can, simultaneously release all their "sexual repressions', thus avoiding the danger of terrible neuroses, but they can become great artists as well.

Only a Jew could have unleashed such a poisonous theory on the gentile community to further confuse and destroy it. Despite Freud's theories, scientists today have begun to doubt that there really is such a thing as a "homosexual impulse'. Instead, they lean to the finding that there are sexual impulses which, in the absence of a member of the opposite sex, tend to turn to a member of the same sex, as in prison, the army or private schools. Such a finding, of course, is devastating to the "gay" community, which has sought to turn perverse impulses into a modern religion.

We could be accused of oversimplification if we sought to condemn the entire "science" of psychotherapy because its two principal foundations, Freud's theory of repressed homosexuality and the Oedipus complex, have been shown to be little more than the products of his cocaine-stimulated imagination.

Realizing from the outset that Freud's theories might be subject to serious challenge, later practitioners of psychotherapy have sought to erect an even more complex superstructure of psychological theories to bolster their basic technique of 'talk'. In this campaign, they have produced millions of words, but not a single workable theory. As Thomas Szasz points out:

> "Psychotherapy is secular ethics. It is the religion of the formally irreligious—with its language which is not Latin but medical jargon; with its codes of conduct, which are not ethical but legalistic; and with its theology, which is not Christianity, but positivism."

For several years, before fixing upon his theories of psychotherapy, Freud had experimented with various other 'treatments', such as electrotherapy, baths and massages. The German Dr. Wilhelm Erb (1840-1921), in his Handbuch der Elektrotherapie, described his technique for applying electric shock to the genitals, which later became a favorite form of torture in Latin America. Erb "assumed" that the victims on whom he practiced this technique had 'neurosis'. During World War I, the most notorious practitioner of electric shocks was Dr. Julius Wagner-Jauregg, professor of psychiatry at the Vienna Medical School and a former teacher of Freud. Wagner-Jauregg was fond of using heavy doses of electric shock on soldiers who suffered nervous breakdowns during artillery barrages in combat zones. Despite heavy criticism, Wagner-Jauregg continued to use electric shock on soldiers throughout the war. Freud defended him against his critics, calling the soldiers 'malingerers'.

In 1920, the Austrian War Ministry, in response to the public outcry against Wagner-Jauregg, conducted a lengthy investigation of his mistreatment of soldier patients. Freud wrote a long memorandum Defending Wagner-Jauregg's torture technique of electrotherapy. "I know," wrote Freud in Wagner-Jauregg's defense, "that the motivating force in his treatment of patients is his humaneness'. This was a typical Jew view of humaneness.

Electrotherapy was later replaced by chemotherapy, although Freud continued to use some electrotherapy on his patients. He explained it as "pretense treatment', which he used to "keep in touch" with his patients.

Throughout his career, Freud was obsessed by sexual imaginings, which ranged from the ludicrous to the obscene. In one of his letters to Ludwig Binswanger, he wrote: "I have always lived on the ground floor in the basement of the building... I already found one for religion when I stumbled on the category neurosis of mankind." One of his last writings (July 12, 1938) contained this "gem': "As a substitute for penisenvy, identification with the clitoris; neatest expression of inferiority, source of all inhibitions." During the erecting of his psychotherapy empire, Freud was on the lookout for a suitable heir apparent. At one time he had selected a young non-Jewish doctor, Jung, after quarreling with his Jewish disciples. Jung spent much time with him, but found himself unable to accept Freud's wild theories, and he finally dismissed Freud's work as "too Jewish'.

IN MEMORIES, DREAMS AND REFLECTIONS, Jung wrote (p.149):

> "Above all, Freud's attitude towards the spirit seems to me highly questionable. Wherever in a person or in a work of art, an expression of spirituality (in the intellectual, not the supernatural senses) came to light, he suspected it, and insinuated that it was repressed sexuality."

It took Jung several years to realize that the earthbound Jew was unable to comprehend anything spiritual, having to interpret it in the grossest physical sense, and he finally parted company with him.

It was Thomas Szasz, in THE MYTH OF PSYCHOTHERAPY, who writes most revealingly of Freud's creation of "the science of psychotherapy" as an instrument of the Jew to be used to gain power over the gentiles. Szasz titled his chapter, "Sigmund Freud, the Jewish Avenger'. (editor's note: Mr. Mullins uses the word "gentile" meaning all non-Jews, not just Christians).

Freud himself was born a Jew, was given the Jewish name of Schlomo after his grandfather, a rabbi, and remained a Jew.

Szasz further comments: 'The inconsistency between Freud's passionate anti-religious tirades and his profound commitment to Jewishness significantly highlights an important aspect of Freud's personality and predilections, namely, his anti-gentilism. The popular image of Freud as an enlightened, emancipated irreligious person who, with the aid of psychoanalysis, 'discovered' that religion is a mental illness is pure fiction."

Szasz then defines the Freudian psyche permanently by writing: "Freud was throughout his life, a proud, chauvinistic, even vengeful Jew." Thus Freud's famed "irreligiousness" was merely his anti-Christian, antigentile bias. In his "science" of psychoanalysis, Freud focused the hatred of centuries which the biological parasite had cultivated against the host, a hatred irreconcilably rooted in the biological situation of the parasite that must live off the host, and that can have no existence without this relationship. Certainly the State of Israel typifies this relationship, as the entire budget of Israel is built on 'loans', 'grants', 'gifts', and the sale of worthless Israeli bonds.

David Bakan writes of Freud's Jewishness:

"Freud believed that anti-Semitism was practically ubiquitous in either latent or manifest form; the broad masses of England were anti-Semitic 'as everywhere'; he refused to accept royalties of Hebrew and Yiddish translations of his works; he was sympathetic to Zionism from the first days of the movement and was acquainted with and respected Herzl. (Editor's note: Herzl died of syphilis, his entire dream of a Jewish empire in Palestine being the product of the decaying brain of a Jew in the last and most violent stages of paresis). Freud's son was a member of the Kadimah, a Zionist organization, and Freud himself was an honorary member of it." Szasz further notes:

"In addition, Freud displayed his devotion to Judaism in the letters he wrote, the friends and enemies he made, and, last but not least, in his anti-gentilism. His interpretations of Western civilization, Oedipus was not a king, but a complex; Leonardo was not a heroic painter but a homosexual pervert." The final statement of Szasz on Freud's racial bias is the most important (p.146). "One of Freud's most powerful motives in his life was the desire to inflict vengeance on Christ." At last we get to the meat of the matter! Psychoanalysis is the creation of a hate-filled Jew whose life was devoted to vengeance against Christ. Could any more definitive analysis of the satanic origins of "the science of psychotherapy" be made?

The sick theories of this modern anti-Christ did not long remain theories. They were quickly put to use by the Jews, not only in treating the "mentally ill', but in the techniques of attaining and holding political power.

The psychiatrists, interviewing the patients, most of them from wealthy and influential gentile families, learned trade secrets and political information invaluable to the Jewish dreams of enslaving the gentiles.

These secrets were quickly turned to advantage in their war against the Christians. They spawned a host of "psychiatrists" that rapidly infested all of the gentile nations, and then turned up as the directors of mental institutions.

The hapless patient who revealed an attitude critical of the Jews, or who was even suspected of such thoughts, was treated mercilessly. The mental institutions provided the Jews with the ideal laboratory for their wildest dreams of power over the non Jews. They now had an endless supply of victims, completely helpless, whose screams would never be heard by the outside world. What tortures, what murders, have gone on in these institutions in the fifty years since the Freudians took over their operations can only be imagined. Most of the victims will never talk—they are dead. The survivors are "insane'; their stories of their sufferings at the hands of the Jews are merely the products of disordered minds. Nevertheless, we do know that not even the highest government officials have been immune from Freudian "correction" when they strayed from Jewish programs. We have only to remember that when our first Secretary of Defense, James Forrestal, hesitated to commit our entire military power to the support of the State of Israel, within a few hours he suffered a 'breakdown'. He was taken to Bethesda Naval Hospital and soon went out the window to his death. In April 1936, Congressman Marion Zioncheck, denounced J. Edgar Hoover on the floor of Congress. Already known as a 'maverick', Zioncheck had gone too far. Soon afterwards, he was taken under mysterious circumstances to a Washington, D.C., mental hospital, St. Elizabeth s (where the patriot Ezra Pound was held as a political prisoner for thirteen years without trial, and then released because of pressure from his friends). Zioncheck was kept incommunicado at St. Elizabeth s, and treated by several of the nation s leading psychiatrists. After several attempts to escape, he was released in what his friends described as a 'drugged, zombie-like condition'.

He returned to Seattle, and soon fell to his death from the fifth floor of the Arctic Building. The verdict was suicide, but most people interviewed in Seattle believed he had been pushed. He was succeeded by Warren G. Magnuson, who enjoyed a long political career in Washington, and who was very careful not to offend the Jews.

Shortly after the Crash of 1929, when many gentiles had been impoverished by Jewish money manipulation, the psychiatrists began to show their hands as the new masters. In May, 1930, an International Congress on Mental Hygiene was held in Washington, D.C. Four thousand psychiatrists from fifty-three countries were welcomed by the President of the United States, Herbert Hoover. The new masters drafted a charter stating that they alone had the knowledge to "understand and control human behavior... Psychiatry must now decide what is to be the immediate future of the human race." The new pronouncement also boasted that "Psychiatrists alone possess the superior intelligence and knowledge to alter materially and permanently human behaviors." Many of the bureaucrats got the message, and promptly signed up for lengthy series of "analysis'. Soon afterwards, a number of Communist cells were established in the government bureaus, chief among them the Harold Ware cell. Ware was merely the office boy for Felix Frankfurter, who masterminded this Communist group, placing Communist agents high in the official levels of every government department in Washington.

One of the principal speakers at the Washington Congress of Psychiatrists was Dr. Donald A. Nicholson, a psychiatrist from Seattle who was the president of the Washington State Medical Assn.

Nicholson was later to examine Congressman Zioncheck shortly before his "suicide'. He committed thousands of Americans to mental hospitals, all of them on his unsupported testimony that they were "insane'. Few of them ever saw freedom again. His most famous victim was the great Hollywood actress Frances Farmer.

Frances who? A curtain of silence has been rung down on one of America's greatest talents.

When she flashed across the Hollywood screen, she became known as "the American Garbo'. Today her movies are never shown on television or in the theatres. Those Hollywood figures who knew her refuse to mention her name. They are terrified that they, too, might have to endure the sufferings visited on her.

What happened to Frances Farmer? A reporter spent five years investigating her story, which he recently published, *Shadowland*.

As a beautiful young woman in Seattle, Washington, Frances Farmer, was known as a brilliant, outspoken person. She won a newspaper essay contest for a free trip to Russia. Despite warnings from her mother and her friends, she insisted on taking the trip. When she returned, the reporters tried to get her either to praise or condemn the Communist experiment, but she replied, quite honestly, that in such a brief trip she had not seen enough to make a decision. The Communists decided that this meant she was really sympathetic; but did not want to declare herself. Soon afterwards, she was "discovered" by talent scouts, and went to Hollywood. Her radiant beauty proved to be very photogenic, and her movies were an immediate sensation. Because of her famous trip to Russia, she was supposed to be a rabid Communist sympathizer, although she had said or done nothing to support such a theory. The large community of Jewish Communists in Hollywood, who completely controlled the making and distribution of movies, entertained her and raved about her beauty. She was then asked to become a Communist courier. She indignantly refused, being an extremely proud and intelligent White girl who had no interest in Communism. The Hollywood Jews were infuriated and frightened by Frances Farmer's refusal. They had supposed she was one of them, and had taken her into their confidence. Now she knew the identity of every prominent Communist in Hollywood. At a secret conference, they resolved that she must be disposed of. An "accident" to such a prominent star would be too risky. The Jews decided that "psychoanalysis" was the answer to their dilemma. She would be railroaded to an insane asylum. Any accusations she might make would then be ignored.

At the very height of her fame, while everyone was predicting she would win an Academy Award, Frances Farmer was invited to a party at the home of a Jewish producer. She was given a drug during this party.

When she drove away, she was soon stopped by a policeman, who claimed she had committed a minor traffic violation. Instead of giving her a ticket, he immediately took her before a judge, although it was late at night. The judge claimed that she was "confused", and in what could only have been a prearranged plan, he committed her to a mental asylum. Reporters made a complete reversal of their usual practice when a movie star gets into trouble. Instead of headlining Frances Farmer's predicament, they were told not to write about it! From that day on, her name was rarely mentioned in the press.

For six years, Frances Farmer was forced to endure horrors which, even without the drugs and shock treatments which she was given on a daily basis, would have destroyed anyone's mind. After a few days in a California mental hospital, she was transferred to a state mental hospital, Steilacoom, near Seattle, Washington, ostensibly so that her mother could visit her, but actually to remove her from any contact with anyone in Hollywood. Many years later, a reporter, William Arnold, spent five years tracing the record of Frances Farmer during her years in Steilacoom. He discovered that the orderlies at Steilacoom were mostly convict trusties from McNeill Island Penitentiary on the other side of Puget Sound. He also discovered that Steilacoom was known as "the brothel of Ft. Lewis'. Each evening, drunken soldiers from Ft. Lewis paid the convicts five dollars each and were admitted to certain wards. Here the convicts held down the women chosen by the soldiers, who then took their will. Arnold found inmates who could recall seeing Frances Farmer, easily the most beautiful and desirable of the inmates, being held down by the convicts while she was being gang-raped by the drunken soldiers. Even the most diseased Jewish mind has never claimed that such horrors went on in the German concentration camps as were nightly enacted at Steilacoom.

To nullify any complaints from Frances Farmer, the orderlies regularly gave her bad reports, claiming that she was 'uncooperative'. Since she was being forcibly held down during these outrages, her cooperation or lack of it does not seem to have presented any problem, but the Jewish doctors were eager to get this diagnosis. The entry of 'uncooperative" by the name of any patient in a mental institution means that any and every possible form of drugs, "treatment" and other punishment is necessary. Frances Farmer was given massive doses of electric shock treatment every week. She was forced to endure medieval form of hydrotherapy by which she was thrown into a tub of ice water for periods of six to eight hours.

During the agony of these ordeals, she chewed her lips to pieces. After four months of 'treatment', her spirit had been broken. She appeared before the psychiatrists and agreed to 'cooperate'. A careful Dr. Nicholson immediately held a press conference to display his latest triumph. In a typical example of Communist "selfticism" and 'confession', Frances Farmer gave her performance. "I was rude and disrespectful," she told the reporters. "I was very, very sick."

"I think this case demonstrates how successfully antisocial behavior can be modified," stated Dr. Nicholson.

"Three months ago, this woman was mentally unresponsive, and today she is being returned to her family completely cured. This marks a significant victory for the mental hygiene movement in Washington."

Because of her fame as a movie star, Frances Farmer was chosen to be publicly exhibited as an example of the triumph of Freudian theories. The power of the psychiatrists had mushroomed during the war, as psychiatrists were stationed with each unit, just as Communists commissars were placed in each combat unit of the Red Army to identify and arrest any dissenters. As the sole victors of World War II, the Jews rapidly extended the influence of psychotherapy over every aspect of American life. In 1946, Harry Truman signed the National Mental Health Act, which brought "mental health" organizations into almost every community in America. These organizations quickly became local outposts of the State of Israel, seeking out and punishing those Americans who were afflicted with 'the running sores of anti-Semitism', as the Jewish Gestapo group, the Anti-Defamation League, characterized anyone who criticized the subversion of the American government by the State of Israel.

No sooner had Dr. Nicholson released Frances Farmer than he received anxious messages.

The news that their victim was no longer imprisoned terrified the Hollywood Communists. Dr. Nicholson was instructed to seize her and return her to Steilacoom. Her freedom had lasted less than two weeks. She was now to endure six years of concentrated treatment intended for only one purpose: To destroy her mind so that she would never be able to identify the Hollywood Communists. She was immediately put back on the weekly schedule of shock treatments. This medical boon to mankind came about when two Italians watched the convulsions of a pig after it had been accidentally electrocuted. At first they were merely amused; but they suddenly realized it would be great sport to try this technique on human beings, and electroconvulsive shock treatment was born. The technique called for sending 70 to 130 volts of electricity through the temples of the victim for a tenth of a second. This destroys large numbers of brain cells, and causes years of headaches, permanent loss of memory, and other unpleasant side effects. The benefits of this treatment, as years of experimentation on many thousands of patients has proved beyond all question, are nonexistent. For this reason, electric shock treatments have been outlawed in most European countries for many years. The United States, being firmly in the grip of the Jews, is the only developed nation which still practices this form of barbarism.

Besides enduring the weekly shock treatments, Frances Farmer, who had been consigned back to Steilacoom at a court hearing at which she was not even present, now became the victim of a new operation, the CIA LSD experiments. It was recently revealed that she was the first person chosen to receive the LSD dosages. A Bronx Jew, Dr. Sidney Gottlieb, joined the CIA to direct the LSD program, which he personally operated from 1951-1956. Through Teddy Kollek, a Jewish terrorist who was a close friend of Allen Dulles, Gottlieb obtained Dulles' direct approval of the entire scheme. Kollek, presently mayor of Jerusalem, was at that time in this country illegally to raise money for the Jewish terrorist organization, Haganah.

He lived in Manhattan in a rent-free apartment, above the Copacabana night club, provided by its Jewish owners. Kollek was the only non-official person invited to Allen Dulles' home for parties, and at one of these gatherings, he was introduced to Jim Angleton, later director of Special Operations for the CIA, who became a "Zionist" director of the CIA. Through this alliance, CIA funds were used to pay the entire budget of the Israeli Intelligence Service, while CIA agents all over the world were instructed that Israeli interests came first. They were directed to turn over all information on Arab economic and military operations to the Jews. With this inside information, which the Arabs themselves furnished to the CIA under an agreement set up by Allen Dulles, the Israelis were able to win each confrontation with the Arabs. The CIA also paid King Hussein one million dollars a year for his private spending on blondes, airplanes and fast cars, as his country, Jordan, was penniless. In return, Hussein furnished the CIA complete information on all conferences of the Arab leaders. It was in retaliation for these CIA operations that the Arabs formed the OPEC alliance and raised the price of their oil. Had we not gone out of our way to make enemies of the Arabs, we would still enjoy low prices for oil. Every dollar we spend at the gas pumps is a fine which we pay for helping the Israelis, but your friendly local newspaper is not going to give you this information.

Richard Helms now became Gottlieb s immediate superior in the LSD program. Because this program severely compromised the highest officials of the United States, Helms was later able to have himself appointed Dulles' successor as Director of the CIA. When he faced dismissal and perjury charges, the personal file of this program enabled him to resign without punishment and to become Ambassador to Iran.

On April 3, 1953, Helms sent a memo to Dulles, requesting "the covert use of chemical and biological materials" to develop controls over possible agents, foreign officials and other targets of CIA infiltration. In Nov. 1953, Dr. Gottlieb entertained a group of gentile scientists from the Army Chemical Corps, Special Operations Division, Ft. Detrick, MD. He secretly gave them large doses of LSD in their drinks.

One of the scientists, Frank Olson, leaped to his death after taking the dose. Twenty-five years later, his widow, learning of the true circumstances of his death, sued the government and obtained a three-million-dollar settlement.

Gottlieb also hired George White, a former narcotics agent, to operate a house of prostitution on Telegraph Hill in San Francisco. CIA officials and other government personages watched the activities through one-way glass and photographed the more unusual scenes. White's assistant in this operation was one Ike Feldman. This operation proved so successful that a second house was opened in Marin County, Calif., and a third in New York City. When Gottlieb retired in 1973, he had most memoranda concerning his activities destroyed. He had spent more than fifty million dollars without a trace.

For more than a year, Frances Farmer received daily doses of LSD, as well as the weekly shock treatments.

Despite this cruel regimen, her tormentors were dismayed to find that her brain had not been destroyed. There remained one final horror for her, a treatment which was guaranteed to destroy the brain of anyone. This was prefrontal lobotomy, which in every case had totally destroyed the rational capacity of its victims. A Portuguese doctor, Edgar Muniz, developed this technique for "curing mental illness" in 1935. For this contribution to human well-being, he received the Nobel Prize in 1949.

Hundreds of thousands of lobotomies were performed in Europe and the United States. Dr. Walter Freeman, head of the Dept. of Neurology at Georgetown University, became an enthusiastic advocate of prefrontal lobotomy after studying with Muniz. He refined Muniz' technique by inserting an ice-pick type of instrument under the eyelid into the brain, and severing the nerve from the cortex to the thalamus which directed rational thought. This turned the human victim into a vegetable. Presto! No more anger, no more protest.

Instead, there was meek compliance with any order. Deciding it might be more prudent to practice his technique away from

Washington, Dr. Freeman went to Spencer State Hospital at Spencer, W. Va. The Jewish doctors at this institution lined up thirty-five women patients, and in a brilliant display of virtuosity, he lobotomized them one after the other.

Learning of this triumph, the CIA asked him to go to Steilacoom to lobotomize Frances Farmer.

As a cover, he first lobotomized twelve other women patients. Frances Farmer was then brought in, and told that the doctor wished to examine her. To attendants seized her by the arms, and Dr. Freeman quickly inserted the ice pick into her brain. Two seconds later, Frances Farmer had become a human vegetable, her memory destroyed and her brain barely functioning, she was no longer a threat to the Hollywood Communist conspirators.

A few months later, satisfied that her memory was gone, the CIA authorized Dr. Nicholson to release Frances Farmer. Her years of horror were over. On March 23, 1950, she left Steilacoom. She was only thirty-six years old. Despite her ordeal, some traces of her former beauty remained, but when she tried to resume her acting career, she found she could not remember lines or follow directions. She died alone and in poverty in Indianapolis a few years later. Yet, even today, those who ordered her torture and destruction still fear the mention of her name. Not only does the blackout of her films remain in effect, but William Arnold found no one in Hollywood willing to be quoted about her fate.

We know the fate of Frank Olson and Frances Farmer only because those dedicated to their memories spent years fighting to uncover their tragic stories. We do not know the fate of many thousands of other victims of the Jewish pseudo-science of psychotherapy, because no one mourns them or remembers their names. They, too, were done to death by drug overdoses, shock treatments, or the Freeman ice-pick treatment. We must act at once to save thousands of other potential victims from the Jewish terrorists. We must outlaw electric shock treatments as humane nations have done; we must outlaw the practice of pseudo-therapy such as psychoanalysis, ice-pick in the brain, and indiscriminate use of LSD and other drugs in the mental institutions. Unless we act quickly, thousands more will die, the victims of Jewish sadism and Freud's poisonous legacy. This Jew converted the shameless charlatanism of a few eighteenth-century necromancers into a worldwide system for "treating the mentally ill', solely because of his anti-gentilism and his hatred of Christ. Freud gave the Jews their most powerful weapon against us. We must stop them now.

BIBLIOGRAPHY:

THE MYTH OF PSYCHOTHERAPY—by Thomas Szasz.

SHADOWLAND; THE SEARCH FOR FRANCES FARMER—by William Arnold, McGraw Hill, New York City, N.Y. 1978.

"SEX, DRUGS, AND THE CIA", Saturday Review, Feb. 3, 1979.

One single columnist spoke up in her behalf. That was John Rosenfield, at the time of her initial arrest, [quoting:] WHAT HAPPENED TO FRANCES FARMER SHOULDN'T HAVE HAPPENED AT ALL!

Just when the movie industry is winning the public's admiration, Hollywood breaks out in a rash of petty scandals. It is not a tribute to a part of the press that some of these episodes have been played well beyond their merits as news.

It was the lesser of sagacity that the industry permitted some of these affairs to get out of hand. The Frances Farmer Incident should never have happened. This unusually gifted actress was no threat against law and order or the public safety. Something that began as merely a traffic reprimand grew into a case of personal violence, a serious charge and a jail sentence.

And all because a sensitive high-strung girl was on the verge of a nervous breakdown.

Miss Farmer, who is no prodigy of emotional stability or sound business management, needed a lawyer one unhappy night last winter. A helping hand might have extradited her immediately from nothing more than a traffic violation. The terrible truth is that she stood alone, and lost. [End quoting] Rosenfield s was the only note of compassion. Tile rest of the press coverage followed the lethal lead of

Lolly Parsons, who snickered: "Hollywood Cinderella Girl has gone back to the ashes on a liquor-slicked highway"

PSYCHIATRISTS' TESTIMONY SAID WORTHLESS IN COURT

by Gene Blake

LOS ANGELES—Testimony of psychiatrists should not be permitted in court because they do not know any more about their subject than laymen, a National Homicide Symposium was told here recently. Jay Ziskin, a psychologist and professor of counseling at California State University, Los Angeles, said psychiatric testimony about the prior mental condition of a criminal defendant was worthless. (Psychiatrists are medical doctors who specialize in mental disorders, whereas psychologists are specialists in human behavior who approach the subject from a non-medical viewpoint.)

"It does not meet the requirements of law of expert testimony," he told the symposium sponsored by the California District Attorneys Association. "It is highly unreliable, highly inaccurate."

"A psychiatric diagnosis is more likely to be wrong than right. It is even more likely wrong when trying to assess the mental condition at some time previous to the examination."

Ziskin said he hopes that the American Psychiatric Association would consider it unethical for psychiatrists to offer testimony in court on a prior mental condition because "they don't have the competence to do so."

"If you need a psychiatrist to tell you that the defendant is crazy," Ziskin said, "he isn't."

Ziskin added that studies had shown the experts are not better at making such diagnoses than are amateurs.

Taking issue with Ziskin was Dr. Seymour Pollack, a noted psychiatrist who has given expert testimony in criminal cases including that of Sirhan Sirhan, the convicted assassin of Senator Robert F. Kennedy.

Pollack accused Ziskin of raising a 'strawman'. Although conceding that medicine—including psychiatry—is an art rather than a science, Pollack said the average layman recognizes that there are people who are 'crazy'.

"They recognize there are a few offenders who are crazy as well, mentally impaired enough to justify some excuse from criminal responsibility," Pollack said. Taken from The Los Angeles Times—1977.

WHO OWNS THE TV NETWORKS

Many observers have noticed the striking similarity of the programs offered to the public by the three "independent" television networks. For the first time, we present a detailed study of the directors of the three networks, revealing their interlocking banking and industrial connections, indicating that, instead of three major networks, we actually have only one.

NBC, a subsidiary of RCA, has the following directors:

John Brademas, president of New York University, chairman of the Federal Reserve Bank of New York (which dominates the other Federal Reserve Banks by its control of the money market), and director of the Rockefeller Foundation. Brademas has received the George Peabody Award (George Peabody established the Peabody Educational Fund which later became the Rockefeller Foundation), and he was named Humanist of the Year in 1978.

Cecily B. Selby, born in London England, national director of the Girl Scouts, director of Avon Products and Loehmann's, a dress firm. She is married to James Coles, president of Bowdoin College since 1952.

Peter G. Peterson, former head of Kuhn, Loeb Co., and ex-Secretary of Commerce.

Robert Cizik, chairman of Cooper Industries (sales of $1.5 billion), and director of RCA and First City Bancorp. First City was identified in Congressional testimony as one of the three Rothschild banks in the United States.

Thomas O. Paine, president of Northrup Co., a large defense contractor. Paine is a director of the influential Institute of Strategic Studies in London, director of the Institute of Metals, London, American Ordnance Assn., and many other professional munitions associations.

Donald Smiley, chairman R.H. Macy Co. since 1945; he is also a director of Metropolitan Life and U.S. Steel, known as Morgan-controlled firms, and director of Ralston-Purina Co., and Irving Trust.

David C. Jones, president of Consolidated Contractors, director of U.S. Steel, Kemper Insurance Co. Thornton Bradshaw, chairman of RCA, director of Champion Paper Co., Atlantic Richfield Oil Co., Rockefeller Brothers Fund, and the Aspen Institute of Humanistic Studies.

Although not listed as a director of NBC, Andrew Sigler is a director of its parent company, RCA. Sigler is chairman of Champion Paper Co., and director of General Electric, Bristol Myers, and Cabot Corp. (which traditionally has had heavy CIA involvement).

Thus we find that NBC has many Rothschild and J.P. Morgan connections among its directors, who include the chairman of the key to our monetary control, the Federal Reserve Bank of New York and other directors associated with such Rothschild operations as Kuhn, Loeb Co., First City Bancorp, and the Institute of Strategic Studies in London.

ABC-TV includes among its directors not one, but two, directors of J.P. Morgan Co.: Ray Adam, director of Metropolitan Life, Cities Service, Morgan Guaranty Trust, and chairman of the $2 billion NL Industries a petroleum field service concern; and Frank Cary, chairman of IBM, director of Merck, J.P. Morgan Co.,

Morgan Guaranty Trust, and Merck Drugs. Chairman of ABC is Leonard Goldenson who is a director of Allied Stores, and the Advertising Council, and Bankers Trust. Other directors are Donald C. Cook, general partner of Lazard Freres banking house, director of General Dynamics, and Amerada Hess; Leon Hess, chairman of Amerada Hess; John T. Connor, of the Kuhn Loeb law firm, Cravath, Swaine & Moore, who was former Asst. Secretary of the Navy, president of Merck Drugs, U.S. Secretary of Commerce 1965-67, chairman of Allied Chemical from 1969-79, director Chase Manhattan Bank, General Motors, Warner Lambert, and chairman of J. Henry Schroder Bank, and Schroders Inc. of London; Jack Hausman, vice chairman of Belden-Heminway, a large goods manufacturer which was founded by Samuel Hausman of Austria; Thomas M. Macioce, chairman of Allied Stores, director of Penn Central and Manufacturers Hanover Trust, one of the Rothschild banks in the United States; George P. Jenkins, chairman of Metropolitan Life (a J.P. Morgan firm), director of Citibank, which has many Rothschild connections, St. Regis Paper, Bethlehem Steel, and W.R. Grace Co.; Martin J. Schwab, chairman of United Manufacturers, and director of Manufacturers Hanover, a Rothschild bank; Norma T. Pace, who is also director of Sears Roebuck, Sperry, 3M and Vulcan; Alan Greenspan, consultant to the Federal Reserve Board, director of J. P. Morgan, Morgan Guaranty Trust, Hoover Institution, Time and General Foods; Ulric Haynes Jr., director of the Ford Foundation, Marine Midland Bank (which is owned by the Hong Kong Shanghai Bank), Cummins Engine Co., and the Association of Black Ambassadors.

Thus we see many J.P. Morgan and Rothschild associations among the directors of ABC which was recently purchased by Capital Cities Communications Co., whose chairman is Thomas S. Murphy. He is a director of Texaco, whose most prominent director is Robert Roosa, senior partner of Brown Bros. Harriman, a firm with close tics to the Bank of England. Roosa headed the "Roosa Brain Trust" at the Federal Reserve Bank of New York which produced Paul Volcker. Roosa and David Rockefeller were credited with selecting Volcker to be chairman of the Federal Reserve Board. John McKinley, chairman of Texaco, is director of Manufacturers Hanover Bank and Manufacturers Hanover Trust, identified as Rothschild controlled in Congressional testimony. Other directors of Texaco are the Earl of Granard; Willard C. Butcher, chairman of Chase Manhattan Bank; and Thomas Aquinas Vanderslice, who is chairman of the electronics firm GTE, and a former Fulbright Scholar who is now trustee of the Aspen Institute of Humanistic Studies.

Of the three major networks, CBS is the pillar of the "Establishment." Its financial expansion for years was directed by Brown Bros. Harriman, whose senior partner, Prescott Bush, was a longtime director of CBS. (His son, George, is now Vice-President of the U.S.) When General Westmoreland sought to recover damages from CBS for a vicious personal assault on his reputation, Westmoreland seemed certain to win a stunning victory, until CBS brought in former CIA officials who testified that Westmoreland's claims had no basis. George Bush was formerly head of the CIA. Westmoreland surrendered, and withdrew his suit.

Ted Turner's expressed intention of buying control of CBS was applauded by millions of patriotic Americans, who had endured its vicious assaults on decent Americans with no means of protest. However, Turner's campaign was viewed in London as a direct attack on the power of the Bank of England and its American subsidiary, Brown Bros. Harriman. Turner was finally deterred from his goal by a clever maneuver which diverted him into purchasing MGM-United Artists, one of whose directors is Alexander Haig, former White House intimate and Secretary of State, later chairman of United Technologies. Turner believed he was buying MGM's extensive library of films for his WTBS channel, but the *Wall Street Journal* later chortled that he had been tricked, and that most of the film library had been sold before he negotiated for MGM. To finance his purchase of MGM-United Artists, Turner intended to borrow $1.5 billion through Drexel Burnham Lambert, the American branch of Banque Bruxelles Lambert, the Belgian branch of the Rothschild operations.

CBS is a $4.5 billion a year operation, which banks through the Morgan Guaranty Trust Co. William S. Paley, heir to a cigar fortune, has been chairman of CBS for many years. To those who do not know of CBS's many CIA and British Intelligence connections, he is supposed to run it as a one-man operation.

Directors of CBS are:

- Harold Brown, who was Secretary of the Air Force from 1963-69, Secretary of Defense from 1977-81, and is now executive director of the Trilateral Commission
- Roswell Gilpatric, who has been with the Kuhn Loeb law firm of Cravath Swaine and Moore since 1931, and served as director of the Federal Reserve Bank of New York from 1973-76
- Henry B. Schacht, chairman Cummins Engine Co., director of AT&T, Chase Manhattan Bank, Council on Foreign Relations, Brookings Institution, and Committee for Economic Development
- Michael C. Bergerac, chairman Revlon, director Manufacturers Hanover
- James D. Wolfensohn, former head of J. Henry Schroder Bank
- Franklon A. Thomas, head of the Ford Foundation
- Walter Cronkite; Newton D. Minow, director of Rand Corp., Pan American, Foote Cone & Belding
- Marietta Tree, director of Winston Churchill Foundation, Ditchley Foundation, U.S. Trust, and Salomon Bros. She is a granddaughter of Endicott Peabody, founder of Groton, which trains America's elite. She married Ronald Tree, a high official of British intelligence, and godson of Marshall Field. She and her

husband gave an ancestral estate, Ditchley Park, to the Ditchley Foundation. Located near Cambridge, it was W. Averell Harriman's headquarters during World War II when he coordinated the partnership of Franklin D. Roosevelt and Winston Churchill, who actively disliked and distrusted each other. They usually checked with Harriman before agreeing to any action. The Ditchley Foundation serves as a conduit for instructions to many American groups from the Tavistock Institute, an arm of the British Army Institute for Psychological Warfare. Marietta Tree's career gave rise to the term "beautiful people," to describe members of a glittering international set that represented the operations of the World Order. She began working for Nelson Rockefeller in 1942, and later served as Ambassador to the United Nations.

One victim of the CIA-British Intelligence operations at CBS was Roger Mudd, generally considered the brightest star among television reporters. A direct descendant of Dr. Samuel Mudd, who spent years as a political prisoner after the Civil War, Roger Mudd had a brilliant 19 year career at CBS, but was passed over as successor to Walter Cronkite in favor of Dan Rather. The excuse was that he was not "vicious enough," but the real reason was that he had "sand-bagged his chances" (according to the *Wall Street Journal*), in 1980 when he conducted a revealing interview with Teddy Kennedy which destroyed Kennedy's chances of being elected President.

Because of continuous Tavistock Institute - British Army Institute of Psychological Warfare control over the major television networks in the United States, ABC, CBS, and NBC present many programs heavily slanted in favor of psychiatry. They also emphasize the current "liberal" preoccupation with racial integration, crippled persons (who represent less of a threat to the mewling parasites), sports programs, and jiggle shows (also known in the trade as "t and a shows").

Although the three networks are supposedly in bloodthirsty competition with each other, viewing of the daily evening news programs reveals that each of the competing networks shows exactly the same items of news each evening, usually in the same order. Almost all of the "news" stories are propaganda items intended to further current World Order goals. The only variations permitted in the iron control over network TV news is the final item, which is a "human interest" story. It usually praises a child who has collected considerable sums of money for UNICEF, or some other World Order operation.

For many months, the three "independent" networks have emphasized a hate campaign against South Africa on their evening news presentations. One could hardly believe that they are attempting to "conquer" South Africa for the World Order, because the Rothschilds and Oppenheimers won control of the rich South African gold and diamond fields in the Boer War of 1899. Today, DeBeers, the diamond monopoly, is operated by Oppenheimer and the Rothschilds, as is the gold mining, exemplified by their ownership of the giant Anglo-American Corp. of South Africa, Ltd. Apparently, the parasites would like to exterminate the Boer population of South Africa, which has lived there for three centuries, and replace it entirely with black workers. Some observers might call this "genocide." Each evening, the three networks outdo each other in their campaign of vilification of the white citizens of South Africa. The rioting and looting committed by the blacks, as well as the vicious murders of their fellow blacks, are glossed over by the news reports as inevitable results of "white oppression." As usual, there is a more immediate benefit gained from this continuous propaganda barrage. The Rothschilds have profited enormously from currency speculations in the rand, i.e. the South African dollar. In a few months, they were able to drive the rand down from a value of $1.35, to thirty-five cents, selling short all the way. On September 2, 1985, they ran it back up to a full ten cents, from thirty-five to forty-five cents. his might seem small change to non-investors, but it has paid off handsomely for the speculators. The fact that the network hate campaign continues unabated suggests that there is still plenty of money to be made in the rand.

On July 31, 1985, the Chase Manhattan Bank announced it would not renew any loans to South Africa. *Businessweek*, Aug. 12, 1985, reported that this threw South African business into a panic. The bankers then demanded that South Africa give blacks the vote. Gavin Relly, chairman of the giant Oppenheimer-Rothschild conglomerate, Anglo-American Carp., tried to force Botha's government to acceded to these demands. Botha refused. Relly then went to Zambia to negotiate with the Communist-dominated African National Congress, preparatory to turning South Africa over to them.

The similarity of the major networks evening "news" programs has given rise to a report that, each day, a list of ten or twelve "acceptable" news stories is prepared by British Intelligence in London for the networks, teletyped to Washington, where the CIA routinely approves it, and then delivered to the networks. The "selectivity" of the broadcasters has never been in doubt. Edith Efron, in "The News Twisters," (Manor Books, N.Y., 1972) cites *TV Guide's* interview with David Brinkley, April 11, 1964, with Brinkley's declaration that "News is what *I* say it is. It's something worth knowing by my standards." This was merely vainglorious boasting on Brinkley's part, as he merely reads the news stories previously selected for him. Efron concludes this important book, which was refused by all the major New York publishers, as follows:

- The networks actively slanted their opinion coverage against U.S. policy on the Vietnam war.
- The networks actively slanted their opinion coverage in favor of the black militants and against U.S. policy on the Vietnam war.
- The networks largely avoided the issue of violent radicals.

- The networks actively favored the Democratic candidate, Hubert Humphrey, for President over his Republican opponent, Richard Nixon.

Efron could not foresee in 1972 that, having lost the election to Nixon, the networks would engage in a successful bid to negate the election and drive him from the White House through their trumped up "Watergate" campaign.

It seems incredible that there are literally thousands of interesting and vital news items from all over the world available to the networks' evening "news" programs, and yet they are restricted to the ten or twelve stories approved by London. The American public has known for years that something was amiss. As cable programs became available, there were mass defections from the networks propaganda vehicles. Some authorities report that the three networks have lost 40% of their viewing audience, although they are desperately trying to conceal this. If forced to revise their advertising rates according to their actual viewing audience, they would be technically bankrupt, as their revenues would not cover operating expenses.

Television is a medium of light. It is a reflection upon all of us that we have allowed it to be taken over by the forces of darkness. What has been taken from us can be regained. Taxation is the medium by which the parasites maintain economic control over us because we refuse to admit the obvious fact that "TAXATION IS THE PRICE WE PAY FOR IRRESPONSIBILITY."

We advise Americans to go to the United States Attorney and ask for an investigation of Criminal Syndicalism. We have exposed in great detail the interlocking Rockefeller Foundation, Ford Foundation and Federal Reserve control of television and the goals of the World Order which they espouse. There are adequate laws on the books which forbid all of these activities. Corpus Juris

Secundum 46, Insurrection and Sedition, sec. 461c, "Sabotage and syndicalism aiming to abolish the present political and social system, including direct action and sabotage." Corpus Juris Secundum 46:462b, "Statutes against criminal syndicalism apply to corporations as well as to individuals organizing or belonging to criminal syndicalist society; evidence of the character and activities of other organizations in which the accused is a member or is affiliated is admissible." This means that any of the networks presenting a program inimical to the interests of the American nation, and socking to change its character to that of a "1984" style dictatorship, can be charged under the law of the United States.

Corpus Juris Secundum 22A identifies Criminal Syndicalism: *"In a prosecution for being a member of an organization which teaches and abets criminal syndicalism, evidences of crimes committed by past or present members of the organization in their capacity as members is admissible to show its character,"* People v. LaRue, 216 P 627 CA 276. This means that you can introduce into a charge of criminal syndicalism any information about activities of any organization with which any director of any television corporation is involved.

THE REUTERS CONNECTION(S)

We recommend to the student of political science, if there is such a science, a volume which has come to our attention, the autobiography of Sir Roderick Jones, entitled *A Life in Reuters*, Hodder and Stoughton, 1951. This book gives us much authoritative information on news distribution. Sir Roderick was Chief of Reuters News Agency for many years, assuming command of that agency when it was still at its historic address of 24 Old Jewry, London.

It is difficult to approach journalism without taking into account its companions of a trinity, propaganda and espionage, and we find in this book many instances of their relationship. On page 200, Sir Roderick relates a bit of history which will not be found in the universities. It describes a luncheon given by him for General Smuts, Sir Starr Jameson, and Dr. Walter Hines Page. He says:

"We dined in a private room at the Windham Club, the one in which twenty years later the terms of the abdication of King Edward VIII were settled. We drifted on to the question of the United States entering the war, for which Britain and France so patiently waited. Dr. Page then revealed to us, under seal of secrecy, that he had received from the President that afternoon a personal communication upon the strength of which he could affirm that, at last, the die was cast.

Consequently it was not without emotion that he found himself able to assure us that the United States would be at war with the Central Powers inside a week from that date. The Ambassador's assurance was correct to the day. We dined on Friday, March 30. On April 2, President Wilson asked Congress to declare a State of War with Germany. On April 6, the United States was at war."

Sir Roderick tells us that Baron Julius de Reuter was born Israel Ben Josaphat Beer, the son of Rabbi Samuel Beer of Caase, Germany. Like so many of his co-religionists, Beer saw that the British Empire was ripe for plucking. He emigrated, set up a news agency, came to the attention of the House of Rothschild, and the rest is history. In 1859, now Baron de Reuter, Beer signed a Covenant with his two rivals in Europe, Havas of France and Wolff of Germany. Havas was a French Jew, Wolff was a German Jew, and these three divided up the world between them. Havas was to have South America, the three were to share the continent of Europe, and Reuter was to have the rest of the world. The arrangement, providentially concluded just before the outbreak of the Civil War in the United States, endured until the First World War for Zionism.

Sir Roderick Jones began his career as Assistant to the Chief Correspondent in the Transvaal, one Leo Weinthal, before the Boer War. On page 38, we find some interesting background on that conflict, as follows:

"Towards the end of 1895, smoldering and unsubstantial fires of political discontent in Johannesberg were fanned by the Transvaal National Union and by the gold mine owners into an outwardly presentable flame of revolution. An Uitlanders Reform Committee was established, with an inner executive consisting of John Hays Hammond, Lionel Phillips (one of the heads of the gold and diamond mining firm of Eckstein -- The Corner House), George Farrar, head of East Rand Property Mines, and Colonel Frank Rhodes, brother of Cecil Rhodes, Prime Minister of the Cape. Percy Fitzpatrick, also of the Eckstein firm, was the Secretary. The General Committee consisted of sixty other prominent citizens, including Abe Bailey and Solly Joel."

Sir Roderick, although he freely relates the role of the House of Eckstein in promoting that war, does not reveal the importance of the House of Rothschild. John Hays Hammond was chief mining engineer for the Rothschilds, later being employed by the Guggenheims at a salary of five hundred thousand dollars a year, and finally becoming Washington lobbyist for the Rothschild policy group, the Council on Foreign Relations. Sir Abe Bailey was the principal angel of its sister group in Britain, the Royal Institute of International Affairs. Almost any biography of Cecil Rhodes will inform the reader that he was financed in his African empire by the House of Rothschild.

On April 28, 1915, Baron Herbert de Reuter, Chief of the Agency, shot himself. The cause was the crash of the Reuters Bank, which had been built up by Baron Julius de Reuter to handle foreign remittances without their being subjected to inspection. It was felt by the directors to be unwise to replace the Baron with another German Jew, there being a war going on with Germany, and Sir Roderick Jones who had served Leo Weintal faithfully and well, was chosen as a more respectable front for the international operations of the agency. On page 363, he tells us:

"Shortly after I succeeded Baron Herbert de Reuter in 1915, it so happened that I received an invitation from Mr. Alfred Rothschild, then the head of the British House of Rothschild, to lunch with him in his historic New Court, in the City."

We are not favored with an account of the conversation, Sir Roderick limiting himself to a description of the formalities attending upon a visit to the Rothschild. After this, the Chief of Reuters toured the world, being received everywhere with a display usually reserved for royalty. In India he was entertained by the Viceroy, Lord Reading, whose name had been entered at the synagogue as Rufus Isaacs. Isaacs told him that on his first visit ti India, he had been a lowly ship's boy, and on his second visit he was a Viceroy, whereupon Sir Roderick remarked that only in the British Empire could such a thing have happened. His observation is a slight to America.

The Gentle Art of Thought Control

When I was a child, during the 1930's depression, my school teacher often commented to our class about the sufferings of our native state, Virginia. She spoke not only of the rigours of the Civil War, but of its even more devastating aftermath, the Reconstruction and the carpetbagger empire. She pointed out that, since the conclusion of the Civil War, or the War Between the States, as we termed it, Northern bankers had continued to exercise a dominant role over our businesses and our government.

Some fifty years later, Gary Arnold asked me to look into a firm which had been opposing his conservative philosophy in California. The firm, Media General, was a familiar one to me. It was the result of an expansion by Virginia's leading newspaper monopoly, RICHMOND NEWSPAPERS, which had become an empire composed of newspapers, radio and TV, cable-vision, newsprint manufacturers, and financial services. From its power base at the seat of the state government in Richmond in the carpetbagger era, it had become the state's primary news monopoly.

Richmond Newspapers (now Media General) is a $500 million a year operation which was founded by Joseph Bryan in the heyday of the carpetbagger empire. His son, John Stewart Bryan, ran the newspapers from 1900 until his death in 1944. John Stewart Bryan was a lieutenant commander in Naval Intelligence, chairman of the 5th Federal Reserve District, and to prove his stellar liberal credentials, he was appointed to the board of overseers of Harvard University.

John Stewart Bryan's son, David Tennant Bryan, took over Richmond Newspapers in 1944, after his father's death. He is now the chairman of Media General. Like his father, he is a director of Southern Railway. He is mentioned on p. 180 of THE WORLD ORDER as a director of the Hoover Institution, the supposedly "rightwing" thinktank at Stanford University which spark-plugged Ronald Reagan's political career, and which furnished 95% of his staff when he became President in 1980. David Tennant Bryan married into the Standard Oil hierarchy, when he married Mary Harkness Davidson, heiress of the ESSO fortune. Like most of Reagan's principal advisers, such as Secretary of State Shultz (also heir to Standard Oil) and Secretary of Defence Weinberger, Bryan is a member of the exclusive Bohemian Club of San Francisco.

Senior vice president of Media General is James A. Linen IV. Formerly vice president of *National Enquirer* (long reputed to be a CIA operation), he is the son of James A. Linen III, who was the publisher of TIME for many years. James A. Linen IV is also chairman of the board of American Thai Corp. Thailand has long been known as the marketing area of the drug empire known as "The Golden Triangle," in which CIA has been heavily involved since World War II. So deep was this commitment, that Secretary of State John Foster Dulles appointed William Donovan (founder of OSS - later CIA) as Ambassador to Thailand on Aug. 12, 1953.

Directors of Media General are J. Stewart Bryan III, cousin of David Tennant Bryan; and Douglas H. Lodeman, president of United Virginia Bank (which is Media General's bank), and also director of the Lane Corp., a large furniture manufacturer, and the Chesapeake Corp., a $273 million firm which also has former Governor of Virginia John Dalton as a director.

Other directors of Media General include insurance tycoon George T. Stewart III, who is president of First Colony Life Insurance Co., chairman of United Virginia Bank shares, a subsidiary of United Virginia Bank, of which he is also a director; chairman of Jamestown Life Insurance Co., and American

Mayflower Life Insurance Co.; and director of the $1.74 billion petroleum operation, Ethyl Corp., of which former Governor Dalton is also a director. Stewart was a former partner of investment banker Shelby Cullon Davis, who is also mentioned on p. 180 of THE WORLD ORDER as director of Hoover Institution. Davis is also the financial angel of the "conservative" Heritage Foundation, another of the "counterfeit conservative" groups which has guided the Reagan Administration into financial disaster.

More directors of Media General are Archie K. Davis and R. L. Ireland III. Davis, of the North Carolina banking empire (Wachovia Bank), is not only a director of Southern Railroad and Chatham Manufacturing (the textile empire), but he exercises great financial power as chairman of the huge Duke Endowment. He is on the board of the Federal Reserve Bank of Richmond and Norfolk Southern Railroad. Another director of Norfolk Southern is R. L. Ireland III of Brown Brothers Harriman, who is mentioned on p. 77 of THE WORLD ORDER. Brown Brother Harriman has direct connections to the Bank of England through its London branch, Brown Shipley & Co.

Yet another director of Media General is J. Harvie Wilkinson Jr., who for many years has been considered the Kingmaker of Virginia politics, and the state's leading financier. Wilkinson has been a director of many leading Virginia firms which have been known since the Civil War as dominated by Wall Street interests. He is director of Richmond Hotels, Richmond Corp., Life Insurance Co. of Virginia, Philip Morris Co., Miller & Rhoads, Richmond Newspapers, and Garfinckel Brooks Bros. He has the obligator Rockefeller connection as a director of Colonial Williamsburg. As director of Freeport Sulphur, he interlocks with the principal Wall Street financiers, including Brown Brothers Harriman. He is now president of United Virginia Bank shares, a $5.42 billion operation whose other directors include former Governor Dalton and Hugh Cullman of the New York tobacco fortune. His son, I. Harvie Wilkinson III, was assistant attorney general in charge of civil rights at the Department of Justice, and cause consternation when, with no previous judicial experience, he was appointed a federal judge.

The last director of Media General, whom we find of great interest, is Paul Manheim. Now 80 years old, Paul Manheim has been a general partner of Lehman Brothers bankers since 1928. In *SECRETS OF THE FEDERAL RESERVE*, I quote Arthur Howden Smiths -- "Men Who Rule America," on the Lehman bankers: (p. 112)

> "(During the Civil War), they were often agents, fixers for both sides, intermediaries for confidential communications and handlers of the many illicit transactions in cotton and drugs for the Confederacy, purveyors of information for the North. The Lehmans, with Mayer in Montgomery, the first capital of the Confederacy, Henry in New Orleans, and Emanuel in New York, were ideally situated to take advantage of every opportunity for profit which appeared. They seem to have missed few chances."

After the Civil War, these "fixers" became tycoons in many fields, among them Cuban sugar, and later, the movie industry. Paul Manheim arranged the merger of Postal Telegraph and Western Union. As an art adviser he directed the multi-million dollar collection of his boss, Robert Lehman, which is now at the Metropolitan Museum. Manheim is trustee of the Metropolitan Museum, the Brooklyn Museum, and president of the Robert Lehman Foundation. Although Richmond Newspapers was supposedly the property of the Bryan family, for many years Paul Manheim was chairman of the board, because of Lehman Brothers investments in the operation. Manheim also is a trustee of Fordham University, chairman of Vertientes Camaguey Sugar Co., director of General Sugar Estates, Cuban Sugar Plantations, and the One William Street Fund.

It was as the financial director of Paramount Pictures that Paul Manheim exercised so great an influence over the American mind for several generations. Lehman Brothers was the principal financier for the major Hollywood producers. Manheim's brother Frank, also of Lehman Brothers, was director of Warner Bros. during the years that Paul was a director of Paramount. During these years, Hollywood churned out relentlessly leftwing pictures. While Congress "investigated" a few Communist Party members who were writers, actors or directors, no Congressman ever stopped to consider that no matter how Communistic these people were, they had no money. They had to turn to Lehman Brothers to finance their pictures, and Lehman Brothers never refused financing for any of them. However, Lehman Brothers saw no reason to finance any anti-Soviet pictures during this period, or since. Paul Manheim was also a director of Bankers Trust Co. of New York.

Paul Manheim's brother Frank, also a general partner of Lehman Brothers, and now head of A. Manheim Co., New York, financed the postwar growth of Mercedes-Benz Company. He is now director of Mercedes-Benz of North America, Mercedes-Benz Ltd. of London, Insilco (International Silver), and chairman of Amex Bank., Ltd. Of London, and Amex Ind. Ltd. of London. He is director of Finance and Building Investments Ltd. of London.

Thus we see that Media General typifies the "dogged determination" of the carpetbaggers and their heirs to maintain ironbound thought control over the citizens of our Republic, through their financial sway over newspapers, television and the movie industry.

MONEY AND FREEDOM
A BOOK BY HANS SENNHOLZ REVIEWED
BY EUSTACE MULLINS

Much of my forty year writing career has been spent in combating the flood of disinformation with which the minions of the World Order poisons the minds of the captive populace. During those decades, I have seldom come across a more flagrant example of disinformation than a current work *Money and Freedom* by a reputedly "conservative" professor, Hans Sennholz. On p. 12, under the amazing heading, "Federal Reserve Independence", Sennholz writes, "The Fed's commander in chief is the President of the United States; no one in the System can resist his wishes and suggestions." Sennholz cites not one instance of the "commander in chief" making known a wish or suggestion to the Fed, nor can he. This is scholarship?

Sennholz could be excused such misconceptions if he is bemused by the quasi-governmental setup which Paul Warburg (a name apparently unknown to Sennholz) invented during his conspirtorial authorship of the Federal Reserve Act. Warburg decreed that the President should name the members of the Federal Reserve Board of Governors. From this Warburg invention, Sennholz naively concludes that the President who has power to name these Governors retains total power over their subsequent decisions. He is blissfully unaware that the power which directs the naming of the Federal Reserve Board of Governors also directs the selection of Presidential candidates and their subsequent election or defeat, according to their plans. Sennholz seems not to have read my "Secrets of the Federal Reserve". On p. 179, I quote the *New York Times*, July 26, 1979, "David Rockefeller, the chairman of Chase, and Mr. Roosa were strong influences in the Mr. Carter (not

President Carter - editor's note) decision to name Mr. Volcker for the Reserve Board chairmanship." I go on to point out that not only did Rockefeller and Roosa "influence" Carter to name their protégé chairman of the Federal Reserve Board; they also had previously selected Carter as the Trilateral Commission candidate for President, David Rockefeller being the founder of the Trilateral Commission and Roosa its executive secretary.

Without knowing these facts, how does Sennholz presume to mislead American citizens on "Money and Freedom"? Sennholz continues, "He (the President) has the power to direct its policies; he appoints the seven governors and designated the chairman and vice-chairman. It is obvious that this power of appointment affords the President the power to direct the course of monetary policies." Sennholz totally misunderstands the operation of the present World Order and its direction of the American bureaucracy. The President, presently starring Ronald Reagan in his best role to date, has become a largely honorary figure, like the Queen of England, perhaps more honorary, since he does not head the world drug trade, as the present Queen is reputed to do. As an actor whose every "opinion" and statement is scripted and reviewed for him, our President can do little but echo the desires of those who have surrounded him with such powerful members of the World Order as Frank Carlucci, Casper Weinberger, William Casey, and George Pratt Shultz. These too are names which Sennholz forbears to discuss in his book. However, Sennholz asks us to believe that this President has the power to direct the course of monetary policies, even if this President had any notion of what [hose policies should be, which he does not. He has proved that by becoming the biggest spender ever to occupy the Governorship of California, and the biggest spender ever to occupy the White House.

In his efforts to convince us of the President's power to direct monetary policy, Sennholz offers another strange omission. He neglects to mention the Federal Advisory Council, a group of carefully chosen bankers (chosen by the banks, we must emphasize, not by the President) who meet with the Federal Reserve Board four times a year in Washington. It is at these meetings (closed to the public and the President of the United States) that monetary policy is decided. Early members of Federal

Advisory Council included J.P. Morgan and Paul Warburg, who directed its policies during the crucial first ten years of the Federal Reserve System. Sennholz states that the Chairman of the Board of Governors is like an advisor to the President. There is no record that any chairman of the Board of Governors has ever functioned in this capacity.

Sennholz claims that the Federal Reserve System was drafted in 1917 for the purpose of financing government expenditures for World War I. I proved in my work that it was secretly drafted in 1910 by Paul Warburg at the behest of the Rothschilds in order to finance World War I and provide capital for the various belligerent powers, not merely the United States. Here again, one is appalled at the consistent disinformation.

Sennholz claims that the Federal Reserve System differs materially from all other central banks, another misleading conception. In my work, I define the central bank as a bank of issues, controlling the nation's money and credit, owned by private individuals who would benefit from ownership of shares, and providing war finance for international adventurists. I showed in *The World Order* that the same interest control all of the major central banks for their own purpose. Sennholz would have us believe that our central bank exists virginal and pure for the sole interest of "the people". In his chapter on the "The Monetarists", Sennholz identifies Milton Friedman as a disciple of Henry C. Simons. In "The World Order", I give Milton Friedman's true origins, apparently unknown to Sennholz, as stemming from the Royal Colonial Society, a group financed by English bankers who later centralized their world drug profits in the Hong Kong Shanghai Bank. The staff economist of the Royal Colonial Society was Alfred Marshall, inventor of the monetarist theory which Milton Friedman peddles under the aegis of the Hoover Institution and other supposedly rightwing think-tanks. Marshall, through the Oxford Group, became the patron of Wesley Clair Mitchell, who founded the National Bureau of Economics Research for the Rockefellers in the United States, and became the teacher of Pan Europe, the latest incarnation of the Austrian School of Economics financed by the Rothschilds as an integral plank in their World Order. All of this is carefully ignored by Sennholz. Why?

Sennholz gets down to the real purpose of his book in Chapter 5, "Advocates of Social Credit". This is a frenetic attack on those who have been influenced by the scholarly work of Ezra Pound, including one "H. S. Kenan". Sennholz's scholarship may be rated by the fact that he seems unaware the "H. S. Kenan" was the pen name of one of the nation's most notorious plagiarists, who reprinted the text of my book, "The Federal Reserve Conspiracy" under that name, and made one million dollars during years of active promotion of this stolen book. Incredibly, Sennholz concludes that these advocates of social credit echo Marxist and Leninist lines.

Finally, "Money and Freedom" is a ripoff, selling for $5.95 plus $2.00 handling for an 83 page pamphlet which is an indirect attack on many conservatives who are genuinely interested in freeing our nation from the control of the international syndicalists. Its real purpose may be better understood when we realize it has been backed by a notorious centimillionaire whose malign influence was concentrated for years on destroying me and my work. He hired the two most influential law firms in Virginia to despoil me of the proceeds of "Secrets of the Federal Reserve" through "legal" procedures, while continuing to pose as a "philanthropist". It was just this type of malignant philanthropy which saddled us with the conspiratorial activities of the Carnegie, Rockefeller and Brookings foundation. Sennholz may be an unwitting tool of this "philanthropist", but his book peddles the "Establishment" theory that the Federal Reserve System is what he claims it to be, and not what Paul Warburg set it up to be. You should get the facts, but you won't get them by paying $7.95 for this pamphlet.

AMERICA'S NEW ROBBER BARONS

To make money in the stock market, you need to use the same tools which the big operators use; that is, capital, and information. The amount of capital which you can lay your hands on may be limited. It is for most people. But the amount of information you can obtain, may be limited only by your desire to get the facts, and your willingness to reject previous misconceptions or misinformation. Then you may begin to understand what is going on in the market.

You must first recognize that fundamental changes have been taking place in our capital structure, and in money-making properties. For more than a century, the American tradition had it that to achieve great wealth, you must have the good fortune to strike it rich with a gold mine, to strike oil, or to own your own bank. In the past decade, we have witnessed the amazing phenomena of millionaires, and even billionaires, who owned vast wealth in the form of gold mines, oil wells, or banks, and who suddenly were declaring bankruptcy. What was happening to the American dream? The answer is that capitalization, or debt structure, was now overcoming capital assets. The cash flow, even from a gold mine, an oil well or bank, was no longer sufficient to pay interest charges, much less to handle the payment of the principal of the debt structure.

This dilemma was not inevitable, nor did it arise from optimism, or over optimism, the courage to take risks which made America the most productive and the wealthiest nation in the world. The debt structure vs. capital assets dilemma was deliberately created by a small group of capital managers, or financiers, who cleverly used their phalanx of money-creating central banks to overcome rival groups and rival nations. This situation directly affects stock transaction which takes place on the world exchanges. Your problem now is how do I translate this debt structure -- capital assets conflict into profitable transactions for myself? The basic problem is similar to that of a poker game -- how do you find out what cards the other fellow is holding? Despite the great secrecy which shrouds major financial transactions, almost every financial move is telegraphed in some way, due to the continuing and growing concentration of financial power in a few hands. Today, a shadowy (but not unknown) financial network achieves its goals through relatively few participants. In some thirty-five years of research, I have narrowed these participants down to the major players. They not only bring tremendous pressure on the exchanges through their power to buy or sell enormous blocks of stock, but they also exercise a daily effect on the prices and daily volume of the exchanges through their control of the faucets, the turning on or off of the money creating flow of the central or pseudo government banks.

Here again, there are always some indicators of major moves in either direction, although the exact decisions remain the secret of the major players. The tremendous power exercised by these creators dwarfs the power earlier exercised by such stock market plungers as Bet A Million Gates, bank pioneers such as George F. Baker of First National Bank (now Citibank), or oil magnates such as the late H.L. Hunt. The 42-year-old heir of the Hunt empire, Ray Hunt, recently told *Fortune* (July 8, 1985): *"We'll never go back to the good old days of the oil industry."* It is not only the good old days of the oil industry, but also the empire building days of the Vanderbilts in railroads, Carnegie in steel, or Baker in finance, which have disappeared. They have been transmuted into new types of financial operations, such as mergers, leveraged buyouts, and other forms of takeovers. Here again, the major players either originate these operations, or they move in and take them over at crucial moments.

Yet we rarely are told the exact identities of the major players. The financial papers such as the *Wall Street Journal* and *Forbes* write about the "raiders," the modern financial buccaneers who supposedly loom out of the fog as lone wolf operators and seize control of major corporations. The financial reporters don't tell us that when the Belzbergs buy control of the Scovill Corp., they are merely acting as agents of the Rothschilds, or that the Bronfmans, in buying a large share of DuPont, are also merely carrying out the instructions of the Rothschilds from London.

Forbes recently identified Seagrams of Canada as the No. 1 foreign investor in the United States. It wholly owns the $2.4 billion Joseph Seagrams and Sons of New York, and 23% of the $14 billion DuPont Corp. And Seagrams of Canada is wholly controlled by the Bronfman family. Right? Wrong. The Bronfmans own large blocks of stock in Seagrams (*US News* recently gushed that Edgar Bronfman may be the most powerful man in America), but the Seagram empire is controlled by the law firm of Vineberg and Phillips through Trizec Corp., which in turn is controlled by Eagle Star Holdings PLC of London. And who controls Eagle Star? Evelyn de Rothschild.

When Seagrams faced a 30% drop in volume, due to the dwindling market for hard liquor in the United States, who guided the firm into Conoco, and then masterminded the purchase of Conoco by DuPont? If you suppose that Edgar Bronfman anticipated all this, and worked to bring it about, then you don't know who really makes the big decisions. Seagrams' stake in DuPont is currently worth $3.2 billion, or 80% of Seagrams net worth. In 1984, DuPont profits were 73% of Seagrams' earnings.

The second largest foreign investor in the U.S., again according to *Forbes* 1985 listings, is Anglo-American Corp. In 1985, it owned 21% of Philbro-Salomon, and 29% of Engelhard Corp. Anglo-American is the gold mining arm of the world diamond trust,

DeBeers, which is owned by the Oppenheimer and the Rothschild families. The principal director of DeBeers, again, is Evelyn de Rothschild.

Forbes lists the largest foreign owned corporation in the world as Royal Dutch Shell. Formerly controlled by the Samuel family, it is now another Rothschild property, controlled through their subsidiary, Shell Transport & Trading Co.

The fourth largest foreign investor in the U.S. is British Petroleum, which owns Standard Oil of Ohio, and British Petroleum of North America. One of the directors of British Petroleum is Sir Alastair Pilkington, who is also a director of the Bank of England.

The sixth largest foreign investor in the U.S. is B.A.T. Industries, a $12.9 billion a year operation which was formerly known as British-American Tobacco Corp. BAT owns 100% of BAT US, 100% of Peoples Drug Stores, Hardee's Fast Foods, and Eagle Star Insurance, the Rothschild holding company, which controls the Bronfman empire. Sir Jasper Hollom, who has been a director of the Bank of England since 1936, is a director of BAT; also on the board of BAT is Sir Denis Mountain, who is chairman of Eagle Star Insurance, and Eagle Star Holdings, a principal Rothschild holding company. Another director of BAT is Sir Michael Palliser, who married the daughter of Paul Henri Spaak, former director general of the United Nations. Sir Michael was a career officer with the British Foreign Office, being named head of planning in 1946. He served with the Foreign Office from 1946 to 1964 as Minister to Paris, and Minister to Brussels, the two leading headquarters on the Continent of the Rothschild operations. Sir Michael is now chairman of the influential think tank, the Institute for Strategic Studies in London. He is also vice chairman of the oldest merchant bank in London, Samuel Montagu & Co., and interlocks with other Rothschild interests as director of Eagle Star, and Shell Transport & Trading Co.

Going on down the list, we find the 76th largest foreign investor in the U.S., is Olympia & York Co., which has been buying up large sections of Manhattan. Olympia & York has acquired the Rouse Co., a large developer; Trizec Corp. which controls the Seagram empire; and Abitibi-Price, a billion dollar producer of newsprint. Olympia & York is supposedly controlled by the well-publicized Reichmann brothers, Albert, Paul and Ralph, but here again, we have the paper "cutouts" for the real owners, the Rothschild family.

Far-reaching consequences are indicated by the foreign takeover of a number of large American supermarket chains. This could be crucial in view of projected food shortages around the end of this century. General Occidentale now owns 100% of Grand Union stores, as well as 25% of Crown Zellenbach. The *Wall Street Journal* will tell you that General Occidental is Sir James Goldsmith, but will neglect to tell you that Sir James was until recently one of the six partners of Banque Rothschild of Paris. He also owns Caveham Foods. The popular British TV series, "To the Manor Born," featured a foreigner who had taken the name of Sir Richard de Vere, and who owned a large supermarket chain, Cavendish Foods. The character was a direct takeoff on Sir James Goldsmith and Cavenham Foods.

The Brussels firm, Delhaize de Lion, is now the 32nd largest foreign investor in the U.S. It owns the Food Giant and the Food Lion chain of supermarkets. The German firm, Tengelmann Group, has purchased 52% of A & P Stores. One of the directors of A & P is Barbara Haupthfuhrer. She is a trustee of the Markle Foundation, which interlocks with the Carnegie Corp., the German Marshall Fund, and the American Council on Germany. The last two groups exercise total control over the militarily occupied nation of West Germany. During the past one hundred and fifty years, the Rothschild fortunes have been centered in the Bank of England, and four family controlled firms, Sun Alliance Assurance, Rio Tinto, DeBeers, and Eagle Star. Rio Tinto is the 41st largest foreign investor in the U.S., owning 100% of U.S. Borax and 100% of Indal U.S. It also has holdings in other U.S. companies. The Rothschilds also control Copperweld, Federal Express, and other U.S. firms. In the *Forbes* list of the 500 largest foreign corporations Sun Alliance Assurance is 332nd; Banque Bruxelles Lambert, the Belgian branch of the Rothschild bank, is 431st; and another family holding, Societe Generale de Banque, is number 224th.

A gentleman recently called me from Dallas, and said, *"I always knew that the stock market is controlled, but until I read your books, I did not realize how absolute the control really is."* Of course, control, to be effective, must be absolute, or as absolute as possible. This is why the financiers must control all political parties, not merely the majority party. Realizing the extent of this control does not mean that you are helpless. On the contrary, you can turn it to your advantage. Knowing who exercises control and why can be a potent weapon in your hands. However, you must know who is actually in charge. You cannot be deceived by the pathetic stooges, the flotsam and jetsam dredged up by the financiers from the lowest elements of the population, and who ostensibly exercise control for the benefit of the real powers. Only children believe that clowns are the most important part of the circus.

Certainly it is better to know than not to know. You can read all the major financial journals for years, and you will not get the information which is being presented here. With this information you can decide where the market is going, plan your strategy. Ask yourself why stock prices, metals, and food prices have been held down at ruinous levels for the past quarter of a century. Economist William H. Meckling of the University of Rochester was quoted on the editorial page of the *Wall Street Journal*, Aug. 20, 1985, as pointing out that the Dow Jones averages, to accurately reflect inflationary trends and monetary developments, should have reached 5600 on Jan. 1, 1983, instead of the actual 1047. He observes that in the eighteen year period from Dec. 1964 to Dec. 1982, the real value of Dow Jones stocks fell by 62%. Obviously, it is to someone's advantage that stocks should be hovering in the 1300 range today, instead of selling at their true value of 5600. By keeping these prices depressed, the major players have forced out much of the stock buying and stockholding public. They are now executing mergers and buyouts to grab these under priced stocks for themselves. The leveraged buyouts also play into the hands of the financiers because they suddenly convert a debt-free corporation into one which is mortgaged to the full value of its holdings, and which is committed to paying heavy interest on its new loans.

Texaco borrowed $4 billion from a consortium of banks, Barclays, Chase Manhattan, Lloyds, Manufacturers Hanover, Midland Bank, and National Westminster Bank, to purchase Getty Oil. Norfolk Southern borrowed $1.3 billion from Morgan Guaranty Trust to buy Conrail; Nestle borrowed $2.5 billion from Citibank to buy Carnation. By creating these huge new debts, which take priority payment from the earnings of these firms, the banks can pay their way out of the dilemma of their disastrous Third World loans. In the financing of these mergers, we find the new leaders of Wall Street. For almost a century, Wall Street was dominated by two Rothschild representatives. Although J.P. Morgan Co. is still going strong, Kuhn, Loeb Co., as well as Lehman Brothers, have been combined into a new operation, known as SLAM, or Shearson Lehman American Express. It is closely linked with First Boston Corp. in handling many of the large mergers. A double page spread in the *Wall Street Journal*, Aug. 15, 1985, hails First Boston Corp. for "Leadership in Mergers, Acquisitions and Divestitures." The advertisement cites twelve recent mergers involving large firms, including Dunlop Tire,

Revco, Cowles Media, Gulf, Allied Corp., Sara Lee, and Castle & Cooke.

The co-chairmen of First Boston are Pedro Paul Kuczynski and Yve Andre Istel. Kuczynski was born in Lima, Peru in 1938; his mother was a Godard. He was educated at Oxford, Cambridge, and Princeton. He served with the World Bank from 1961-67 and was named senior economist there 1971-73. He was with the Banco de Venezuela and the Central Bank of Peru from 1957-69, and with the International Monetary Fund in Washington from 1969-71. He joined Kuhn, Loeb Co. in 1975, staying until 1977. He became president of Halco Mining Co. in 1977, a Pittsburgh aluminum firm doing $277 million a year. Kuczynski was Minister of Energy of Peru from 1980-82. He joined First Boston in 1982. Richard Mellon Scaife, scion of the Mellon fortune, is a director of First Boston.

Kuczynski's co-chairman at First Boston, Yve Andre Istel, also came from Kuhn Loeb Co. Born in Paris, he worked for his family banking house, Andre Istel and Co. of Paris and New York. He married Nancy Lazarus, and later joined Kuhn, Loeb Co. He is now manager of Shearson Lehman American Express. His brother Jacques Istel, is manager of Andre Istel & Co., and director of the Dreyfus Fund of New York. SLAM, or Shearson Lehman, is actually the continuation of the old Kuhn, Loeb Co., which was set up by Jacob Schiff as the secret American representative of the Rothschild family. Schiff had been born in the Rothschild house on Judengasse in the Frankfurt ghetto. The present directors of Shearson Lehman include Peter Cohen, president; George Sheinberg, director, who is also chairman of American Express Credit Corp. and director of Warner-Amex Cable, Franks Broadcasting System; ex-President Gerald Ford; Kenneth J. Bialkin of the law firm of Willkie, Farr and Gallagher, director of Gulf, E.M. Warburg Pincus and Municipal Assistance Corporation of New York, which bailed the city out of bankruptcy; Howard L.

Clark, Jr exec. VP American Express, director Magic Chef, and Palm Beach Co.; Roger S. Berlind, chairman Berlind Production Co., Financial News Network, and Etz Lavud Inc., an Israeli firm and James S. Robinson III, chairman of American Express, director of Union Pacific Railroad (Harriman), Coca Cola, and Bristol Myers Co.

American Express, a $9.77 billion a year operation, is in a very profitable business, the business of printing and circulating money. It is mind-boggling to think how many billions of dollars worth of American Express travelers checks are printed and sold each year. Judging from the volume of its television advertising it finds it worthwhile. Directors of American Express include the chairman, James D. Robinson III, mentioned above; ex-president Gerald R. Ford, who is also director of a large defense contractor, G.K. Technologies; Anne Armstrong, former Ambassador to England, chairman of the Reagan-Bush campaign, and director of the Texan axis of the Rothschild fortune, First City Bank Corporation. She is also a trustee of the Atlantic Council, Guggenheim Foundation, Hoover Institution, and the Council on Foreign Relations; Henry Kissinger, former Secretary of State under Nixon and Ford, now partners with Lord Carrington of England in a public relations firm (Lord Carrington is related by marriage to the Rothschilds).

Kissinger is also a director of Chase Manhattan Bank, trustee of Aspen Institute and the Rockefeller Brothers Fund; his brother Walter, also a refugee from Germany, is director of Manufacturers Hanover, another of the Rothschild banks, and the National Council on U.S.-China Trade; Joseph H. Williams, chairman of the Williams Companies, a $2.17 billion a year oil operation, director of American Petroleum Institute, and Peabody Coal Co.; Martha Wallace, management consultant, member Trilateral Commission, chairman Rhodes Scholar Selection Committee, American Council of Germany (which rules West Germany in the name of the financiers), and the Japan Society. She formerly was with RCA, Time, Fortune, and the Henry Luce Foundation, now director Chemical Bank NY, Bristol Myers, New York Stock Exchange, New York Telephone, National Council on U.S.-China Trade, British North American Committee, and International House; Rawleigh Warner, chairman of Mobil Corp., director of AT & T, Chemical Bank and Signal Co. (a $6.67 billion company which interlocks with Rothschild interests in Texas and Rothschild interests in Canada through another director, Philip Beckman, president of Seagrams); Robert V. Roosa, partner of Brown Bros. Harriman, chairman of Brookings Institution, Trilateral Commission, director Texaco; Peter Cohen, president Shearson Lehman Bros.; Charles W. Duncan, Chairman Coca Cola Europe, director United Technologies, former deputy Secretary of Defense, 1977-79, Secretary of Energy, 1979-81; Richard M. Furlaud, chairman Squibb Pharmaceutical, director of munitions firm Olin, trustee Rockefeller University; Magnus Bohm; David Culver, president Alcan, director of Seagrams, Canadair and American Cyanamid.

Through Seagrams, Culver interlocks with the giant Rothschild complex, Eagle Star Holdings PLC, which controls their Canadian and American operations; Robert Genillard, chairman of Thyssen-Bornemiza, the giant European holding company formed from the former Thyssen Steel complex of Germany, also director Corning Glass and Swiss Aluminum; Fred Kirby, the Woolworth heir who is chairman of the Alleghany Corp.; and Archie McCardell, director of Honeywell, General Foods, and Harris Bancorp.

The presence of such well known political figures as Gerald Ford and Henry Kissinger illustrates the fact that what we know as Big Business is inextricably linked with the wielding of total political power in America. The Central Intelligence Agency, known to its employees as *The Company*, and to those familiar with its operations as "The Central Investment Agency," is headed by William Casey, who made a fortune while working with Leo Cherne at the Research

Institute of America. Cherne has long been associated with such leftwing institutions as the New School for Social Research in New York. He was chairman of the board of Freedom House from 1946-75. As head of the CIA, Casey has devoted much of his time to managing his extensive stock portfolio. He was recently involved with one of his wartime OSS pals, Joe Rosenbaum, in a huge Middle East pipeline deal.

It is not coincidental that political power and international finance go hand in hand. All economic problems are eventually solved by the barrel of a gun. Money cannot own anything; it can only serve as the medium by which to transfer ownership. In the history of mankind, property has been transferred by the power of the gun perhaps as often as by any other technique. This is the unspoken reason for the frantic struggle to enact gun control legislation in the United States. As long as American citizens possess some 200,000,000 guns, the financiers have to put on hold their five thousand year old dream of seeing all of the world's wealth fall into the hands of a small group of parasites.

The previously cited economist, William H. Meckling, has proposed that Congress and the state legislatures be abolished, and that all statutes be put to public referendum. This "revolutionary" solution would return the world to the pure Greek democracy of some five thousand years ago. It would also destroy the program of the parasites. Meckling's proposal to abolish Congress is somewhat redundant, because the Congress of the United States has had no independent existence since 1945. It has been a rubber stamp Duma for the international financiers, and it has routinely enacted into law the most vicious acts against the interests of the American people. The state legislatures have served as a rubber stamp for the financial interests since the Council of State Governments was set up by the Rockefellers in the mid-1930s. Nevertheless, the American colony, although still under complete control, shows unmistakable signs of unrest, because of the ruthless war which has been waged against it since 1945 by the subversive interests.

A gun is being held to the heads of the American people. Their reaction must take place before they are completely overwhelmed by the vast number of aliens whom the parasites are importing into the U.S. to carry out their final solution. The parasites intend that these aliens shall make up 80% of the American population before the year 2000. This will insulate the parasites against any possible reaction from the outraged American people. An investment program must reflect these political developments that will offer higher taxes and inflation in the immediate future.

WARNING — THE DEPARTMENT OF JUSTICE IS DANGEROUS TO AMERICANS

Although the Department of Justice, Washington, D.C., is not yet a serious challenge to the old Mack Sennatt comedies, or the leers and sneers of the "funnyman", Charlie Chaplin, its antics concern many Americans, who do not know whether to laugh or cry, as each new revelation of the department's ventures into insanity are laid before the American public.

We have recently witnessed the spectacle of a "Special Prosecutor" from the Justice Dept., Lawrence Walsh, spending forty million dollars of taxpayers money to find out whether Col. Oliver North paid for two tires. This is more money than the Credit Bureau has spent in its entire existence! We also witnessed the ludicrous spectacle of a black man, William Lucas, who was appointed by President Bush to the Civil Rights Division of the Justice Department, being harried and torn by the most fanatical leftwing Senators from the Democratic Parry.

They turned him down flat, sending a clear message that the black man had better stay in his place. Lucas' offense was not that he was black, but that he had strayed off the plantation, until he was picked up by the "patterole", as the old slave chasers were known. There is a clear understanding in Washington that the "civil tights" movement not only is limited to blacks, (no whites need apply for relief under its stringent protection but it is also the private preserve of the old hard line Stalinist-Communist wing of the national Democratic Party. It maintains its private army of Stepin Fetchits, who cringe and laugh whenever the Democratic leaders, such as Senator Edward (Chappaquiddick) Kennedy, bark, and no "civil rights" effort is allowed unless it is authorized by the party of Bella Moscovitz and the secret Harold Ware cell of Communist government officials in Washington. Lucas not only ran away from the plantation, he actually joined the Republican Party, and attempted to take office in Washington under its auspices. This was not to be. Amazingly enough, Bush refused to appoint Lucas to the civil rights post anyway, giving it to him as an "interim" appointment until 1990, on the cowardly excuse that to make such an appointment might "offend" the Democratic leaders in Congress. They had already trashed Lucas in public, for the entire nation to see, and Bush dared not rob them of their Muscovite victory by going over their heads. As King George IV, representing the Bank of England, Bush has served notice that he will observe all the bylaws of "bipartisanship", meaning that whenever the interests of Republican voters, who elected him President, conflict with the wishes of the old Stalinist leaders of the Democratic Party, he will ignore the people who elected him, and will vote for the Democratic program. No doubt he has good reason for doing so; there is not only the central bank policy of "bipartisanship", which has been imposed by force upon the American people; there are also the unpleasant reminders of what happens to Presidents who refuse to go along with the Moscow line. Nixon was hounded from office, directly negating the Presidential election which had put him in the White House; there was an attempted assassination of Ronald Reagan shortly after he took office, to remind him that certain people were still extremely displeased that he had defeated the Democratic candidate, What's His Name, for the Presidency. Reagan got the message, and never again challenged the Stalinist Communists of the Democratic Party during his two terms in office.

Some of his followers, who had failed to be baptized in the new religion of bipartisanship, sought to bypass Congress by funding the Nicaraguan rebels, the Contras, against the Nicaraguan Communists by private fund-raising. It was not to be. Israel got the funds, and North got the blame. The fact that he and his associates were merely faceless stooges for Henry Kissinger did not save them from the stake; it meant only that the fire was lower and burned much longer during their ordeal. The Department of Justice, as we have mentioned, functioned as the Inquisition which made the ritual executions possible.

In the light of its persistent efforts to function as a super KGB in the United States, it is difficult to recall that we have not always had a "Department of Justice". Such an operation was never envisioned by the Founding Fathers, who believed that they had made adequate provision for judicial and police departments in the Constitution, and in the Judiciary Act of 1789. Almost a hundred years later, subterranean influences in Washington, working upon the sensibilities of Congress, claimed that there was now a public demand (inaudible to all but the conspirators) for a Department of Justice. By means as yet undisclosed, Congress was persuaded to create a "Department of Justice" in 1870. The first century of this nation's existence had seen unparalleled growth and prosperity for all Americans. This began to change, and not subtly, soon after the department began to operate. The century since its creation has been one of steadily accelerating decline for our people. How did this happen? America had begun its existence as something for which the entire world longed, a nation of freedom, a nation of opportunity, a nation which had not been stifled by the stealthy machinations of the Canaanites and the Black Nobility. America was also intended to be a land where justice would prevail. In fact, it did prevail, until the Department of Justice was established. After 1870, the new department, as the ultimate tool of the monopolists and their spoils system, served to remove the possibility of obtaining justice in the courts beyond the reach of Americans who were not in on the scam. Justice since that time has been only for the fortunate few, for those who conspired to create the Department of Justice, and who have since been the sole beneficiaries of that creation.

Because of these sinister origins, the Department of Justice exists solely to serve the directors of the PIP, the Party in Power, which is known more accurately as "the Perverts in Power", because of their strange desires, and also for their compulsion to pervert every aspect of American existence. Although all government departments in Washington are permanently tainted by political opportunism, the Department of Justice remains the most reprehensible, because it advertises itself as the final arbiter of justice. Thus it is the most flagrant prostitute of our national government, boldly flaunting its commitment to do anything for its pimps.

The present writer has routinely advised the Department of Justice, over the past forty years of grievous criminal acts which have been committed, and whose prosecution falls within the purlieu of this department. These letters have been sent Certified, and with Return Receipt Requested; therefore the department has regularly answered these letters, and has as regularly refused to take any action. Reported violations of civil rights are met with the Department of Justice response, usually in an ill-concealed sneer, that if I really think my civil rights have been violated, I should hire a private attorney! Notifications of interstate theft, using the mails to defraud, and conspiracy to defraud, all amply documented, have met with the identical response, that I should hire a private lawyer. This is the same Department of Justice which will spend millions of dollars to prosecute a political dissident.

On one complaint of copyright violation, Oliver (Buck) Revell, acting director of the FBI wrote to me on May 28, 1986 that "the FBI pursues criminal investigations and prosecution of copyright matters generally in the areas of sound recordings, motion pictures, and audiovisual works .... the FBI will not institute a criminal investigation in this matter."

Few Americans are aware that for years the vast resources of the FBI have been diverted to protect the profits of a few Hollywood film moguls, who are also the largest donors of funds to political campaigns. The resources of the FBI are dedicated to protecting the profits of these film moguls, and to conducting black bag criminal break-ins for the ADL. The five thousand lawyers employed at the Department of Justice carry out the most humiliating errands for the party bosses; when they are not conspiring with the dread KGB to commit atrocities against American citizens, they indulge in their most consuming passion, volunteering to carry out hatchet jobs against any critic of the State of Israel.

Since the advent of Franklin Delano Roosevelt in 1933, and a staff of government officials personally selected by Bella Moscovitz, the secret boss of the top secret Harold Ware cell in Washington, the Department of Justice has been unrelentingly pro-Communist in its bias.

When Bella Moswvitz fell, or was pushed, down the stairs a few days before Roosevelt's inauguration, the leadership of the Harold Ware cell was taken over by none other than Roosevelt's other mentor, the sinister Felix Frankfurter, who had been denounced by Roosevelt's own cousin, former President Theodore Roosevelt.

The long parade of Republican White House staff members convicted and sent to prison reflects not only the powers delegated to the Department of Justice attorneys, but also the political clout of the Democratic Congress. Like the Supreme Court, the Department of Justice can be said to have read the election returns, but its actions occur on a much lower and more petty level. The dedication of the Justice attorneys to the aggrandizement of statism, more properly known as Marxism, has never been a secret in Washington. However, in recent years, two conflicting philosophies have clashed in the department, as the adherents of fanatical sects sought to attain absolute control of the department for their own sinister ends. In 1933, with the advent of the Roosevelt regime, the Stalinist wing of the world Communist party, through Bella

Moscovitz, and later through Felix Frankfurter, seized total control of the Democratic Party. Our government officials now vied with each other in demonstrating their newfound loyalty. Large posters of Lincoln and Stalin suddenly appeared in the homes of leading government officials; the Internationale was now routinely and prayerfully sung at exclusive weekend parties hosted by their friends, and earnest clerks could be seen poring over the latest edition of Stalin's speeches from International Publishers.

However, these were only token gestures. These officials were not token Communists; they were actively engaged in espionage activities in every department of the government.

Frankfurter placed his ubiquitous proteges, who were nicknamed "the happy hot dogs," in obeisance to their mentor, in key positions. At the War Department, he sent over to Secretary Henry Stimson two of his most eager followers, Harvey Bundy and John J. McCloy. McCloy later became the Gauleiter of a defeated Germany, and the personal lawyer of the Rockefeller fortune. Native born government employees, who had served ably and well at very low salaries, were quickly shunted to the background, irreversibly tainted as "good Americans".

They could not ever boast a foreign accent.

Meanwhile, the Republican Party was taken over by the descendants of Trotsky's revolutionaries, who had nested in the Rockefeller-financed League for Industrial Democracy. Now calling themselves "neo-conservatives", and boasted of their absolute loyalty to the State of Israel.

As the "neo-cons" took over the various government departments, during the "Reagan Revolution", loyalty to Stalin was met by equal loyalty to Trotsky. The Department of Justice was taken over by a small group of activists, a coalition of bankers, radicals, and Zionist fanatics who became known to each other as members of "Nesher", the Hebrew word for "eagle". The origins of Nesher are to be found in "Chekisty: A History of the KGB", by John J. Dziak, the official historian of the Defense Intelligence Agency. Dziak exposed the world-wide espionage and assassination bureau run by the KGB through Dr. Max Eitington, a close associate of Sigmund Freud. It was Eitington who introduced psychiatry and drugs as principal tools of the espionage trade. Eitington also prepared the documents for the 1937 show trials, which resulted in the nine top generals of Stalin's army being executed. These documents were later found to have been prepared by the Gestapo, with which Eitington worked closely. He had long been an intimate of Reinhard Heydrich.

The Eitington technique of preparing forged documents for use in political show trials have recently been employed with great success in the Office of Special Investigations of the Department of Justice, persecuting American citizens, and having them deported and executed by the KGB on "war criminal" charges. The evidence in these cases was prepared by the KGB, special "witnesses" were dredged up from Soviet concentration camps, their testimony purchased by offers of release from life imprisonment, and our citizens were convicted on accusations prepared jointly by the KGB and Mossad. The "trials" took place almost a half century after the alleged "crimes" outside American jurisdiction. Its equivalent would be the prosecution of Soviet leaders today for mass murders committed during the 1930s in the Stalin purges.

Among the many assassinations arranged by Max Eitington were the murder of Trotsky's son, Leon Sedov, in a Paris hospital; Rudolf Kleist, a German Trotskyite whose decapitated body was found in the Seine; and Walter Krivitsky, a KGB defector who was found shot in a Washington hotel room, only a few feet from the halls of Congress. Eitington's brother ran foreign espionage operations of the KGB, expenses being paid by the income from the Soviet Fur

Trust. Max Eitington set up the Berlin Psychiatric Institute whose graduates later were sent to the United States to establish cells of the Tavistock Institute (the British Army Dept. of Psychological Warfare operation), which now systematically sets up brainwashing curricula at which the leading officials of the major U.S. foundations, government departments, and educational institutions are forced to attend.

The Eitington group, known by the nickname, "the killerati", because they were self-styled intellectuals and doctors dedicated to secret conspiracies, became the nucleus of the British Secret Intelligence Service, and its more recent subsidiary, the Central Intelligence Agency. The Department of Justice takeover by Nesher created a mutually satisfactory meeting ground for the ostensibly hostile forces of Mossad and the KGB. Provided with unlimited funds by the American taxpayer, they were enabled to carry out their sinister worldwide campaigns of murder and sabotage. Nesher is known to have financed hit teams to assassinate Palestinians who were cooperating with the United States government, and thereby assured the continuing chaos in Palestine, the basis of Israeli policy. In retaliation for Nesher operations, which were known to be financed by the American government the Arabian forces began to take American hostages, creating an even more fortuitous situation for the Israelis, who could now demand further appropriations from Congress to fight the "terrorists". Nesher then ousted Duvalier in Haiti, creating chaos in that suffering nation. Meanwhile, Nesher's principal operative mole in government offices, Jonathan Pollard, was daily removing thousands of pages of crucial U.S. documents from secret files for his Israeli employers, assuring more economic chaos and future diplomatic catastrophes for our nation. Pollard operated under the aegis of Under Secretary of Defense Fred Ikle, whose Swiss connection is now involved in another international financial scandal. Ikle's two principal aides were also prominent in Nesher, Richard Perle and Stephen Bryen They set up yet another front group, the Jewish Institute for National Security Affairs, as the cover for their furtive operations, working closely with Moscow Procurator Natalya Koleznikova, and the mastermind of the Irangate imbroglio, David Kimche, who was director of Mossad.

When Pollard was exposed, a massive coverup was initiated by Nesher conspirators, Dep. Atty Gen Arnold Burns and Nate Lewin of Nesher initiated desperate "damage control" techniques to cover up for Pollard and prevent his prosecution. Burns' law firm had handled the books for the Lansky Syndicate financial operations through the Sterling National Bank. Burns also set up fifteen illegal tax shelters through Israeli connections, which resulted in the criminal evasion of some forty million dollars in taxes. Investigation into Burns' operations was stopped by William Weld, head of Justice's Criminal Division. Weld is a member of the prominent Wall Street investment family whose control of the Bank of Boston funnelled the payments to Pollard for his Israeli espionage operations.

The Nesher group continues to work closely with Swiss espionage and conspiracy operators, one of whose proctors, Tibor Rosenbaum, had financed the Israeli takeover of Palestine.

Swiss law enforcement was headed by Elizabeth Ikle Kopp, cousin of the aforementioned Fred Ikle at Defense. Her husband, Hans Kopp, headed a billion dollar holding company, Shakarchi Trading Co., which handled the funds for worldwide espionage groups, principally, the CIA and Mossad. Ten million dollars of the Iran-Contra proceeds from illegal sale of arms to Iran was first deposited in the Chase Manhattan Bank (read Kissinger) by Arab wheeler-dealer, Adna Kashoggi; the money was then transferred to Credit Swisse, and later was laundered by Shakarchi executives. This ten million dollars paid for the purchase and delivery of one thousand TOW missiles by the CIA for clandestine transfer to Iranian terrorists. As a result of information revealed during the Iran-Contra investigation, both Kopp and his wife are now under investigation, while Kashoggi was arrested and thrown into a Swiss prison. He was recently transferred to the United States, but a trial is unlikely, because it would directly involve too many highly placed Defense and Department of Justice officials.

During the Reagan Revolution, the Department of Justice was headed by Edwin Meese III, who publicly denounced the American Civil Liberties Union. He was then hounded from office, and forced to hire Nate Lewin, of Nesher, to defend him against a host of charges, none of which were ever proved. Meese was replaced by a longtime pillar of the Eastern Establishment, Dick Thornburgh, the former Governor of Pennsylvania. Thornburgh is a former director of the ACLU! As head of some 77,000 employees at Justice, Thornburgh has announced his intention of dismantling fourteen regional strike forces which had been set up to fight organized crime. He had previously begun the same process of dismantling while working in the Gerald Ford administration. Thornburgh developed a cozy relationship with the firm of Merrill Lynch while serving as Governor of Pennsylvania. His largest expenditure during his term of office was the authorization of an $807 million bond issue to patch up the decaying Pennsylvania Turnpike. The issue was handled by Merrill Lynch. He then became a director of Merrill Lynch, for $35,000 a year. He also became the political protégé of Donald Regan, former head of Merrill Lynch, who was now Reagan's chief of staff.

Although Thurnburgh's predecessor, Edwin Meese III, left office under a cloud, having been drawn into the notorious Wedtech scandal with the State of Israel, his record may be surpassed by Thornburgh. A Yale graduate! and longtime personal friend of President Bush, Thornburgh not only has a long association with the firm of Merrill Lynch; he is also a director of the scandal ridden Rite Aid Co., the nation's largest retail drug firm. Rite Aid's president, Marty Grass, was recently arrested in Room 158 of Cleveland's Sheraton Airport Hotel.

Detectives seized him as he was handing a $33,000 check to Melvin Wilcynski, a voting member of the state pharmacy board. According to the *Wall Street Journal*, Grass was trying to remedy problems caused when Rite Aid bought out Gray Drug Fair, acquiring 162 stores in Ohio. The stores had been fined for allowing non-pharmacy employees access to prescription drugs, failing to install proper security alarm systems, and other violations. Marty's father had married Lois Lehrman, whose family owns 100 million of Rite Aid stock. Her brother, Lewis Lehrman, is the well known "conservative" who funds Buckley's CIA agitprop organ, the *National Review*, the Lehrman Institute, and Jack Kemp's abortive Presidential bids.

As a front for the Nesher operation, Thornburgh can be trusted to continue the role of the Department of Justice as the enforcement arm of Mossad operations in the United States. The identification of this department as an Israeli operation reinforces a long felt conviction among Washington insiders that the time is ripe to abolish the Department of Justice and the FBI. As the 1988 Libertarian candidate for President, Ron Paul had called for closing the FBI, but he neglected to focus on the festering sore at Justice which produced such FBI outrages as the notorious Cointelpro operation. It is time to clean house in Washington.

HOW TO BE A UNITED STATES SENATOR

The Hiding Place

When one surveys the present crop of United States Senators, it is obvious that that body no longer provides the melodrama on Capitol Hill. During the 1930s, the Senators, particularly those from the Southern states, outdid themselves in colorful language, plantation owner attire, complete with wide brimmed Panama hats, and a cold-blooded approach to political dominance which has not been seen since they vanished like the dinosaurs of old. Today, we have such creatures as Senator Metzenbaum of Ohio, making $300,000 deals over his office phone, his colleague, Senator-Glenn, still reeling from the after effects of his trips through outer space, and, in the historic State of Virginia, Senator Warner, who parlayed his advantage of being born into a good family by marrying two of the wealthiest women in the United States.

In the 1930s, no one in the United States Senate more successfully wielded political power than Senator Harry Byrd, the senior Senator from Virginia. His career on Capitol Hill remains the howto-do-it Bible for would-be politicians, even though no one today has either the temerity or the ruthlessness to follow in his footsteps.

From the very outset of his career, Harry Byrd knew where the power lay, and he went after it. In reviewing his personal history, one finds few mistakes, despite flaws of personality which effectively prevented him from attaining the supreme prize, one which was often near his grasp, the office of President of the United States.

Although he was born into a distinguished political family, Harry Byrd was not even a Virgin ian. He was born in Martinsburg, West Virginia, where his closest childhood friend was a little Jewish boy named Lewis Lichtenstein Strauss, of whom more later. Byrd attained supreme political power in the State of Virginia by closely following the outstanding political career of the dominant figure of the twentieth century, Josef Stalin, Master of all the Russias. Byrd realized that Stalin, after the strange death of Lenin, reaped the benefits of efforts made years earlier, when he had carefully stacked the membership of local Soviets across Russia with his personal henchmen, sworn to support him.

As the crow flies, it is but a short distance from Martinsburg, West Virginia to Washington.

However, Harry Byrd realized at an early age that the road to Washington lies through the state capitol of Virginia, Richmond. That road, since the end of the Civil War, is known as the Carpetbagger Trail, because of the pervasive influence of alien infiltrators who came in the wake of the Federal troops, bribing their commanders to allow them to set up business in the devastated countryside. Byrd's own career began shortly after one of the most brazen robberies ever to occur on the Carpetbagger Trail, in 1893, when control of the state legislature of Virginia was purchased openly, as at a cattle auction, by the state's political boss, Senator Thomas Martin. Martin's war chest came from his activities as the lawyer for the Wall Street firms of J.P. Morgan and Kuhn, Loeb Co. of New York, both firms being active in the United States as the secret representatives of the House of Rothschild. As the paid lackey of the Morgan, Schiff and Belmont railroad interests, the Chesapeake and Ohio Railroad, and the Norfolk and Western Railway, Martin was advanced funds from these Rothschild firms in 1893 to buy the controlling interest in the state legislature, by bribing nine key members of the Virginia body for the sum of one thousand dollars each. His assistant in this bribery was the chief counsel for the Norfolk and Western, one William A. Glasgow Jr, who later had a town named after him to memorialize his brilliant achievements of bribery and corruption.

Martin's chief enforcer in controlling the votes of the state legislature was Senator Hal Flood, the grandfather of Harry Byrd, whose middle name, Flood, memorializes his mentor. With such advantages of birth, young Harry Byrd left school at the age of fifteen. He already had enough education to achieve what he planned to do with his life. He might later say, as did Commodore Vanderbilt, "I seen my chances, and I took'em." Senator Martin died in 1919, having successfully consolidated absolute power in Virginia through his Martin machine. It was the up and coming Harry Byrd who was to transform this political cabal into the even more successful Bird machine. Byrd would rule without a single serious challenge in Virginia for more than fifty years. The iron hand of the Byrd machine was oiled by whatever funds he needed to maintain his power. He had continuing access to money for political control from the greatest carpetbaggers of them all, the House of Rothschild. That access came through his childhood friend, Lewis Lichtenstein Strauss. After an unpromising beginning as an itinerant shoe salesman, Strauss suddenly showed up in Washington during the First World War as a key member of the Wilson bureaucracy, also known as the Baruch-House bureaucracy. His tribal connections allowed Strauss, with no previous experience, to take over the recently named U.S. Food Administration, as deputy to the "engineer", Herbert Hoover.

After being banned from dealing on the London Stock Exchange because of a notorious swindle, Herbert Hoover had promptly been recruited by the Rothschilds as just the man they had been looking for. Like J.P. Morgan and many others, he became an undercover Rothschild agent, with such success that he was named a director of the family firm, Rio Tinto. After successfully carrying out the Rothschild assignment of keeping the First World War going a full two years after the Germans begged for peace, by providing them with food and fuel through his mis-named "Belgian Relief Administration", Hoover was sent to the United States to become the Food Czar in the Baruch bureaucracy. Strauss was the person you had to see if you wanted to do business with the U.S. Food Administration.

Because he performed his job well for his masters, Strauss was rewarded at the end of the war by being appointed a director of the powerful Rothschild banking house, Kuhn, Loeb Co. Thus his longtime friend, Harry Byrd, now had a personal pipeline into the richest mother lode in modern history, the gold of the House of Rothschild. With the Byrd machine in control of the state; the partners of Kuhn, Loeb Co. lost no time in becoming Virginia squires. Freddie Warburg bought a huge estate at Middleburg, where he became famous for his lavish parties during the 1920s, while Lewis Strauss bought a vast property at Brandy Station, Virginia, a historical monument famed as the sight of the last cavalry charge in the United States.

After seizing the reins of power in Virginia from the fallen Senator Martin in 1919, Byrd's personal fortune mushroomed, while the state itself began to suffer from what was to be known during the next fifty years as "the Byrd blight". His financial sacrifices while serving the nation brought Harry Byrd an immense empire of orchards, warehouses, banks, newspapers and stock holdings, while the personal income of most Virginians continued to steadily decline. All of Byrd's holdings have been gained since he entered the Virginia Senate in 1915. The Byrd millions historically were sweated from cheap labor, which explains why he deliberately converted vast areas of Virginia into regions of hopeless poverty, the famed Appalachian pockets of depression which remain essentially unchanged today. At the same time, neighboring states, such as North Carolina, enjoyed unparalleled prosperity. He and his minions in the Byrd machine fought off all efforts of the national government to intervene with relief programs. Byrd refused to allow federal funds to be spent in Virginia because he was fearful of losing control. The government poured billions of dollars into slums in Chicago and New York, while Byrd's victims continued to exist in hopeless poverty.

The Byrd machine was able to retain power for a half century because of the twin evils of poverty and ignorance. He kept the people in poverty, while the Byrd-controlled press kept the people in ignorance of what was being done to them. The party line was laid down by the newspapers personally owned by Byrd in Winchester and Harrisonburg. A 1950 survey among professors of journalism ranked the Virginia press forty-ninth in the nation in its record of public service. Other Virginia newspaper publishers aspired to the Byrd image, hoping to be accepted by the local squirearchy, while they cynically continued to print editorials denying that there was a "Byrd machine" in Virginia. The machine's "Fifty Years of Shame" continued without any political opposition.

Following the example of Josef Stalin, Byrd put into place the most successful Soviet type of bureaucracy ever seen in the United States. In each of the one hundred Virginia counties, every office was held by a succession of Byrd look alikes, elderly, whitehaired, hard-drinking men who carefully cultivated the voice modulations of a cotton headed keeper of the men's room at an exclusive Southern country club. It was well known in the state that even the janitor in the county courthouse must be a reliable Byrd supporter, and willing to kick in with a suitable contribution to the Democratic Party when election time approached.

A key department in this state control was Byrd's invention of the Alcoholic Beverage Control Board. In the ancient Byzantine Empire, the Emperor maintained a personal monopoly on the sale of all alcoholic beverages, using the profits to pay his enormous palace expenses.

Emperor Byrd used the liquor monopoly to finance the enormous costs of maintaining his political machine. He had rammed the ABC law through the state legislature while he was Governor in 1933, in a typical Byrd plebiscite. The statute was later found to have been copied word for word from the Soviet statute setting up the Soviet State Liquor Trust in Russia! Today, the ABC Board still maintains a statewide network of Gestapo agents whose activities are vital to the health of the Byrd machine. Despite Byrd's huge Socialist bureaucracy in Virginia, his Soviet-style liquor monopoly, and other Soviet style state trusts, he always claimed to be a political conservative and an avowed anti-Communist. In the neighboring environs of the District of Columbia, free enterprise liquor stores offered longer hours, greater variety, and an average of twenty per cent less prices than Byrd's Soviet type state liquor stores. Visitors returning from the District of Columbia frequently had their cars stopped and searched, as Byrd's deputies sought to seize "contraband", that is, bottles of liquor purchased in the District of Columbia which had not been charged Byrd's state tax. A liquor distributor complained that it was very expensive to get on Byrd's purchase list, but worth it because of access to the Byrd monopoly stores. ABC agents still maintain iron control over restaurants, convenience stores and other outlets which handle any type of alcohol.

For eight years, Byrd kept Senator Carter Glass in the Senate of the United States, although it was known that he was totally senile. Socialist bureaucracies often maintain senile and disabled persons in government offices, because they are more easily controlled. Most Virginians refused to speak out against the Byrd dictatorship, because retaliation was swift. A Richmond physician who criticized the brutal murder of a patient in a state institution, was summoned on the following day for a compete examination of his tax returns.

"Deficiencies" were found, and he was compelled to pay a large sum in additional state taxes.

After cynically running Carter Glass for re-election to the Senate, Byrd lost no power when the old man finally died. He chose the most subservient member of his entourage to take Glass' place. Newsman at the National Press Club joked that Senator Robertson could not go to the men's room unless he asked Byrd for the key. Robertson attained some status in the Millionaire's Club, as the Senate was known, when he was quickly appointed to the powerful Senate Banking Committee. Now he was answerable to the international bankers, as Byrd had been throughout his political career. Robertson's son, Pat, later became a national figure by operating his own television network.

Byrd himself had followed a devious road to the Senate, attaining his seat by appointment rather than by election. The Federal Reserve bankers needed to ramrod some changes in the Federal Reserve Act through Congress. The original Act had bore Carter Glass' name, and had been signed into law by another Virginian, Woodrow Wilson. Now Byrd's mentors, the Rothchilds, decreed that Byrd be given a seat in the United States Senate in order to update the Federal Reserve Act without opposition. However, this posed a problem, as the incumbent Senator from Virginia, Claude Swanson, refused to vacate. The dilemma was solved by having Franklin D. Roosevelt appoint Swanson to his Cabinet. Byrd then took his Senate seat, and the changes to the Federal Reserve Act were passed without discussion.

Indeed none of the Senators had any idea how the Federal Reserve System worked what the changes portended. To avoid any Senate discussion, Byrd quickly obtained pro forma approval, and the Federal Reserve Act was amended.

Meanwhile, Byrd's childhood friend, Lewis Lichtenstein Strauss, had used his position as partner in Kuhn, Loeb Co. to have himself appointed to a number of key government posts, including head of the Atomic Energy Commission. Although lacking any military experience, he somehow became an Admiral along the way. As the financier of the huge Industrial Rayon Corporation, an Ohio firm which produced most of the fibre for the entire U.S. tire industry, Strauss named the son of his old friend, Harry Byrd Jr., as director of this firm. When Harry Byrd's failing health forced him to retire, it was Strauss who forced the reluctant son to take his place in the Senate. It was at this point that a petulant voice was heard in a hotel lobby in Richmond, "You know I don't want to run! Daddy's making me do it!" To ensure that young Byrd would not lose heart and withdraw, Strauss appointed himself as his campaign chairman. In the face of the Rothschild billions, all political opponents silently folded their tents, and young Byrd took his father's Senate seat, as though it were an hereditary post, to be handed down from father to son. In his declining years, old Harry's personal fortune was declared to be $28,791,618.42, yet he had never had any employment in private business.

Despite his reputed anti-Communism, Byrd had received a personal telephone call from Bernard Baruch during the tense hearings on the appointment of Anna Rosenberg as Assistant Secretary of Defense during the Korean War. She had been identified in testimony before the Senate Armed Services Committee as a Communist, which was not remarkable, because she had long been the Rockefeller empire's specialist in labor relations, and it was the Rockefellers who had dispatched Leon Trotsky from New York to bring about the successful Communist Revolution in Russia in 1917. As the senior figure on the Armed Services Committee, Byrd informed his colleagues that they must vote for the confirmation of Anna Rosenberg as Assistant Secretary of Defense. So much for his anti-Communism.

Byrd's political machine remained invulnerable because of the allegiance of the statewide Masonic lodges, which had been in place in the state of Virginia for some two hundred years. They controlled every business and every state and local office in each of the Virginia counties and hamlets. No one could expect any advancement or preferment, or a bank loan, without approval of the local lodge. The academic historian, Allen Moger, writes that "Byrd's power amazed observers .... it was explained by friends as an association of like-minded men." However, Moger prudently refrains from telling us the common denominator of these likeminded men, namely, that they were "the determined men of Masonry" to whom Disraeli referred in his writings. Mager's supposedly definitive history, "Virginia: Bourbon to Byrd", Univ. of Va. Press 1958, does not even mention Masonry in the Index. Despite Byrd's importance to the Federal Reserve bankers, the Federal Reserve System is mentioned by Moger only twice.

After Byrd's passing, one might suppose that the State of Virginia would move into a new era of political freedom, as is customary once a dictator vanishes. However, this failed to happen, because the Byrd state bureaucracy continued to function solely in its own interest. The people remained effectively shut out of their own government. Byrd's son left the Democratic Party, supposedly because of its extreme leftwing composition, and was elected as an independent, but this had no effect on the Byrd legacy, the Soviet style bureaucracy in Virginia. It has continued to operate with business as usual, with Jewish and black governors cynically elected by the insiders to protect their power.

The victory of Governor Wilder, hailed as the first black governor elected anywhere in the United States since the Reconstruction era, conveniently ignores the fact that for the Southern states, the Reconstruction Era has never ended. Although the Federal troops were withdrawn in 1877, the state governments were left firmly in the hands of the carpetbaggers. No others need apply for office. Wilder's election was a sop to the growing discontent of blacks in Virginia, who realized they, like everyone else in the state, continued to be robbed by the rapacious Soviet bureaucracy. It was not a revolution, despite the manipulated press acclaim to that effect. On the contrary, it was more of the same -- business as usual -- and that business will continue, without relief for the hard-pressed citizens who survived fifty years of shame under Harry Byrd, only to find that the yoke is still firmly riveted around their necks.

THE DAY VIRGINIA DIED

The tentacles of the Masonic Canaanite octopus are nowhere more deeply embedded than in the State of Virginia. Known to our traditions as "the Mother of Presidents" and "the Cradle of the Republic", Virginia is credited with having set the standards of Southern living and culture. This is a far cry from the twentieth century reality of Virginia as a degraded, backward state which from the beginning of its history has been invaded and overrun by "the determined men of Masonry". Since the end of the Civil War, the state has been run by a succession of Masonic carpetbaggers. Later it was invaded by a host of Northern millionaires, most of them Masons, who bought out the old families of Virginia and evicted them from their historic homes. In most cases, these showplaces have been turned into advertisements for the type of decor features in "Better Homes and Gardens".

The state of Virginia is dominated by three large residential areas, the northeast, which is a bedroom community for federal government workers in Washington, D.C.; the Richmond axis, which is totally dominated by the burgeoning state bureaucracy, and the Norfolk area, which is dominated by a huge naval base and the defense bureaucracy. Thus, the major part of the state is hostage to the bureaucracy.

On close examination, its much vaunted "culture" vanishes like the morning mist. Its' "great" writers consist of two wealthy dilettantes, James Branch Cabell and Ellen Glasgow, whose unreadable, and unread books languish on library shelves until they are mercifully disposed of at garage sales. These two Establishment figures made little or no impression on the national literary scene. Cabell churned out some eighteen volumes about an imaginary place which he called "Pointesme"; its significance apparently unknown to anyone but himself. Virginia's literary tradition actually was buried with Edgar Allen Poe. In the twentieth century, young writers and artists flee the state like chain gang refugees fleeing across a fetid swamp, before their talents are irrevocably damaged by the noxious vapors emitted by Virginia's prisonlike estate, the result of its longstanding domination by the bureaucracy. These young people never return; thus Virginia nourishes the cultural life of other states, but never its own.

As in the most fearful days of the Reign Of Terror during the French Revolution, the state of Virginia is overrun by hordes of agents and spies, most of whom have no idea that they are actually being "run" by the British Intelligence Service, which totally controls the top officials of the state. The FBI maintains its training school at the Marine base at Quantico, Virginia. Here they are taught techniques for following "subversives", who in most instances turn out to be anyone who professes a belief in the Constitution of the United States. The CIA also has its massive Babylonian headquarters at McLean, Virginia, as well as various training schools and "safe houses" throughout the state, closed off areas such as Vint Hill and other sacrosanct preserves. These agencies maintain a close liaison (read control) over state and local police agencies throughout Virginia. The rube policeman finds it very exciting to be told that he can keep watch while FBI or CIA agents burglarize, or "black bag", the home of "disidents", stealing whatever they might suppose to be valuable in framing him with a criminal charge or committing him to a mental institution. Some of the things which they take, of course, are simply "valuables", which enrich the private purse of the agents. Although there have been thousands of such incidents in the past fifty years, only a few cases challenging these strange intruders have ever come before the controlled curts, where they are promptly dismissed as "paranoia" by a compliant judge. The state also has large numbers of spies in such agencies as the State Liquor Control Board, the Department of Taxation, and other agencies whose zeal stems directly from the worst days of the Reign of Terror. During the Byzantine Empire, the Emperor used the profits from his liquor and wine monopoly to pay for his enormous household expenses. In the state of Virginia, a local Byzantine Emperor, Harry Byrd, who was then Governor, rammed through the ABC law in 1933 in a typical Virginia plebiscite; it was later found to have been copied from the statute setting up the Soviet Liquor Trust in Russia! The patronage and the profits from the Liquor Trust have since become the mainstay of the Party machine. The state-wide network of ABC agents terrorizes small businessmen with their carefully-developed Gestapo-like tactics and constant surveillance. Any unfavorable report means the loss of the business, after the all-important "license" is suspended. This power creates an ideal political climate for totalitarian control, continuous shakedowns, which are euphemistically called "contributions", either to the political machine, or to "collectors" who promise to pass the funds along to the proper parties. Whether this ever occurs is not traceable in any way. With these profits, Byrd built the largest per capita State Socialist bureaucracy in the United States, which effortlessly perpetuated his machine rule throughout his long political career. To maintain the illusion of a "two party democracy", Byrd usually allowed token political opposition in political campaigns for state offices, but he never permitted any serious opponent to challenge his reign. As a result, he never had to campaign, nor did he have to spend the enormous funds which had been raised to pay his campaign expenses. He routinely filled the state offices with lookalike Byrd stooges, elderly, softspoken, white-haired, harddrinking men who spoke slowly and carefully, with the Old South modulation of a wool-topped keeper of the men's room at an exclusive country club.

Byrd himself was merely the heir to a long-standing previous corruption. After the Civil War, the carpetbaggers had swarmed into Virginia, seizing their pitiful remnants of property from the defeated and impoverished Virginians. The corruption reached its apogee in 1893, when control of the state legislature was purchased openly, as at a cattle auction, by Senator Thomas Martin. Martin had long been the lawyer for the Morgan-Belmont interests in Virginia, and represented their substantial railroad holdings, the Chesapeake and Ohio Railroad and the Norfolk and Western Railway. Congressional testimony showed that J.P. Morgan and Kuhn, Loeb Co. between them controlled ninety-two per cent of all the railroad mileage in the United States. Both of them were fronts for the Rothschild operations. The funds advanced for that purpose by the Morgan-Belmont interests (Belmont was the Rothschilds' authorized representative in the United States), were used by Martin in 1893 to buy nine members of the Legislature for $1000 each; this gave him complete control of that body. His assistant in this bribery was William A. Glasgow, Jr., the chief counsel for the Norfolk and Western Railway. Martin's chief ally in controlling the state legislature was his able assistant, State Senator Hal Flood, grandfather of Harry Byrd. With such political prospects, Harry Byrd left school at the age of fifteen. In 1919, Martin died, and Byrd took over the machine. He ruled it with an iron hand for more than half a century. Politically, Byrd had access to all the funds he needed to control the state, that is, the political slush funds which Rothschild agents routinely dispensed throughout the United States to maintain their control of the nation. Byrd had actually been born in Martinsburg, West Virginia; a classmate there had been one Lewis Lichtenstein Strauss. Strauss later became an itinerant shoe salesman. With the advent of World War I, he suddenly showed up in Washington as "Secretary" of the U.S. Food Administration, being named assistant to Herbert Hoover, a longtime Rothschild agent who had been named by them as director of their family firm, Rio Tinto. After World War I, Strauss was named a partner in Kuhn, Loeb Co.; Byrd, with Strauss' money behind him, became Governor of Virginia. Strauss bought a large estate at Brandy Station, Virginia, scene of the last cavalry charge in the United States. He continued his long association with

Byrd during their years together in Washington. When Byrd retired, Strauss became his son's campaign manager.

After Martin's domination of the state of Virginia for some thirty years, Byrd was in place to take power, just as Stalin was waiting when Lenin mysteriously fell ill and died. For the next fifty years, Virginia suffered from what was not humorously called "the Byrd blight", while Byrd's lifelong financial sacrifices to serve his country in the Senate brought him a vast family empire of orchards, warehouses, banks, newspapers and stock portfolios. All of this had been gained since he entered the Virginia Senate in 1915. The Byrd millions historically were sweated from cheap labor, which shed some light on why he converted vast areas of Virginia into hopeless regions of poverty; at the same time, neighboring states such as North Carolina enjoyed unparalleled prosperity. The Byrd blight which resulted in the famous rural poverty area known as Appalachia ensured the Byrd empire an ample supply of cheap labor; he and his minions bitterly fought government efforts to intervene with their various programs. Byrd refused to allow Federal funds to be spent in Virginia unless he retained absolute control over their allotment; they were to go to his political supporters; none others need apply. Byrd realized that dispensation of Federal funds would bring a horde of federal supervisors into his domain, while he fought to remain in position to name every recipient of these funds, guaranteeing his future support from those who had received the "Byrd largesse".

Although he was always dependent upon contributions from the agents of the Rothschilds, Byrd's political machine remained unassailable because of the statewide network of Masonic Lodges, which had been in place for some two hundred years. They controlled every business and every state and local office in each of the Virginia counties and hamlets. No one could expect any advancement or preferment, or even a bank loan, without Masonic approval. Historian Allen Moger writes that "Byrd's power amazed observers"; "It was explained by friends as an association of like-minded men". Moger does not tell us what the like minds were committed to, or that they were "the determined men of Masonry". Moger's book, "Virginia: Bourbon to Byrd", the Univ. of Va., 1968, does not even mention Masonry in the index! Not only that, but Moger only mentions the Federal Reserve Act twice en passant, with no credit given to the fact that this bill was originated in the House by Carter Glass of Lynchburg, coauthored by senator Owen of Lynchburg, and signed into law by President Woodrow Wilson of Staunton. In fact, the Virginian, Woodrow Wilson, left an unsurpassed legacy to the nation; he gave us the income tax, World War I, and the Federal Reserve Act. No other President can claim to have saddled his unfortunate fellow countrymen with so many crushing burdens.

While Byrd kept the state of Virginia in poverty, the newspapers kept the state in igno rance. Having been totally taken over by the Masonic Order of Canaanites, they carefully refrained from printing anything that Byrd's Pravda, or Truth, would disapprove. No censorship was necessary; every editor and reporter in the state knew what was required of their unbiased journalism. The "federal" area, the northeast bedroom community bordering Washington, was dominated by the *Washington Post*, the family property of the Meyers. Eugene Meyer, partner of Lazard Freres international bankers, had purchased the paper cheaply, and gradually drove all of his competition out of business. The political activist, Lyndon LaRouche, also operated in the Washington area. He was allowed free rein until he published a story that the "black widow", Katherine Graham, daughter of Eugene Meyer, had killed her husband, Philip Graham, to prevent him from giving the *Post* to his current girlfriend. Shortly after LaRouche printed this story in his newspaper, 648 federal agents swarmed down on his headquarters at Leesburg, Virginia, seizing all of his documents and carting many of his assistants off to jail. If they were looking for Philip Graham's death certificate, they didn't find it; the concerned agencies had steadfastly refused to release it, or even to let anyone see it. If LaRouche had had any doubts about the power behind the *Washington Post*, he was soon enlightened; his entire operation seemed to have been shattered.

Byrd himself traditionally laid down the party line for the state in his chain of newspapers, which was run from Winchester. A survey by professors of journalism ranked the state of Virginia 49th in the nation in the record of its press' public service campaigns. Byrd's papers, like most of the other Virginia newspapers, were generally considered "the end of the road" by the profession because of their lower pay and working conditions. Most Virginia publishers, Masons to the man, conformed to the image which Byrd cultivated, and aspired only to be accepted into the local "squirearchy". At the same time, they continually printed editorials cynically denying that there had ever been a "Byrd machine" in the state of Virginia.

The eastern press of the state is totally dominated by the conglomerate, Media General, which had been put together from the Richmond newspapers and a Norfolk publication. The Richmond papers had strong scalawag and carpetbagger connections; after World War II they showed powerful CIA direction. Their chairman Joseph Bryan, had served in Naval Intell. during World War I, and chairman of the 5th Federal Reserve district. To prove his stellar liberal credentials, he was appointed to the board of overseers of Harvard University. His son married into the Standard Oil fortune, the Harkness Davidson family. He is also a director of the Hoover Institution, a supposedly right-wing think tank, and a member of the exclusive Bohemian Club of San Francisco. The senior vice president of Media General is James A. Linen IV. Formerly vice-president of the National Enquirer, which is widely reputed to be a CIA or Mafia publication or both, he is the son of James A. Linen III, the longtime publisher of *Time* magazine. James A. Linen IV is also chairman of the

American Thai Corporation, which operates in the marketing area of the drug empire known as "the Golden Triangle", which has been dominated by the CIA for years. The founder of OSS (later the CIA), William J. Donovan, was appointed ambassador to Thailand in 1953.

ELEGY FOR A STATE

As I pointed out in my most recent work, *The Curse of Canaan*,[3] "The tentacles of the Masonic Canaanite octopus are nowhere more deeply embedded than in the State of Virginia." This depressing fact was emphasized when the present Governor of Virginia, Gerald Baliles, organized the Virginia-Israel Commission to promote closer relations between the State of Virginia and the bandit State of Israel. Baliles threw the resources of Virginia's omnivorous tax collectors behind his pet project, one which may have been closer to his heart because of his own background. Although he has coyly refrained from revealing his origins, it is notable that he is the only state governor in *Who's Who* who has left blank the names of his father and mother. *Who's Who* biographies generally lead off with the full name of the father and the maiden name of the mother. It is possible, of course, that Baliles did not include them because he didn't know who they were. In that case, it would not be an omission.

Baliles was the political heir of ex-Governor Charles Robb, son-in-law of Lyndon Johnson, who has been courting the American Israel Political Action Committee for financial and political support for his currentrace for the Senate. Although this grovelling before the most dangerous elements in the nation is hardly unique among our craven politicos, it is more flagrant in Virginia because of the invasion of the leading Rothschild operators in the United States, who have come to Virginia seeking instant squiredom on their vast estates. Lewis Lichtenstein Strauss, partner of Herbert Hoover and of Kuhn, Loeb Co., the American representatives of the Rothschilds, bought an historic estate at Brandywine, Virginia

---

[3] Omnia Veritas Ltd, www.omnia-veritas.com

during the 1930's, from which he ran the notorious Byrd machine for many years, a totalitarian control of Virginia politics which had begun at the turn of the century, when the Rothschild railroad operator, William Glasglow, became the driving force in state politics. Strauss was followed by another Kuhn, Loeb partner, Freddie Warburg, who ignored local politics in favor of throwing great parties at his Middleburg Va. estate. The present Virginia mogul is Edgar Bronfman, another Rothschild stooge who heads Seagram liquor. Bronfman bought a vast estate near Charlottesville, a few miles from Thomas Jefferson's historic Monticello. Bronfman seems less interested in becoming a Virginia gentleman than in making Virginia even more Jewish. As president of the World Jewish Congress, he has been the principal financier of the worldwide hate campaign against the president of Austria, Kurt Waldheim, and the entire population of Austria (which is presently an American ally). Bronfman is also chairman of the notorious terrorist organization, the Anti Defamation League of B'nai B'rith (the Jewish Masonic organization), the American Jewish Congress, the United Jewish Appeal, the Federation of Jewish Philanthropies, B'nai B'rith, and the National Urban League. He is also a primary member of the notorious U.S./U.S.S.R. Trading and Economic Committee, which is desperately trying to salvage the faltering Soviet economy with U.S. taxpayers' dollars. In doing so, it has shrouded its operations in mystery, so that its machinations have become officially protected from public view by the U.S. government, which announces that USTEC, as it is often known, is now Top Secret.

Another prominent Virginia baron and political supporter of Baliles is a refugee from Chemnitz, Germany, the communications mogul, John Kluge. Listed by Forbes magazine as the second richest man in America, with a personal fortune of $2.5 billion, Kluge bought a 5,000 acre estate in the millionaires section of Albemarle County, which he named, properly enough, Albemarle Farms. After emigrating to the United States, Kluge became the partner of

Finkelstein, in Baltimore, in a food brokerage business. The firm of Kluge, Finkelstein is still the cornerstone of his fortune. After noticing the amount of money which Kluge, Finkelstein was spending on radio advertising, Kluge bought the station. This launched him on a career as a radio and television mogul. He now owns Metromedia, of which he is chairman. He is also a member of the advisory commission of the Rothschild bank, Manufacturers Hanover, in New York, a partner of Armand Hammer in Occidental Petroleum, a director of the Waldorf Astoria Hotel in New York, and head of the Shubert theatre empire. His executive vice president at Metromedia, Stuart Sobotnick, is a director of Orion Pictures. Director of Metromedia is Jane Pickens Hoving. A former radio star, Jane Pickens, married department store tycoon Walter Hoving, who was thirty years her senior. A Swedish immigrant, he had married into the Marshall Field department store fortune, later becoming chairman of Tiffany's and president of Bonwit Teller, the two most prestigious stores in Manhattan. Jane Hoving received awards from the Federation of Jewish Philanthropy for her zeal in raising money for Israel, and later she was given the Albert Einstein award.

Kluge has lately been much in the news, because his British-born wife, Patricia, decided to become an "instant lady" by installing a British type driven pheasant shoot on their lavish Virginia estate. In this type of shoot, the peasants drive the pheasants out into the guns of the waiting aristocrats, hoping that the sportsmen will be able to distinguish the pheasants from the peasants. Patricia imported a British baronet as her shoot master, or gamekeeper. She confided to a friend that "Baronets make wonderful house guests, but it's better to have them as employees. Then, if they take the silver, you can ask them to put it back."

The imported gamekeeper then inaugurated a reign of terror in the peaceful Virginia countryside, trying to protect the expensive game birds by shooting the neighbors' dogs, and killing the amazing number of four hundred hawks, an endangered and protected species. The keepers amused themselves by tormenting the wounded hawks with sharp sticks before burying them alive. After months of complaints, officials reluctantly brought charges against the keepers, emphasizing by a personal appearance of the U.S. Attorney for Virginia, John Alderman, that their investigation did not involve Mr. Kluge. It is expected that the criminals will pay a small fine, but Kluge now faces a torrent of lawsuits from neighbors whose dogs were trapped and killed. Such is life among the nested billionaires of Virginia.

As the political creature of these powerful Zionist financiers in Virginia, Governor Baliles discovered that the creation of the Virginia-Israel Commission was the ideal way to ensure his political future after he leaves the Governor's mansion in Richmond. On May 16, 1988, he addressed the powerful American Israel Political Action Committee in Washington, a move which the state's largest newspaper, *The Richmond Times Dispatch*, described as "ingratiating himself with the powerful Jewish lobby" Baliles is also the upcoming chairman of the National Governors' Association, where he intends to use his influence to promote an Israel Commission in each of the other states.

Because of his work with the Virginia-Israel Commission, Baliles was definitely promised a future run for the presidency by AIPAC. *The Richmond Times Dispatch* noted May 24, 1988 that "Gov. Gerald Baliles is readying for a role on the national political stage."

Baliles' Zionist backers rammed an initial grant of $200,000 for the Virginia-Israel Commission through the state legislature, a seemingly illegal use of state funds for personal political propaganda and aggrandizement. Baliles attempted to justify this use of state taxpayers funds by matching it with $200,000 provided by Bronfman and other Jewish propagandists in Virginia.

Governor Baliles made his most impressive move to ensure his political career in April of 1988, when he led a strange hegira of some 150 Virginians to Israel on a "goodwill mission". The trip was apparently inspired by the desire to convince the Palestinians, an oppressed captive people under Israeli military occupation, that the American people approved of Israeli brutality towards them, and that they could expect no help or sympathy from America. This was a powerful propaganda coup for the Israeli government.

The Baliles mission was demanded by the government of Israel because some five months of passive Palestine resistance had been met with the utmost brutality by heavily armed Israeli troops. Hundreds of Palestinian women and children had been murdered by the Israelis in their attempts to stifle all patriotic protest. Women hanging up their washing were shot down by Israelis in their own backyards; small children were beaten and their bodies hastily covered by bulldozers. Not since the horrors attributed to the Nazis had the world been stunned by the revelations of such brutality. In the case of the Nazis, only verbal testimony was available to back up stories of atrocities. In the case of Israel, American television viewers nightly saw armed soldiers beating unarmed children, purposely breaking their arms and wrists, crimes of which even the Nazis had never been accused. Incredibly, Governor Baliles travelled to Israel to offer the terrorist government the official endorsement of the people of Virginia in their terror campaign against unarmed civilian critics, the captive Palestinians.

As a theocratic state and dictatorship, Israel does not recognize the religious rights of any one but the Jewish people. Americans were outraged to see Israeli soldiers invading Arab mosques, dragging out the worshippers and beating them in the street. This activity is heavily subsidized by American taxpayers, who pay each Israeli soldier an amazing $12,000 a year to carry out these atrocities. Because the First Amendment to the Constitution prohibits Congress from enacting any law which abridges the establishment of religion, the Internal Revenue Service annually violates the Constitution of the United States when it collects from Americans money authorized by an Act of Congress to finance the theocratic state of Israel and its oppression of religious minorities in the Middle East. Although no American had previously protested against this violation of the Constitution, many citizens were now moved to write to Congress demanding to know why our tax money was financing these terrorist acts. However, any protest against the atrocities committed against Arab civilians is immediately met by a furious barrage of counter propaganda in the United States raising the specter of "anti-Semitism". Abie Foxman, the national director of the Anti-Defamation League (of which the aforementioned Edgar Bronfman is national chairman) ran a scare story in the *Washington Post*, June 4, 1988, warning against "growing anti-Semitic incidents in the United States." One would suppose this would be the recital of attacks against Jews; instead, Abie Foxman cited the distribution of pro-Palestinian literature in the United States -- specifically -- "Stop the Genocide in Palestine", as "an anti-Semitic incident". This was a strange distortion of ethnic reality, because the Palestinians, by all accounts, are themselves of Semitic origin. In strange contrast, the vast majority of the present Israelis, as I point out in *The Curse of Canaan*, are not even Semitic. They are a Turco-Edomite people from the steppes of central Russia, who are known historically as "Khazars".

The 150 chosen Virginians who accompanied Governor Gerald Baliles to Israel on his propaganda rescue mission were largely drawn from the membership of the Masonic lodges. They included newspaper publishers, businessmen, and a horde of ambitious politicians. They published newspaper accounts that "Israel's hospitality was unsurpassed, as we were wined and dined throughout our visit". They participated in the heavily publicized tree-plantings, a ritual for American politicians ever since 1948, and reported that they had not seen any evidence of brutality during their entire stay. Baliles abruptly dismissed any suggestion that there was a propaganda aspect to his trip. "I'm not interested in discussing political ramifications," he told reporters. He then signed an official pact with Israeli Economic Minister Gad Yaacobi. Just how a state governor is empowered to conclude formal agreements with other nations was not made clear.

On April 28, 1988, the *Richmond Times Dispatch* reported under the dateline "With the Saar Regiment in the Golan Heights, Israel - Gov. Gerald Baliles and more than 140 Virginians became ersatz soldiers yesterday ... they got a demonstration from a tank crew that launched shells and sprayed bullets." These are the same Israeli soldiers who daily commit atrocities against Arab civilians. On his return, Baliles brushed aside feeble protests from a few Arabs residing in Virginia. Their votes would never get him into the White House.

One of the conditions to which Governor Baliles agreed during his sojourn in Israel was a commitment to the Israeli government that he would fly the Israeli flag over the State Capitol each year on the anniversary of Israel's conquest of the Arabs and the establishment of the State of Israel. He also agreed to use his position as chairman of the National Governors Association to persuade the other governors to follow suit. One suspects that he will have little difficulty in persuading them of the political advantages of such treachery against their own state constituents.

As Attorney General of Virginia, Baliles had endeared himself to his co-racialists by ex pending hundreds of thousands of dollars of state funds and years of effort in persecuting a Virginia realtor whose offense was that he had included a small sign of the cross in his advertisements. Although this was not a violation of any known Virginia law, Baliles considered it a direct racial insult that the realtor would let his customers know that he was a Christian realtor. The case dragged on for years, until Baliles was elected Governor. He was quoted in the Richmond Times Dispatch, April 24, 1988, that "He sees a lot of similarities between people of Israel and Virginia." This is undoubtedly true, as the only Virginians with whom he comes into contact are his Zionist allies.

Baliles shrugged off a suggestion from disgruntled Arabs living in Virginia that he should now make a similar state visit to an Arab country, claiming that Arabs have no "freedom of speech". Freedom of speech, of course, is a relative term, as a study of the Virginia press shows no anti-Israel criticism or pro-Arab views. Arabs may be free to establish their own newspaper in Virginia, but one suspects they would find it difficult to fill it with advertisements from such Jewish department stores as Thalhimer's, the state's largest such enterprise. Hard on the five months "days of rage" protest by the captive Palestinians in the Israeli occupied territory, the *Richmond Times Dispatch* carried a lengthy defense of the Israeli atrocities by a Richmond rabbi, Dr. Myron Berman, of Temple Beth-El. In this two page article, Berman maintained the usual nonsense that "Because Israel, like the United States, is a democracy, it fosters many differences of opinion based upon a foundation of an indestructible bond of national loyalty."

This is an ingenious whitewash of the torture and murder of Palestinian children, who have failed to show "national loyalty". In fact, these child victims are loyal, but to their native homeland. As Sameeh Al-Quassem, the Palestinian poet, expresses the grief, rage, and determination of this captive people,

You may put out the light in my eyes.
You may deprive me of my mother's kisses.
You may curse my father, my people.
You may distort my history,
You may deprive my children of a smile
And of life's necessities.
You may fool my friends with a borrowed face.
You may build walls of hatred around me.

You may glue my eyes to humiliations,
O enemy of the sun, But
I shall not compromise
And to the last pulse in my veins I shall resist,
O enemy of the sun
The decorations are raised at the port.

We have forgotten that the Arabs, our traditional friends, are a nation of poets and warriors. History will decide whether this people will vanish beneath the yoke of international bandits and their Babylonian monetary system of debt capitalism. We believe that they will not. The greatest shame which Baliles has visited upon the noble history of the State of Virginia is his sullying of our proud history with the stain of the blood of the murdered Palestinian children. As the great scholar Chang Ch'Ao put it, "A little injustice in the heart can be drowned by wine; but a great injustice in the world can be drowned only by the sword."

The peple of Virginia, who have suffered under the enemy occupation of the Federal troops, the scalawags, and the carpetbaggers, have the greatest sympathy for the suffering of the Palestinian people. Baliles, who has no contact with the people of Virginia, having been put in office by his Zionist allies, has no conception of the depth of this feeling.

The Scandal Unveiled

The *Wall Street Journal* has led the expose of the current financial scandals which have supposedly rocked Wall Street. They have given us endless details about Dennis Levine and Ivan Boesky; they have even been forced to mention the name of Drexel Burnham Lambert, investment bankers extraordinary. What they have not done is to tell the American public just what is going on -- who is doing what to whom.

You will read here for the first time the names of the major players, names which the *Wall Street Journal* dares not mention. The first name is Rothschild. Not once has the *Wall Street Journal*, during its current "expose", dared to mention the vital information that Drexel Burnham Lambert (pronounced Lambeer), is the New York branch of Banque Bruxelles Lambert, of Brussels, Belgium or that the enormously wealthy and powerful Lamberts are the Belgian branch of the Rothschild family. Baron Lambert is regularly listed as an attendee at Bilderberger meetings.

The *Wall Street Journal* would have you believe that a greedy young stockbroker, Dennis Levine, a minor figure at Drexel Burnham Lambert, cut himself in on some upcoming deals at his firm and stashed $12 million in an offshore bank; that he was contacted by one Ivan Boesky, an "arbitrator" (read "rag and bone man" see The World Order by Eustace Mullins for further information), who offered Levine a contract whereby Boesky would pay Levine 5% of profits which Boesky made from stock trades involving inside information provided him by Levine. Said contract, of course was illegal; not only that, but it was a "breach of ethics", only the top officials of these firms being allowed to profit from such information. It was not for the clerks.

Let me tell you what was really going on. While Boesky and Levine were engaged in their penny ante operations, a gigantic financial plot, one might well say swindle, was being conducted to gain control of the major corporations for alien interests. The plot, quite simply, was to "buy" out or leverage these corporations by a consortium of international financiers who had unlimited capital at their command. The beauty of the plan was that, despite their unlimited capital, the conspirators would not put up any capital. Instead, they would create a new type of financial instrument, called a "junk bond", to pay for their seizure of these American corporations. The financial writers of the U.S. routinely refer to Drexel Burnham Lambert as the "creators of the junk bond". This is nonsense. The plan originated in Brussels, Belgium, at the offices of Banque Bruxelles Lambert. It is no accident that Brussels is the headquarters of NATO, which actually rules Europe in the name of the World Order, or that the head of NATO is Lord Carrington, a Rothschild relative, and partner of Henry Kissinger in the notorious international operation known as "Kiss Ass", an irreverent Wall Street title for the firm of Kissinger Associates, wheelers and dealers for the World Order. Nor is it an accident that in the current White House crisis, as Reagan stands convicted in the eyes of the world as an international conspirator caught with his hands in the till with his Israeli co-conspirators, who had to be hastily summoned to "take over" the situation? None other than Lt. Gen. Brent Scowcroft, a partner in Kissinger Associates! Scowcroft is also a trustee of the Rand Corp., Georgetown Center for Strategic and International Studies, Council on Foreign Relations, and the US Air Force University; Lord Carrington has very close ties with the British royal Family, and is a director of continued on page Rio Tinto, one of the three firms on which the Rothschild fortune is based.

Brussels is also the location of the World Computer Center, set up by Bank Rothschild to maintain computer records on every inhabitant of the world, who will thus be ruled from "World

Headquarters". To understand this power, we must go back two hundred years in history. While the American colonists were fighting to win their independence, the British Crown cast about for some top combat troops who could put down the "rebels". The King was offered some seasoned troops, Hessians, by a minor German potentate, the Elector of Hesse. When the Elector received payment for his mercenaries, he entrusted the proceeds to a financial adviser, one Mayer Amschel Bauer of Frankfurt, Germany, later known as Rothschild. Rothschild invested the funds very profitably; the Elector suddenly died, and a new dynasty was born. With their new-found wealth, the Rothschilds developed a new technique, not merely for controlling one nation, but for controlling all nations simultaneously. The technique was simple. They would create a bogeyman, an evil militarist intent on conquering the entire world; the altruistic Rothschilds would finance "allies" to oppose and crush the evil fanatic.

The first "monster" created by the new dynasty of international financiers was Napoleon. He was allowed to march across Europe, winning victory after victory against straw man opponents (the "fight game" has been manipulated by the Jacobs family in the U.S. for decades using the same technique). When the "dictator" had been built up to world class status, a phalanx of nations was financed and armed by the Rothschilds to rise up against him. Napoleon, who had been led to believe he had no serious opposition, was stunned to find at Waterloo that he had been betrayed by his own generals. In 1914, the Kaiser was the "monster" before whom civilization quailed; again benefactors were found to oppose him, the Morgans and Kuhn, Leob Co., acting as lieutenants for the Rothschilds, armed the "Allies" against the German militarists who tossed babies on their bayonets. In 1939, another "monster", Adolf Hitler, financed by the Bank of England, again menaced civilization. Once again, the only victor was the Rothschild family.

The Rothschild technique was a simple one; after setting up a central bank, the Rothschilds controlled a nation by controlling the issuance of money and credit. They then embarked on a ruinous program of armaments, financed by progressively higher and higher taxation, which reduced the citizens to the status of serfs. The munitions program, of course, was absolutely necessary because there would always be a "Rothschild-created monster" on the horizon.

After defeating Napoleon, the Rothschilds brought the victorious allies together at the Rothschild headquarters, Vienna, for the Congress of Vienna in 1515. What has this to do with our current scandal? Be patient. The mastermind of the present Drexel Burnham Lambert operation is a former partner of Banque Rothschild, Sir James Goldsmith. He is married to his third wife, the daughter of the Marquis of Londenderry, Viscount Castlereagh. At the Congress of Vienna in 1815, the negotiations were dominated by her ancestor, Viscount Castlereagh, the famed foreign minister of England. Castlereagh apparently did not understand at the time that his negotiations were designed to create a new ruler in Europe, the Rothschild family. Castlereagh was minister plenipotentiary of the victors at Waterloo, the British Crown. With him was his half-brother and heir, Lord Charles Stewart, British Ambassador to Vienna. At the Treaty of Paris, Castlereagh achieved his principal objective in France, to solidify the control of the Bourbons. Sir James Goldsmith's second wife had been Laure Boulay de la Meurthe, niece of the Comte de Paris, present head of the Bourbon family and pretender to the throne of France.

Viscount Castlereagh owed his spectacular rise to the fact that he was the godson of his uncle, Lord Camden (Charles Pratt), who served as attorney general of England and president of the Privy Council. Lord Camden frequently lent money to the Prime Minister, William Pitt, and became the power behind the Pitt ministry. The Pratt family has also been prominent behind the scenes in the United States. Pratt was John D. Rockefeller's partner in Standard Oil, and gave his New York mansion as the present headquarters of the Council on Foreign Relations.

His descendant, George Pratt Schultz, is now Secretary of State.

In 1822, Viscount Castlereagh realized how he had handed Europe over to the Rothschilds as a result of his actions at the Congress of Vienna. He became extremely depressed, realizing it was too late to rectify his acts. He had an audience with George IV, saying to him, "Sire, it is necessary to say good-bye to Europe." He then went to his home and committed suicide, cutting his catotid artery with a small penknife. There has been considerable speculation about his sudden depression and suicide, notably in "the Strange Death of Castlereagh" by H. Montgomery Hyde, a well-known British historian. Hyde suggests he may have been depressed by a false accusation of an act of homosexuality, or that he may have been given a drug which produced extreme depression.

Because Castlereagh delivered Europe into the hands of the Rothschilds through his diplomacy, Henry Kissinger openly modelled his own diplomatic career after Castlereagh (excepting, of course, the suicide). He reveals this resolve in his book, "A World Restored", Grusset & Dunlap 1964, which he dedicated to McGeorge Bundy of the Ford Foundation.

Kissinger's goal, which he followed as Secretary of State, was to perpetuate the Rothschild world hegemony enthroned at the Congress of Vienna, which had been described by von Gentz, secretary to Prince von Metternich, as follows: "The real purpose of the Congress was to divide among the conquerors the spoils taken from the vanquished." From the Congress of Vienna came the phrases "Austrian School of Politics", and the "Austrian School of Economics" presently epitomized by Milton Friedman, in which

Rothschild financial schemes are used to carry out Rothschild political goals.

Sir James Goldsmith's grandfather was financial adviser to Bismarck during the rise of the German Empire. Goldsmith first married Isabel Patino, heiress to the tin fortune of the Patino family, which had also been backed by the Rothschilds. Isabel Patino died mysteriously; Goldsmith then married the niece of the Bourbon heir, and third, the descendant of Viscount Castlereagh. Goldsmith is now bidding for Channel 5, the French TV station; he owns *L Express*, the biggest news-weekly in France; *Lire*, a major book periodical, and La Cite de France, the largest French book publisher. He also owns a weekly newspaper in Belgium. The *Wall Street Journal* reported that Goldsmith made $93 million profit in a recent $600 million takeover attempt at Goodyear.

The *Wall Street Journal* noted that Goldsmith was a major partner of Boesky in his operations, having invested $3 million of Drexel Burnham Lambert funds in the Boesky deal. Boesky's other major partners were Milton and Joseph Dresner, $10 million; Marty Peretz, publisher of the fanatically pro-Israeli publication, the *New Republic*, $1 million; and Lewis Lehrman, famed "conservative" backer of Ronald Reagan, the Lehrman Institute, and the Heritage Foundation, $1 million.

Boesky was characterized in the *Washington Post* of Nov. 21, 1986 as follows: "Boesky is known for his passion for the State of Israel and Jewish causes." He was appointed to the notorious Holocaust Commission by President Reagan, for whom he had been active as a fund-raiser. These connections stood him in good stead when Sorkin of the Securities Exchange Commission announced a supposedly heavily punitive assessment against Boesky, an unprecedented $100 million, of which $50 million was a fine and $50 million for "restitution" to investors. This seemed a drastic penalty, but the Wall Street Journal promptly pointed out that $25 million of this fine will be allowed as a tax deduction for Boesky. The SEC also outraged Wall Street investors by allowing Boesky to unload $440 million worth of stocks before announcing their punitive action against him. These stocks, principally holdings of Time, CSX and Goodyear which Boesky had been buying for future takeover action, immediately dropped 15% in value, which meant that Boesky picked up about $70 million in profits by unloading them, while other Wall Street investors lost heavily. Merrill Lynch alone lost $40 million because of Boesky's stock dumping. At the same time, Morgan Stanley's real estate division is selling Boesky's Beverly Hills Hotel (Boesky married the daughter of Ben Silberstein, who owned this hotel) for $140 million, of which Boesky will receive half, or $70 million. The SEC also is continuing to allow Boesky to trade stocks until April, 1988, which caused further anger among investors who have been damaged by his manipulations. Boesky also was rumored to have made video tapes of some of his associates while discussing these manipulations, but later stories said he had only made audio tapes of their dealings with him.

A source commented to the Wall Street Journal, Nov. 21, 1986, "First he sold his friends to the government, then he sold his stocks to his friends."

The American public is not likely to be informed that Boesky's profits, large though they may seem, are minuscule compared to the profits made in these takeovers by the major players, Sir James Goldsmith, and his partners, the Rothschilds. Our "investigative reporters" are not allowed to go beyond the straw men, nor have they ever heard of the Congress of Vienna, where these formulae were developed. The American people are misled into concerns about tax reform, while their manipulators prepare the sheep for the shearing, business as usual.

The Secret History of the Atomic Bomb - Why Hiroshima Was Destroyed

The untold story

The world was stunned to learn that India has now tested nuclear weapons. For many years, all nations have been concerned about the proliferation of atomic explosives. Even in their distress, no one seems to be interested in the historic or the psychological record of why these weapons were developed, and what special breed of mankind devoted themselves to this diabolical goal.

Despite the lack of public interest, the record is clear, and easily available to anyone who is interested. My interest in this subject, dormant for many years was suddenly rekindled during my annual lecture tour in Japan. My hosts had taken me to the city of Nagasaki for the first time. Without telling me their plans, they entered the Nagasaki Atomic Bomb Museum. I thought it would be an interesting experience, but, to my surprise, when I walked into the exhibition rooms, I was suddenly overcome by sadness. Realizing that I was about to burst into tears, I moved away from my companions, and stood biting my lip. Even so, it seemed impossible to control myself. I was surrounded by the most gruesome objects, the fingers of a human hand fused with glass, a photograph of the shadow of a man on a brick wall; the man had been vaporized in the explosion.

A NEW MISSION

When I returned to the United States, I knew1 had to unearth the sinister figures behind greatest of human catastrophes. It took many weeks of research to uncover what turned out to be the most far-reaching conspiracy of all time, the program of a few dedicated revolutionaries to seize control of the entire world, by inventing the powerful weapon ever unveiled.

The story begins in Germany. In the 1930s, Germany and Japan had a number of scientists icing on the development of nuclear fission. In both of these countries, their leaders sternly forbade them to continue their research. Adolf Hitler said he would never allow anyone in Germany to work to work on such an inhumane weapon.

The Emperor of Japan let his scientists know that he would never approve such a weapon. At that time the United States had no one working on nuclear fission. The disgruntled German scientists contacted friends in the United States, and were told that there was a possibility of government support for their work here. As Don Beyer tells these immigrants to the United States pushed their program.

"Leo Szilard, together with his long time friends and fellow Hungarian physicists, Eugene Wigner and Edward Teller, agreed that the President must be warned; fission bomb tehnology was not so farfetched. The Jewish emigres, now living in America, had personal experience of fascism in Europe. In 1939, the three physicists enlisted the support of Albert Einstein, letter dated August 2 signed by Einstein was delivered by Alexander Sachs to Franklin D. Roosevelt at the White House on October 11, 39."

CRIMINALS ON DISPLAY

At the Nagasaki Atomic Bomb Museum, photographs of two men are prominently displayed; Albert Einstein, and J. Robert Oppenheimer, who developed the atomic bomb at Los Alamos laboratories, New Mexico. Also on display is a statement from General Eisenhower, who was then supreme Military Commander, which is found in number of books about Eisenhower, and which can be found on p.426, Eisenhower by Stephen E. Ambrose, Simon & Shuster, NY, 1983.

"Secretary of War Henry L. Stimson first told Eisenhower of the bomb's existence. Eisenhower was engulfed by "a feeling of depression'. When Stimson said the United States proposed to use the bomb against Japan, Eisenhower voiced 'my grave misgivings, first on the basis of my belief that Japan was already defeated and that dropping the bomb was completely unnecessary, and secondly because I thought that our country should avoid shocking world opinion by the use (of atomic weapons).' Stimson was upset by Eisenhower's attitude 'almost angrily refuting the reasons I gave for my quick conclusion'. Three days later, Eisenhower flew to Berlin, where he met with Truman and his principal advisors. Again Eisenhower recommended against using the bomb, and again was ignored.

Other books on Eisenhower state that he endangered his career by his protests against the bomb, which the conspirators in the highest level of the United States government had already sworn to use against Japan, regardless of any military developments. Eisenhower could not have known that Stimson was a prominent member of Skull and Bones at Yale, the Brotherhood of Death, founded by the Russell Trust in 1848 as a bunch of the German Illuminati, or that they had played prominent roles in organizing wars and revolutions since that time. Nor could he have known that President Truman had only had one job in his career, as a Masonic organizer for the State of Missouri, and that the lodges he built up later sent him to the United States Senate and then to the presidency.

ATOMIC TERRORISM

The man who set all this in motion was Albert Einstein, who left Europe and came to the United States in October 1933. His wife said that he "regarded human beings with detestation". He had previously corresponded with Sigmund Freud about his projects of "peace" and "disarmament", although Freud later said he did not believe that Einstein ever accepted any of his theories. Einstein had a personal interest in Freud's work because his son Eduard spent his life in mental institutions, undergoing both insulin therapy and electroshock treatment, none of which produced any change in his condition.

When Einstien arrived in the United States, he was feted as a famous scientist, and was invited to the White House by President and Mrs. Roosevelt. He was soon deeply involved with Eleanor Roosevelt in her many leftwing causes, in which Einstein heartily concurred. Some of Einstein's biographers hail the modern era as "the Einstein Revolution" and "the Age of Einstein", possibly because he set in motion the program of nuclear fission in the United States. His letter to Roosevelt requesting that the government inaugurate an atomic bomb program was obviously stirred by his lifelong commitment to "peace and disarmament". His actual commitment was to Zionism; Ronald W. Clark mentions in Einstein; His Life And Times, Avon, 1971, p.377, "He would campaign with the Zionists for a Jewish homeland in Palestine." On p.460, Clark quotes Einstein, "As a Jew I am from today a supporter of the Jewish Zionist efforts." (1919) Einstein's letter to Roosevelt, dated august 2, 1939, was delivered personally to President Roosevelt by Alexander Sachs on October 11. Why did Einstein enlist an intermediary to bring this letter to Roosevelt, with whom he was on friendly terms? The atomic bomb program could not be launched without the necessary Wall Street sponsorship.

Sachs, a Russian Jew, listed his profession as "economist" but was actually a bagman for the Rothschilds, who regularly delivered large sums of cash to Roosevelt in the White House.

Sachs was an advisor to Eugene Meyer of the Lazard Freres International Banking House, and also with Lehman Brothers, another well known banker. Sachs' delivery of the Einstein letter to the White House let Roosevelt know that the Rothschilds approved of the project and wished him to go full speed ahead.

A UNITED NATIONS PROJECT

In May of 1945, the architects of postwar strategy, or, as they liked to call themselves, the "Masters of the Universe", gathered in San Francisco at the plush Palace Hotel to write the Charter for the United Nations. Several of the principals retired for a private meeting in the exclusive Garden Room. The head of the United States delegation had called this secret meeting with his top aide, Alger Hiss, representing the president of the United States and the Soviet KGB; John Foster Dulles, of the Wall Street law firm of Sullivan and Cromwell, whose mentor, William Nelson Cromwell, had been called a "professional revolutionary" on the floor of Congress; and W. Averill Harriman, plenipotentiary extraordinary, who had spent the last two years in Moscow directing Stalin's war for survival. These four men represented the awesome power of the American Republic in world affairs, yet of the four, only Secretary of State Edward Stettinius Jr., had a position authorized by the Constitution. Stettinius called the meeting to order to discuss an urgent matter; the Japanese were already privately suing for peace, which presented a grave crisis. The atomic bomb would not be ready for several more months. "We have already lost Germany," Stettinius said. "If Japan bows out, we will not have a live population on which to test the bomb."

"But, Mr. Secretary," said Alger Hiss, "no one can ignore the terrible power of this weapon." "Nevertheless," said Stettinius, "our entire postwar program depends on terrifying the world with the atomic bomb." "To accomplish that goal," said John Foster Dulles, "you will need a very good tally. I should say a million." "Yes," replied Stettinius, "we are hoping for a million tally in Japan. But if they surrender, we won't have anything." "Then you have to keep them in the war until the bomb is ready," said John Foster Dulles. "That is no problem. Unconditional surrender." "They won't agree to that," said Stettinius. "They are sworn to protect the Emperor." "Exactly," said John Foster Dulles. **"Keep Japan in the war another three months, and we can use the bomb on their cities; we will end this war with the naked fear of all the peoples of the world, who will then bow to our will."**

Edward Stettinius Jr. was the son of a J.P. Morgan partner who had been the world's largest munitions dealer in the First World War. He had been named by J.P. Morgan to oversee all purchases of munitions by both France and England in the United States throughout the war. John Foster Dulles was also an accomplished warmonger. In 1933, he and his brother Allen had rushed to Cologne to meet with Adolf Hitler and guaranteed him the funds to maintain the Nazi regime. The Dulles brothers were representing their clients, Kuhn Loeb Co., and the Rothschilds. Alger Hiss was the golden prince of the communist elite in the united States.

When he was chosen as head of the prestigious Carnegie Endowment for International Peace after World War II, his nomination was seconded by John Foster Dulles. Hiss was later sent to prison for perjury for lying about his exploits as a Soviet espionage agent.

This secret meeting in the Garden Room was actually the first military strategy session of the United Nations, because it was dedicated to its mission of exploding the world's first atomic weapon on a living population. It also forecast the entire strategy of the Cold War, which lasted forty-three years, cost American taxpayers five trillion dollars, and accomplished exactly nothing, as it was intended to do. Thus we see that the New World Order has based its entire strategy on the agony of the hundreds of thousands of civilians burned alive at Hiroshima and Nagasaki, including many thousands of children sitting in their schoolrooms. These leaders had learned from their master, Josef Stalin, that no one can rule without mass terrorism, which in turn required mass murder. As Senator Vandenberg, leader of the Republican loyal opposition, was to say (as quoted in American Heritage magazine, August 1977), "We have got to scare the hell out of "em."

THE JEWISH HELL-BOMB

The atomic bomb was developed at the Los Alamos Laboratories in New Mexico. The top secret project was called the Manhattan Project, because its secret director, Bernard Baruch, lived in Manhattan, as did many of the other principals. Baruch had chosen Maj. Gen. Leslie R. Groves to head the operation. He had previously built the Pentagon, and had a good reputation among the Washington politicians, who usually came when Baruch beckoned.

The scientific director at Los Alamos was J. Robert Oppenheimer, scion of a prosperous family of clothing merchants. In Oppenheimer; the Years Of Risk, by James Kunetka, Prentice Hall, NY, 1982, Kunetka writes, p. 106, "Baruch was especially interested in Oppenheimer for the position of senior scientific adviser." The project cost an estimated two billion dollars. No other nation in the world could have afforded to develop such a bomb. The first successful test of the atomic bomb occurred at the Trinity site, two hundred miles south of Los Alamos at 5:29:45 a.m. on July 16, 1945. Oppenheimer was beside himself at the spectacle. He shrieked, "I am become Death, the Destroyer of worlds." Indeed, this seemed to be the ultimate goal of the Manhattan Project, to destroy the world. There had been considerable fear among the scientists that the test explosion might indeed set off a chain reaction, which would destroy the entire world. Oppenheimer's exultation came from his realization that now his people had attained the ultimate power, through which they could implement their five-thousand-year desire to rule the entire world.

THE BUCK PASSES TO TRUMAN

Although Truman liked to take full credit for the decision to drop the atomic bomb on Japan, in fact, he was advised by a prestigious group, The National Defense Research Committee, consisting of George L. Harrison, president of the Federal Reserve Bank of New York; Dr. James B. Conant, president of Harvard, who had spent the First World War developing more effective poison gases, and who in 1942 had been commissioned by Winston Churchill to develop an Anthrax bomb to be used on Germany, which would have killed every living thing in Germany. Conant was unable to perfect the bomb before Germany surrendered, otherwise he would have had another line to add to his resume. His service on Truman's Committee which advised him to drop the atomic bomb on Japan, added to his previous record as a chemical warfare professional, allowed me to describe him in papers filed before the United States Court of Claims in 1957, as "the most notorious war criminal of the Second World War". As Gauleiter of Germany after the war, he had ordered the burning of my book, *The Federal Reserve Conspiracy*, ten thousand copies having been published in Oberammergau, the site of the world-famed Passion Play.

Also on the committee were Dr. Karl Compton, and James F. Byrnes, acting Secretary of State. For thirty years, Byrnes had been known as Bernard Baruch's man in Washington. With his Wall Street profits, Baruch had built the most lavish estate in South Carolina, which he named Hobcaw Barony. As the wealthiest man in South Carolina, this epitome of the carpet-bagger also controlled the political purse strings. Now Baruch was in a position to dictate to Truman, through his man Byrnes, that he should drop the atomic bomb on Japan.

LIPMAN SIEW

Despite the fact that the Manhattan Project was the most closely guarded secret of World War II, one man, and one many only, was allowed to observe everything and to know everything about the project. He was Lipman Siew, a Lithuanian Jew who had come to the United States as a political refugee at the age of seventeen. He lived in Boston on Lawrence St., and decided to take the name of William L. Laurence. At Harvard, he became a close friend of James B. Conant and was tutored by him. When Laurence went to New York, he was hired by Herbert Bayard Swope, editor of the *New York World*, who was known as Bernard Baruch's personal publicity agent. Baruch owned the World. In 1930, Laurence accepted an offer from the *New York Times* to become its science editor. He states in Who's Who that he "was selected by the heads of the atomic bomb project as sole writer and public relations." How one could be a public relations writer for a top secret project was not explained. Laurence was the only civilian present at the historic explosion of the test bomb on July 16, 1945. Less than a month later, he sat in the copilots seat of the B-29 on the fateful Nagasaki bombing run.

WILL JAPAN SURRENDER BEFORE THE BOMB IS DROPPED?

There were still many anxious moments for the conspirators, who planned to launch a new reign of terror throughout the world. Japan had been suing for peace. Each day it seemed less likely that she could stay in the war. On March 9 and 10, 1945, 325 B-29s had burned thirty-five square miles of Tokyo, leaving more than one hundred thousand Japanese dead in the ensuing firestorm. Of Japan's 66 biggest cities, 59 had been mostly destroyed. 178 square miles of urban dwellings had been burned, 500,000 died in the fires, and now twenty million Japanese were homeless. Only four cities had not been destroyed; Hiroshima, Kokura, Niigata, and Nagasaki. Their inhabitants had no inkling that they had been saved as target cities for the experimental atomic bomb. Maj. Gen. Leslie Groves, at Bernard Baruch's insistence, had demanded that Kyoto be the initial target of the bomb. Secretary of War Stimson objected, saying that as the ancient capital of Japan, the city of Kyoto had hundreds of historic wooden temples, and no military targets. The Jews wanted to destroy it precisely because of its great cultural importance to the Japanese people.

THE HORROR OF HIROSHIMA

While the residents of Hiroshima continued to watch the B-29s fly overhead without dropping bombs on them, they had no inkling of the terrible fate which the scientists had reserved for them. William Manchester quotes General Douglas MacArtbur in American Caesar, Little Brown, 1978, p.437 [quoting:] There was another Japan, and MacArthur was one of the few Americans who suspected its existence. He kept urging the Pentagon and the State Department to be alert for conciliatory gestures. The General predicted that the break would come from Tokyo, not the Japanese army. The General was right. A dovish coalition was forming in the Japanese capital, and it was headed by Hirohito himself, who had concluded in the spring of 1945 that a negotiated peace was the only way to end his nation's agony. Beginning in early May, a six-man council of Japanese diplomats explored ways to accommodate the Allies. The delegates informed top military officials that "our resistance is finished". [End quoting]

On p.359, Gar Alperowitz quotes Brig. Gen. Carter W. Clarke, in charge of preparing the MAGIC summary in 1945, who stated in a 1959 historical interview, "We brought them down to an abject surrender through the accelerated sinking of their merchant marine and hunger alone, and when we didn't need to do it, and knew we didn't need to do it, we used them as an experiment for two atomic bombs."

Although President Truman referred to himself as the sole authority in the decision to drop the bomb, in fact he was totally influenced by Bernard Baruch's man in Washington, James F. Byrnes. Gar Alperowitz states, p. 196, "Byrnes spoke with the authority of—personally represented—the president of the United States on all bomb-related matters in the Interim Committee's deliberations." David McCullough, in his laudatory biography of Truman, which was described as "a valentine", admitted that "Truman didn't know his own Secretary of State, Stettinius. He had no background in foreign policy, no expert advisors of his own."

The tragedy of Hiroshima and Nagasaki was that a weak, inexperienced president, completely under the influence of Byrnes and Baruch, allowed himself to be manipulated into perpetrating a terrible massacre. In the introduction to Hiroshima's Shadows, we find that "Truman was moving in quite the opposite direction, largely under the influence of Byrnes. The atom bomb for Byrnes was an instrument of diplomacy-atomic diplomacy." (p.ix)

Mass Murder

On August 6, 1945, a uranium bomb 3-235, 20 kilotons yield, was exploded 1850 feet in the air above Hiroshima, for maximum explosive effect. It devastated four square miles, and killed 140,000 of the 255,000 inhabitants. In Hiroshima's Shadows, we find a statement by a doctor who treated some of the victims; p.415, Dr. Shuntaro Hida: "It was strange to us that Hiroshima had never been bombed, despite the fact that B-29 bombers flew over the city every day. Only after the war did I come to know that Hiroshima, according to American archives, had been kept untouched in order to preserve it as a target for the use of nuclear weapons. Perhaps, if the American administration and its military authorities had paid sufficient regard to the terrible nature of the fiery demon which mankind had discovered and yet knew so little about its consequences, the American authorities might never have used such a weapon against the 750,000 Japanese who ultimately became its victims."

Dr. Hida says that while treating the terribly mangled and burned victims, "My eyes were ready to overflow with tears. I spoke to myself and bit my lip so that I would not cry. If I had cried, I would have lost my courage to keep standing and working, treating dying victims of Hiroshima."

On p.433, *Hiroshima's Shadows*, Kensaburo Oe declares, "From the instant the atomic bomb exploded, it became the symbol of all human evil; it was a savagely primitive demon and most modern curse.... My nightmare stems from a suspicion that a 'certain trust in human strength' or 'humanism' flashed across the minds of American intellectuals who decided upon the project that concluded with the dropping of the bomb on Hiroshima."

In the introduction to *Hiroshima's Shadows*, we find that "One of the myths of Hiroshima is that the inhabitants were warned by leaflets that an atomic bomb would be dropped. The leaflets Leonard Nadler and William P. Jones recall seeing in the Hiroshima Museum in 1960 and 1970 were dropped after the bombing. This happened because the President's Interim Committee on the Atomic Bomb decided on May 31 'that we could not give the Japanese any warning'. Furthermore, the decision to drop 'atomic' leaflets on Japanese cities was not made until August 7, the day after the Hiroshima bombing. They were not dropped until August 10, after Nagasaki had been bombed. We can say that the residents of Hiroshima received no advance warning about the use of the atomic bomb. On June 1, 1945, a formal and official decision was taken during a meeting of the so-called Interim Committee not to warn the populations of the specific target cities. James Byrnes and

Oppenheimer insisted that the bombs must be used without prior warning."

"Closely linked to the question of whether a warning of an atomic bomb attack was given to the civilian populations of the target cities is the third 'article of fifth' that underpins the American legend of Hiroshima; the belief that Hiroshima and Nagasaki were military targets. The Headquarters of the Japanese Second army were located in Hiroshima and approximately 20,000 men—of which about half, or 10,000 died in the attack. In Nagasaki, there were about 150 deaths among military personnel in the city. Thus, between the two cities, 4.4% of the total death toll was made up of military personnel. In short, more than 95% of the casualties were civilians."

On p.39 of *Hiroshima's Shadows* we find that (at Hiroshima) "strictly military damage was insignificant." How are we to reconcile this statement with Harry Truman's vainglorious boast in Off The Record; the Private Papers of Harry S. Truman Harper, 1980, p.304, "In 1945 I had ordered the Atomic Bomb dropped on Japan at two places devoted almost exclusively to war production." In fact, many thousands of the Hiroshima casualties were children sitting in their classrooms.

The bomb was dropped because (p.35) "The Manhattan Project's managers were lobbying to use the atomic bomb. Byrnes sat in on these meetings. Maj. Gen. Groves seems to have been the author of the claim that the use of the bomb would save a million American lives—a figure in the realm of fantasy."

Truman himself variously stated that the use of the use of the atomic bomb saved "a quarter of a million American lives", a "half-million American lives", and finally settled on the Gen. Groves figure of "a million American lives saved."

Meanwhile (p.64) William L. Laurence, who was writing for the New York Times at full salary while also receiving a full salary from the War Department as the "public relations agent for the atomic bomb" published several stories in the New York Times denying that there had been any radiation effects on the victims of the Hiroshima bombing (Sept. 5, 1945 et seq.) in which he quotes General Groves' indignant comment, "The Japanese are still continuing their propaganda aimed at creating the impression we won the war unfairly and thus attempting to create sympathy for themselves."(p.66) "The Legation of Switzerland on August 11, 1945 forwarded from Tokyo the following memorandum to the State Department (which sat on it for twenty-five years before finally releasing it): 'The Legation of Switzerland has received a communication from the Japanese Government.' On August 6, 1945, American airplanes released on the residential district of the town of Hiroshima, bombs of a new type, killing and injuring in one second a large number of civilians and destroying a great part of the town. Not only is the city of Hiroshima a provincial town without any protection or special military installations of any kind, but also none of the neighboring regions or towns constitutes a military objective."

The introduction to *Hiroshima's Shadows* concludes that (p.lxvii) "The claim that an invasion of the Japanese home islands was necessary without the use of the atomic bombs is untrue. The claim that an 'atomic warning' was given to the populace of Hiroshima is untrue. And the claim that both cities were key military targets is untrue."

A PILOT'S STORY

Corroboration of these statements is found in the remarkable record of Ellsworth Torrey Carrington, "Reflections of a Hiroshima Pilot", (p.9) "As part of the Hiroshima atomic battle plan my B-29 (named Jabbitt III, Captain John Abbott Wilson's third war plane) flew the weather observation mission over the secondary target of Kokura on August 6, 1945." (p. 10) "After the first bomb was dropped, the atom bomb command was very fearful that Japan might surrender before we could drop the second bomb, so our people worked around the clock, 24-hours-a-day to avoid such a misfortune." This is, of course, satire on Carrington's part. (p. 13) "in city after city all over the face of Japan (except for our cities spared because reserved for atomic holocaust) they ignited the most terrible firestorms in history with very light losses (of B-29s). Sometimes the heat from these firestorms was so intense that later waves of B-29s were caught by updrafts strong enough to loft them upwards from 4 or 5,000 feet all the way up to 8 or 10,000 feet. The major told us that the fire-bombing of Japan had proven successful far beyond anything they had imagined possible and that the 20th Air Force was running out of cities to burn. Already there were no longer (as of the first week in June 1945) any target cities left that were worth the attention of more than 50 B-29s, and on a big day, we could send up as many as 450 planes!" "The totality of the devastation in Japan was extraordinary, and this was matched by the near-totality of Japan's defencelessness." (as of June 1, 1945, before the atomic bombs were dropped.) (p. 14) "The Truman government censored and controlled all the war information that was allowed to reach the public, and of course, Truman had a vested interest in obscuring the truth so as to surreptitiously prolong the war and be politically able to use the atom bomb. Regarding the second element of the Roosevelt-Truman atomic Cold War strategy of deceiving the public into believing that Japan was still militarily viable in the spring and summer of 1945, the centerpiece was the terribly expensive and criminally unnecessary campaign against Okinawa.

Carrington quotes Admiral William D. Leahy, p. 245, *I Was There*, McGraw Hill: "A large part of the Japanese Navy was already on the bottom of the sea. The combined Navy surface and air force action even by this time had forced Japan into a position that made her early surrender inevitable. None of us then knew the potentialities of the atomic bomb, but it was my opinion, and I urged it strongly on the Joint Chiefs, that no major land invasion of the Japanese mainland was necessary to win the war. The JCS did order the preparation of plans for an invasion, but the invasion itself was never authorized."

Thus Truman, urged on by General Groves, claims that "a million American lives were saved" by the use of the atomic bomb, when no invasion had ever been authorized, and was not in the cards. Carrington continues, p. 16, "The monstrous truth is that the timing of the Okinawa campaign was exclusively related to the early August timetable of the atomic bomb. J'accuse! I accuse Presidents Franklin Roosevelt and Harry Truman of deliberately committing war crimes against the American people for the sole purpose of helping set the stage for the criminally unnecessary use of atomic weapons on Japan."

Carrington further quotes Admiral Leahy, from *I Was There*, "It is my opinion that the use of this barbarous weapon at Hiroshima and Nagaski was of no material assistance in our war against Japan. The Japanese were already defeated and ready to surrender because of the effective sea blockade and the successful bombing with conventional weapons."

Carrington concludes, p.22, "Truman's wanton use of atomic weapons left the American people feeling dramatically less secure after winning World War II than they had ever felt before, and these feelings of insecurity have been exploited by unscrupulous Cold War Machine Politicians ever since." As Senator Vandenberg said, "We have to scare the hell out of 'em" in order to browbeat the American people into paying heavy taxes to support the Cold War.

DID THE ATOMIC BOMB WIN THE WAR AGAINST JAPAN?

Admiral William Leahy also stated in *I Was There*, "My own feeling is that being the first to use it (the atomic bomb) we had adopted an ethical standard common to the Barbarism of the Dark Ages. I was not taught to make war in that fashion, and wars cannot be won by destroying women and children."

Gar Alperowitz notes, p. 16, "On May 5, May 12 and June 7, the Office of Strategic Services (our intelligence operation), reported Japan was considering capitulation. Further messages came on May 18, July 7, July 13 and July 16."

Alperowitz points out, p.36, "The standing United States demand for 'unconditional surrender' directly threatened not only the person of the Emperor but such central tenets of Japanese culture as well."

Alperowitz also quotes General Curtis LeMay, chief of the Air Forces, p.334, "The war would have been over in two weeks without the Russians entering and without the atomic bomb. PRESS INQUIRY: You mean that, sir? Without the Russians and without the atomic bomb? LeMay: The atomic bomb had nothing to do with the end of the war at all." September 29, 1945, statement.

THE NAGASAKI BOMB

When the Air Force dropped the atomic bomb on Nagasaki, with William Laurence riding in the co-pilot's seat of the B-29, pretending to be Dr. Strangelove, here again the principal target was a Catholic church. P.93, *The Fall Of Japan*, by William Craig, Dial, NY, 1967, "the roof and masonry of the Catholic cathedral fell on the kneeling worshippers. All of them died." This church has now been rebuilt, and is a prominent feature of the Nagasaki tour.

After the terror bombings of Hiroshima and Nagasaki, the victorious Allies moved promptly to try Japanese officials for their "war crimes". From 1945-51 several thousand Japanese military men were found guilty of war crimes by an International Military Tribunal which met in Tokyo from 1946 to 1948. Twenty-eight Japanese military and civilian leaders were accused of having engaged in conspiracy to commit atrocities. The dissenting member of the Tokyo tribunal, Judge Radhabinod of India, dismissed the charge that Japanese leaders had conspired to commit atrocities, stating that a stronger case might be made against the victors, because the decision to use the atomic bomb resulted in indiscriminate murder.

A very popular movie in Japan today is *Pride, The Fateful Moment*, which shows Prime Minister General Hideki Tojo in a favorable light. With six others, he was hanged in 1968 as a war criminal. During his trial, his lawyers stated to the International Tribunal for the Far East, the Asian version of Nuremberg Trials, that Tojo's war crimes could not begin to approach the dropping of the atomic bombs on Hiroshima and Nagasaki. The prosecutors immediately objected, and censored their statements. That was the last time there was any official recognition of the atomic bomb massacres in Japan. Japanese officials have been effectively prevented from taking any stand on this matter because the American military occupation, which officially ended in 1952 with the Treaty with Japan, was quietly continued. Today, 49,000 American troops are still stationed in Japan, and there is no public discussion of the crimes of Hiroshima and Nagasaki.

AMERICAN MILITARY AUTHORITIES SAY ATOMIC BOMB UNNECESSARY

The most authoritative Air Force unit during World War II was the U.S. Strategic Bombing Survey, which selected targets on the basis of need, and which analyzed the results for future missions. In *Hiroshima's Shadow*, the U.S. Strategic Bombing Survey report of July 1, 1946 states, "The Hiroshima and Nagasaki atomic bombs did not defeat Japan, nor by the testimony of the enemy leaders who ended the war did they persuade Japan to accept unconditional surrender. The Emperor, the lord privy seal, the prime minister, the foreign minister, and the navy minister had decided as early as May 1945 that the war should be ended even if it meant acceptance of defeat on allied terms.... It is the Survey's opinion that certainly prior to December 1, 1945 and in all probability prior to November 1, 1945, Japan would have surrendered even if the atomic bombs had not been dropped and even if no invasion had been planned or contemplated."

Both military, political and religious leaders spoke out against the atomic bombing of Japanese civilians. The Federal Council of the Churches of Christ in America issued a formal statement in March 1946 (cited by Gar Alperowitz):

"The surprise bombings of Hiroshima and Nagasaki are morally indefensible. Both bombings must be judged to have been unnecessary for winning the war. As the power that first used the atomic bomb under these circumstances, we have sinned grievously against the laws of God and against the people of Japan."— Commission on the Relation of the Church to the War in the Light of the Christian Faith.

On p.438, Gar Alperowitz quotes James M. Gillis, editor of Catholic World, "I would call it a crime were it not that the word 'crime' implies sin, and sin requires a consciousness of guilt. The action taken by the Untied States government was in defiance of every sentiment and every conviction upon which our civilization is based."

One of the most vociferous critics of the atomic bombings was David Lawrence, founder and editor of U.S. News and World Report. He signed a number of stinging editorials, the first on August 17, 1945.

"Military necessity will be our constant cry in answer to criticism, but it will never erase from our minds the simple truth, that we, of all civilized nations, though hesitating to use poison gas, did not hesitate to employ the most destructive weapon of all times indiscriminately against men, women and children." On October 5, Lawrence continued his attack, "The United States should be the first to condemn the atomic bomb and apologize for its use against Japan. Spokesmen for the Army Air Forces said it wasn't necessary and that the war had been won already. Competent testimony exists to prove that Japan was seeking to surrender many weeks before the atomic bomb came." On November 23, Lawrence wrote, "The truth is we are guilty. Our conscience as a nation must trouble us. We must confess our sin. We have used a horrible weapon to asphyxiate and cremate more than 100,000 men, women and children in a sort of super-lethal gas chamber— and all this in a war already won or which spokesman for our Air Forces tell us we could have readily won without the atomic bomb. We ought, therefore, to apologize in unequivocal terms at once to the whole world for our misuse of the atomic bomb."

David Lawrence was an avowed conservative, a successful businessman, who knew eleven presidents of the United States intimately, and was awarded the Medal of Freedom by President Richard M. Nixon, April 22, 1970.

ANOTHER EISENHOWER SPEAKS

Although Eisenhower never changed his opinion of the use of the atomic bomb, during his presidency he repeatedly voiced his opinion, as quoted by Steve Neal, *The Eisenhowers* Doubleday,

1978. P.225, "Ike would never lose his scepticism of the weapon and later referred to it as a 'hellish contrivance'."

His brother, Milton Eisenhower, a prominent educator, was even more vocal on this subject. As quoted by Gar Alperwitz, p.358, Milton Eisenhower said, "Our employment of this new force at Hiroshima and Nagasaki was a supreme provocation to other nations, especially the Soviet Union. Moreover, its use violated the normal standards of warfare by wiping out entire populations, mostly civilians, in the target cities. Certainly what happened at Hiroshima and Nagasaki will forever be on the conscience of the American people."

During his Presidency, Dwight Eisenhower tried to find peaceful uses for atomic energy. In *The Eisenhower Diaries*, p.261, we find that "The phrase 'atoms for peace' entered the lexicon of international affairs with a speech by Eisenhower before the United Nations December 8, 1953." Control of atomic energy had now given the New World Order clique enormous power, and Eisenhower, in his farewell speech to the American people on leaving the Presidency In Review (Doubleday, 1969), on January 17, 1961, warned, "In the councils of government we must guard against the acquisition of unwarranted influence, whether sought or unsought, by the miliary-industrial complex. The potential for the disastrous rise of misplaced power exists and will persist."

By failing to name the power behind the military-industrial complex, the international bankers, Eisenhower left the American people in the dark as to he was actually warning them against. To this day they do not understand what he was trying to say, that the international bankers, the Zionists and the Freemasons had formed an unholy alliance whose money and power could not be overcome by righteous citizens of the United States.

MACARTHUR'S WARNING

General Douglas MacArthur also tried to warn the American people of this threat, as quoted in *American Ceaser*, by William Manchester, Little Brown, 1978, p.692, "In 1957, he lashed out at large Pentagon budgets. 'Our government has kept us in a perpetual state of fear—kept us in a continuous stampede of patriotic fervor—with the cry of grave national emergency. Always there has been some terrible evil to gobble us up if we did not blindly rally behind it by furnishing the exorbitant funds demanded. Yet, in retrospect, these disasters seem never to have happened, seem never to have been quite real."

This was the restatement of Senator Vandenberg's famous comment, "We have to scare the hell out of'em."

THE NEW ATOMIC AGE

The scientists who had built the atomic bomb were gleeful when they received the news of its success at Hiroshima and Nagasaki. In the book, Robert Oppenheimer, Dark Prince, by Jack Rummel, 1992, we find, p.96, "Back in the United States the news of the bombing of Hiroshima was greeted with a mixture of relief, pride, joy, shock and sadness. Otto Frisch remembers the shouts of joy, 'Hiroshima has been destroyed!' 'Many of my friends were rushing to the telephone to book tables at the La Fonda Hotel in Santa Fe in order to celebrate. Oppenheimer walked around "like a prizefighter, clasping his hands together above his head as he came to the podium".'"

Oppenheimer had been a lifelong Communist. "He was heavily influenced by Soviet Communism ": A New Civilization, by Sidney and Beatrice Webb, the founders of Fabian Socialism in England. He became director of research at the newly formed U.S. Atomic

Energy Commission, with his mentor, Bernard Baruch, serving as chairman. Oppenheimer continued his many Communist Party Associations; his wife was Kitty Peuning, widow of Joe Dallet, an American Communist who had been killed defending Communism with the notorious Lincoln Brigade in Spain. Because Oppenheimer was under Party discipline, the Party then ordered him to marry Kitty Peuning and make a home for her.

Baruch resigned from the Atomic Energy Commission to attend to his business interests. He was replaced by Lewis Lichtenstein Strauss, of Kuhn, Loeb Co. Strauss was apprised of Oppenheimer's many Communist associations, but he decided to overlook them until he found that Oppenheimer was sabotaging progress on developing the new and much more destructive hydrogen bomb. It seemed apparent that Oppenheimer was delaying the hydrogen bomb until the Soviet Union could get its own version on line. Furious at the betrayal, he asked Oppenheimer to resign as director of the Commission. Oppenheimer refused. Strauss then ordered that he be tried. A hearing was held from April 5 to May 6, 1954. After reviewing the results, the Atomic Energy Commission voted to strip Oppenheimer of his security clearance, ruling that he "possessed substantial defects of character and imprudent dangerous associations with known subversives".

Oppenheimer retired to Princeton, where his mentor, Albert Einstein, presided over the Institute for Advanced Study, a think tank for refugee "geniuses", financed by the Rothschilds through one of their many secret foundations. Oppenheimer was already a trustee of the Institute, were he remained until his death in 1966.

THE REBIRTH OF ISRAEL

Einstein considered the atomic age merely as a stage for the rebirth of Israel. On p.760 of *Einstein; His Life And Times* we find that Abba Eban, the Israeli Ambassador, came to his home with the

Israeli consul, Reuben Dafni. He later wrote, "Professor Einstein told me that he saw the rebirth of Israel as one of the few political acts in his lifetime which had an essential moral quality. He believed that the conscience of the world should, therefore, be involved in Israel's preservation." by Ronald W. Clarke, Avon Books 1971.

On March 1, 1946, Army Air Force Contract No. MX-791 was signed, creating the RAND Corporation as an official think tank, defining Project RAND as "a continuing program of scientific study and research on the broad subject of air warfare with the object of recommending to the Air Force preferred methods of techniques and instrumentalities for this purpose." On May 14, 1948, RAND Corporation funding was taken over by H. Rowan Gaither, head of the Ford Foundation. This was done because the Air Force had sole control of the atomic bomb, RAND Corp. developed the Air Force and atomic bomb program for the Cold War, with the Strategic Air Command, the missile program, and many other elements of the "terror strategy". It became a billion dollar game for these scientists, with John von Neumann, their leading scientist, becoming world famous as the inventor of "game theory", in which the United States and the Soviet Union engaged in a worldwide "game" to see which would be the first to attack the other with nuclear missiles. In the United States, the schools held daily bomb drills, with the children hiding under their desks. No one told them that thousands of schools children in Hiroshima had been incinerated in their classrooms; the desks offered no protection against nuclear weapons. The moral effect on the children was devastating. If they were to be vaporized in the next ten seconds, there seemed little reason to study, marry and have children, or prepare for a steady job. This demoralization through the nuclear weapons program is the undisclosed reason for the decline in public morality.

In 1987, Phyllis LaFarge published *The Strangelove Legacy, The Impact Of The Nuclear Threat On Children*, chronicling through extended research the moral devastation wreaked on the children by the daily threat of annihilation. She quotes Freeman Dyson, who stated the world has been divided into two worlds, the world of the warriors, and the world of the victims, the children. It was William L. Laurence, sitting in the co-pilot's seat of a B-29 over Nagasaki, and the children waiting to be vaporized below. This situation has not changed.

THE LEGAL ASPECTS OF NUCLEAR WARFARE

Because Japan was occupied by the U.S. Military in 1945, the Japanese Government was never allowed any opportunity to file any legal charges about the use of the atomic bombs on Hiroshima and Nagasaki. Although Japanese leaders were tried and executed for "war crimes" no one was ever charged for the atomic bombings. It was not until 1996 that the World Court delivered an opinion on the use of nuclear weapons, (p.565, Hiroshima's Shadows) "In July 1996, the World court took a stand in its first formal opinion on the legality of nuclear weapons. Two years earlier, the United Nations had asked the Court for an advisory opinion. The General Assembly of the United Nations posed a single, yet profoundly basic, question for consideration. It the threat of use of nuclear weapons on any circumstances permitted under international law? For the first time, the world's pre-eminent judicial authority has considered the question of criminality vis-a-vis the use of a nuclear weapon, and, in doing so, it has come to the conclusion that the use of a nuclear weapon is 'unlawful'. It is also the Court's view that even the threat of the use of a nuclear weapon is illegal. Although there were differences concerning the implications of the right of self-defense provided by Article 51 of the U.N. Charter, ten of the fourteen judges hearing the case found the use of threat to use a nuclear weapon to be illegal on the basis of the existing canon of humanitarian law which governs the conduct of armed conflict. The judges based their opinion on more than a century of treatise and conventions that are collectively known as the 'Hague' and 'Geneva' laws."

Thus the Court ruled that nuclear weapons are illegal under the Hague and Geneva conventions, agreements which were in existence at the time of the Hiroshima and Nagasaki bombings. They were illegal then, and they are illegal now.

GANDHI SPEAKS

Among world leaders who spoke out about the United States' use of atomic weapons in Japan, Mahatma Gandhi echoed the general climate of opinion. P.258, Hiroshima's Shadow: "The atomic bomb has deadened the finest feelings which have sustained mankind for ages. There used to be so-called laws of war which made it tolerable. Now we understand the naked truth. War knows no law except that of might. The atomic bomb brought an empty victory to the Allied armies. It has resulted for the time being in the soul of Japan being destroyed. What has happened to the soul of the destroying nation is yet too early to see. Truth needs to be repeated as long as there are men who do not believe it."

Memorial Day, 1998

CAST OF CHARACTERS:

The House of Rothschild; international bankers who made enormous profits during the nineteenth century, and used their money to take over governments.

Bernard Baruch: New York agent of the Rothschilds who at the turn of the century set up the tobacco trust, the copper trust and other trusts for the Rothschilds. He became the grey eminence of the United States atomic bomb program when his lackey, J. Robert

Oppenheimner, became director of the Los Alamos bomb development, and when his Washington lackey, James F. Byrnes, advised Truman to drop the atomic bomb on Hiroshima and Nagasaki.

Albert Einstein; lifelong Zionist who initiated the United States' atomic bomb program with a personal letter to President Franklin D. Roosevelt in 1939.

BIBLIOGRAPHY:

The Private Lives Of Albert Einstein, by Roger Highfield, St. Martins Press, NY, 1993.

The Wizards Of Armageddon, by Fred Kaplan, Simon & Shuster, NY, 1993.

Albert Einstein, by Milton Dank, Franklin Watts, 1983.

Off The Record; The Private Papers Of Harry S. Truman, Harper & Row, 1980.

The Eisenhowers, by Steve Neal, Doubleday, 1978.

The Eisenhower Diaries, W.W. Norton, 1981.

In Review, Dwight D. Eisenhower, Doubleday, 1969.

Eisenhower, Stephen E. Ambrose, Simon & Schuster, 1983.

The Strangelove Legacy, Phyllis LaFarge, Harper & Row, 1987.

Einstein, His Life & Times, Ronald W. Clark, Avon books, 1971.

Robert Oppenheimer, Dark Prince, by Jack Rummel, 1992.

The Manhattan Project, by Don E. Beyer, Franklin Wat, 1991.

The Great Decision, The Secret History Of The Atomic Bomb, Michael Amrine, Putnams, NY, 1959.

Eisenhower At War, by David Eisenhower, Random House, NY, 1986.

The Fall Of Japan, by William Craig, Dial, NY, 1967.

Oppenheimer, The Years Of Risk, Jas W. Kunetka, Prentice Hall, 1982.

Target Tokyo, Gordon W. Prange, McGraw Hill, 1984.

Hiroshima's Shadow, edited by Kai Bird, Pamphleteer Press, 1998.

The Decision To Use The Atomic Bomb, by Gar Alperowitz, Knopf, NY, 1995.

Was Einstein Right? by Clifford M. Will, Basic Books, 1986.

THE COURT OF INTERNATIONAL JUSTICE

Eustace C. Mullins, Ezra Pound World Peace Foundation Japanese-American Friendship Society and the People of Japan, Plaintiffs,

The United States Government, Defendant.

The plaintiffs bring this action before the World Court of International Justice to resolve the following charges:

1. Defendant conspired to commit war crimes against the people of Japan during World War II.

2. Defendant conspired to commit atrocities against the people of Japan during World War II.

3. Defendant conspired to subsequently evade and cover up these crimes by militarily occupying the nation of Japan, effectively preventing the people of Japan from seeking legal recourse for the actions of defendant. Defendant continues to militarily occupy Japan today, with 49,999 troops stationed there, on the pretext that the Soviet Union might attack. This pretext ignores the geopolitical fact that the Soviet Union collapsed in 1989 and does not pose a threat to anyone.

4. Defendant conspired to commit crimes of genocide against the people of Japan, motivated by racial hatred and religious bigotry.

5. Defendant violated the Hague agreements and the Geneva Convention, as determined by the World Court in June 1996, by making war against civilians and inflicting millions of casualties by firebombing Japanese cities and the atomic bombing of Hiroshima and Nagasaki during World War II.

6. After committing these crimes, defendant conspired to cover up these crimes by issuing a number of false statements, denying war crimes, and distortions of fact to evade any punishment for these war crimes.

7. Defendant also conspired to conceal from the American people the circumstances behind the commission of these war crimes, that a small group of conspirators, refugees from Europe, came to the United States and infiltrated the government of the United States, and in total secrecy launched the project to manufacture an atomic bomb for use against Germany and Japan. At no time during this conspiracy were the people of the United States aware of what was taking place, nor consulted for their approval, in violation of republican' principles and the Constitution of the United States.

8. Since World War II, defendant has conducted a worldwide program of atomic terrorism, called atomic diplomacy, to ensure that its program continues unabated, and without punishment.

9. Although Japan had been reduced to ashes by June 1945, defendant insisted that an invasion was necessary, while ignoring peace tenders from Japan since May 1945, and defendant further claimed that the American military would suffer one million war dead while invading Japan, and that it was necessary to drop the atomic bombs on Hiroshima, August 6, 1945, and Nagasaki, August 9, 1945. In fact, as Admiral William D. Leahy pointed out in his book, *I Was There*, "the invasion itself was never authorized." General Dwight D. Eisenhower, Supreme Military Commander, Admiral William D. Leahy, Air force General Curtis LeMay, and many other American military leaders, made public statements that it was not necessary to drop the atomic bombs. Political considerations dictated that it be dropped on Japan, in order to test it on a living population, and, if possible, to "tally" a million or more victims with the bombs, for the purpose of postwar intimidation of all other nations.

10. The atomic bomb was the creation of a small group of European refugees, whose efforts to develop such a bomb in Europe had been indignantly rejected. Albert Einstein, the physicist, wrote a personal letter to President Franklin D. Roosevelt, August 2, 1939, recommending that this bomb be built by the United States. His letter was hand-delivered to Roosevelt by Alexander Sachs, a Wall Street speculator. The atomic bomb program was directed from behind the scenes by another Wall Street speculator, Bernard Baruch, an agent of the Rothschilds. Baruch selected Major General Leslie Groves as the director of the project, and J. Robert Oppenheimer as science director of the program. Baruch continued to issue directives throughout the program, insisting to Major General Groves that the city of Kyoto be the primary target of the atomic bombs. Military leaders opposed this selection, pointing out that Kyoto was the ancient capital of Japan, and a religious center with more than two hundred ancient temples. Hiroshima and Nagasaki were finally chosen, although neither of these cities offered a primary military target. Baruch continued to dictate decisions on the atomic bomb, through the President's National

Defense Research Committee, chaired by Baruch's Washington representative, James F. Byrnes.

11. After the devastation of Hiroshima and Nagasaki, defendant perpetrated a number of outright falsehoods to avoid blame for these massacres of civilians. The first was that the inhabitants were warned by leaflets dropped over the city that an atomic bomb would be used. In fact, the leaflets were not dropped until August 10, after the bombs had exploded. The President's Committee had resolved on May 31, 1945 that "we could not give the Japanese any warning." The second falsehood was that an invasion of Japan would be necessary if the atomic bomb was not used; this would cost a million American lives. Many leading American military authorities state this is absolutely false. The third falsehood was that both cities were "key military targets". President Truman boasted in his private papers that "in 1945 I had ordered the atomic bomb dropped on Japan at two places devoted almost exclusively to war production."

In fact, more than 95% of the dead at Hiroshima and Nagasaki were civilians. Only 4.4% of the death toll was made up of military personnel. A fourth falsehood, printed in the New York Times September 5, 1945, was that the victims had suffered no radiation damage. This story was written by William L. Laurence, the paid propagandist for the War Department with exclusive rights to material on the atomic bomb. Laurence quoted Major General Groves that the Japanese "are attempting to create sympathy for themselves".

12. The Legation of Switzerland in Tokyo forwarded to the defendant a statement from the Japanese government, the complaint that "the city of Hiroshima is a provincial town without any protection or military installations of any kind, but also none of the neighboring regions or towns constitutes a military objective." Observers on the scene recorded that "strictly military damage was insignificant."

13. The most authoritative official United States unit during World War II was the U.S. Strategic Bombing Survey, which selected targets and analyzed the results of the bombings for the benefit of future missions. Their report of July 1, 1946 states, "the Hiroshima and Nagasaki bombs did not defeat Japan, nor by the testimony of the enemy leaders who ended the war did they persuade Japan to accept unconditional surrender. The Emperor, the lord privy seal, the prime minister, the foreign minister, and the navy minister had decided as early as May 1945 that the war should be ended even if it meant acceptance of defeat on allied terms... It is the Survey's opinion that certainly prior to December 1, 1945, and in all probability prior to November 1, 1945, Japan would have surrendered even if the atomic bombs had not been dropped and even if no invasion had been planned or contemplated."

14. This proves that the destruction of Hiroshima and Nagasaki were war crimes deliberately committed, with foreknowledge that it was not necessary to drop the atomic bombs on these two cities. As David Lawrence, founder and editor of U.S. News And World Report, wrote in his editorial November 23, 1945, "the truth is we are guilty. Our conscience as a nation must trouble us. We must confess our sin. We have used a horrible weapon to asphyxiate and cremate more than 100,000 men, women and children in a sort of super-lethal gas chamber—• and all this in a war already won or which spokesman for our Air Forces tell us we could have readily won without the atomic bomb."

15. The world leader and pacifist Mahatma Gandhi spoke sadly about the tragedy of Hiroshima and Nagasaki. "The atomic bomb has deadened the finest feelings which have sustained mankind for ages. There used to be so-called laws of war which made it tolerable. Now we understand the naked truth. War knows no law except that of might.

The atomic bomb brought an empty victory to the Allied armies. It has resulted for the time being in the soul of Japan being destroyed. What has happened to the soul of the destroying nation is yet too early to see."

16. Defendant is in violation of the Geneva Convention. Protocol 2, Scope of Application of Humanitarian Law, states: 1. "International humanitarian law is applicable to international armed conflicts. The international law of peace existing between the states concerned will thus be large superseded by the rules of international humanitarian law.... A state can not, therefore, be allowed to invoke military necessity as a justification for upsetting that balance by departing from those rules."

17. IV. Humanitarian Requirements and Military Necessity. "In war, a belligerent many apply only that amount and kind of force necessary to defeat the enemy. Acts of war are only permissible if they are directed against military objectives, if they are not likely to cause unnecessary suffering, and if they are not perfidious." The bombing of Hiroshima and Nagasaki clearly falls outside the scope of this ruling, being civilian targets, the bombing caused unnecessary suffering, and defendant's attempted justification was openly perfidious.

18. 129. If an act of war is not expressly prohibited by international agreements or customary law, this does not necessarily mean that it is actually permissible. The so-called Martens Clause, developed by the Livonian professor Friedrich von Martens (1845-1909) delegate of Tsar Nicholas II at the Hague Peace Conferences, which has been included in the Preamble to the 1907 Hague Convention IV and reaffirmed in the 1977 Additional Protocol I as stated below, will always be applicable. In cases not covered by the Protocol or by other international agreement, civilians and combatants remain under the protection and authority of the principles of international law derived from established custom, from the principles of humanity, and from the dictates of public conscience. (Artl., pars. 2 AP 1; see also Preamble pars. 4 AP II)

19. Protocol I—Part IV. Section i. "....the obligation of the Parties to the conflict to 'at all times distinguish between the civilian

population and combatants'."Article 48—Basic rule, "the prohibition of 'indiscriminate attacks'." Article 51—Protection of the civilian population, paragraph 4, in particular "an attack by bombardment by any method or means which treats as a single military objective a number of clearly separated and distinct military objectives, located in a city, town, village or other area containing a similar concentration of civilians or civilian objects" (Article 51—Protection of the civilian population paragraph 5 (a) and "an attack which may be expected to cause incidental loss of civilian life, injury to civilians, damage to civilian objects, or a combination thereof, which would be excessive in relation to the concrete and direct military advantage anticipated (article 51—Protection of the civilian population, paragraph 5 [b]).

20. Protocal I—Part IV, Section 1. "Protection of civilians from arbitrary and oppressive enemy action, outlined in 1899, and later in 1907, was expressed in its most complete form in the Fourth Geneva Convention of 1949, which is now supplemented by this Protocol.

WHEREFORE, the plaintiffs respectfully move this Court to hear these charges of conspiracy to commit war crimes and atrocities, conspiracy to cover up their crimes, motivated by racial hatred and religious bigotry, and having intimidated the government of Japan and prevented them from seeking any redress for these crimes, and by defendant's ongoing program of atomic terrorism, perfidious falsehoods, and their continuing conspiracy to cover up crimes of genocide, mass murder and undue suffering among their victims, and that the Court shall hear these charges, decide upon appropriate damages, and punishment for the offenders.

Respectfully submitted Eustace C. Mullins as a citizen in party, the movant, having firsthand knowledge of the facts. Eustace C. Mullins 126 Madison Place Staunton, VA 24401

WASHINGTON DC CITY OF FEAR

A famous self hating white liberal, the late Sen. Alan Cranston of California, was held up by three armed blacks as he walked the few feet from his car to his office in the Senate Office Building. Perhaps in deference to his well known bias in favour of blacks the bandits did not shoot him down and leave him to die in the gutter, as they did to others.

At that time the city schools were about to close because of a strike by the school custodians. The Asst. U.S. Atty. for the District of Columbia was indicted for taking bribes and the first Jewish Governor of Maryland, which embraced some of Washington's suburbs, was on trial for bribery and corruption. A few days later, the nude, stabbed body of a Congressional aide and holder of a number of official positions in Washington, was found dead at the Iwo Jima Memorial, which was one of the most famous homosexual trysting places in the world.

It was a typical week in the most dangerous, of the world's big cities. Washington's crime rate is three times that of Buenos Aires, and several times that of London. The D.C. Police Dept. regularly falsifies its figures so that only one third of all robberies and rapes are recorded. Washington is one of the most heavily policed cities in the world, with its Metropolitan Police, U. S. Park Police, U. S. Capital Police, Secret Service, and with agents of the Treasury, the CIA, and FBI, walking about heavily armed, to say nothing of thousands of members of the Armed Forces. However, the presence of these armed legions his no effect on the burgeoning crime rate. At one time the metropolitan police was an all-white force, then it was fully integrated, with the predictable result that black policemen simply turn their backs when they see a "brother" robbing or beating a white person. They also turn their backs when they see their soul brothers robbing and killing each other, because they are only too familiar with the innate savagery of their own kind, and they know it would be fatal to interfere.

The Canon of Washington Cathedral, an imposing edifice where many of the nation's leading officials attend services, pronounced in a sermon that Washington had become a "human slaughter house". For this he was immediately denounced on all sides as an "alarmist" and, most terrible of all, a "racist". He purposely did not mention blacks in speaking out as a concerned Christian leader against the City of Fear in which his parishioners lived. However, everyone knew that he was referring to the slaughter of whites by black terrorists. The nation's press picked up his sermon, and he was asked to resign.

The ceding of the nation's capital to black terrorists by the United States government was the biggest story in the 1970's. Fifty years later it is still the biggest story which, is still suppressed by the news media. In the very centre of this black Hell is the headquarters of the most influential newspaper in America today, the Washington Post.

It is owned by the Jewish Meyer banking family. Eugene Meyer, purchased the newspaper with the proceeds from his enormous profits as head of the War Finance Corporation. Although serving as a "dollar a year" man during World War I, Meyer had made the simple discovery that Liberty Bonds, being merely paper, could be printed in duplicate for each number sold. He divided them up evenly, one for you, and one for me. The government bonds were sold to the public through the War Finance Corporation, where his fellow Jewish friend, Bernard Baruch had appointed him Director.

The duplicates were sold through Bernard Baruch, who was head of the War Industries Board and found time apart from his duties to, as he so well put it, "take the profits."

In a sworn testimony before the Senate Finance Committee, Meyer said he used his war profits to purchase the Allied Chemical & Dye Corp. and the Washington Post.

His daughter Katharine inherited the Post, and placed her husband in nominal charge. Philip Graham soon found that he had difficulty in carrying out his duties as publisher of the Post, because he had become very depressed.

The white pressmen's union had succeeded in keeping most blacks out of their Union.

Graham found that even though he was publisher of the Post, he had little influence with the pressmen's union.

Disturbed that he could not integrate the union, Graham became more and more depressed. He finally drove out to the splendid Meyer estate, and blew his head off with a shotgun.

The story did not end there. Katharine Meyer Graham took over as active head of the Washington Post. She continued to bring pressure on the union to hire more blacks. As a Jewess, she had an emotional attachment for blacks stemming back thousands of years when they intermixed in the slave quarters of Egypt. The union stubbornly resisted her efforts, remaining a white island in the black hell of Washington. When she brought, more blacks into the pressroom in 1973, the white pressmen smashed the presses and almost put the Post out of business. As Jews are accustomed to such setbacks, this did not faze Katharine Graham, who proceeded undaunted with her plans to force the President of the United States, Richard Nixon, out of office. Washington Post reporters have won many awards for their journalistic "scoops", but none for exposes of black terrorism in Washington, because they have not written one. Eighty years ago, Washington was a sleepy Southern town in which the inhabitants went to bed without locking their doors. This stable existence was rudely shattered when the Supreme Court outlawed racial clauses in real estate contracts which excluded blacks from buying in quiet white residential areas. The white residents of the District of Columbia hurriedly packed and fled to all white suburbs in Virginia and Maryland, while. Washington soon became the largest black city in the world. The beautifully maintained homes became rat warrens in which cockroaches waved to and fro, and in which black children sat placidly eating the paint off the decaying walls. Today the worst crime a landlord can commit in the District of Columbia is to, put lead paint on a wall, as the black children, who are always unattended, eat it and become ill. Garbage was piled in the front yards, along with broken furniture and plumbing which the blacks ripped out and threw out the windows.

The buildings of the Federal bureaucracy became veritable fortresses in which the white workers left only in large groups, going to their cars to drive back to the suburbs at the end of the day. Despite armed guards stationed at all entrances, the Senate and the House office buildings became favoured haunts of black criminals, who roamed the halls, entering and robbing the staffs during broad daylight and occasionally raping a secretary. Extremely stringent security procedures were set up, with the result that Congressmen accustomed to frolic late at night in their offices now had to take comely staff members of either sex to a hotel or to the members' apartments. They now became vulnerable to black mail.

In 1967, President Lyndon B. Johnson administered what was to prove to be the final blow to the District of Columbia when he appointed Walter Washington as Mayor (left).

An easy-going, simple person, Washington had genially presided over the complete disintegration of the city government, while serving as the alter ego of his hard driving and ambitious wife. Bernetta. An intimate of the Washington's.

His wife explained the situation, "Ole Walltuh, now, HE'S all right, don't nuthin' bother him, ..."

There were two distinct classes of blacks in the Old South, the illiterate, simple minded blacks who worked in the fields, and the more intelligent and arrogant blacks who worked in the Big Houses and who literally ran the lives of the field blacks. There is no question that "Aint Nettie" was one of the real powers in Washington. With their combined incomes and official "perks", the Washington's were one of the wealthiest black couples in America. Their home was robbed many times, and on one occasion a passing reporter snapped a picture of a burglar hastily leaving the premises. However, the burglar was never apprehended.

In Washington hundreds of thousands of blacks have their every need taken care of by the Federal government, with subsidized schools, hospitals, welfare, food stamps and many other benefits.

During the riots of 1968, Washington telephoned President Johnson and informed him that there could be no counterattack against the black rioters. "If you let one black get shot, we're marching on the White House!" he yelled, and then slammed down the phone. Watching the burning capital city from his office, Johnson realized that he too could be burned out by the mobs. He hastily issued orders that the National Guard could march only if they carried UNLOADED guns. Hundreds of white youths were marched out into the rioting mobs with no protection. Washington had the radio stations inform the mobs that the soldiers had no bullets, and the looting proceeded without interference. After the stores had been emptied, the blacks set fire to them. Today, many of the destroyed areas have not been rebuilt, and block after block has a desolate bombed out look. Although. the Federal government has appropriated many millions of dollars to rebuild these areas, it has disappeared into the bottomless pockets of the city officials.

Years later, Walter Washington was disturbed by 'sudden' shooting pains in his body. When the doctors could find no cause, he immediately deduced their origin. J. Edgar Hoover was surprised when Washington called him and demanded that he find out who was practicing voodoo on him. Since Hoover, unlike most Federal officials, still lived in the District, he wished to placate the Mayor, and he assigned an agent to the case. After weeks of fruitless investigation, Hoover and the agent conspired to deport a Jamaican fortune teller from the 14th Street who was illegally in this country. Washington was given the results of this arrangement and the pains disappeared. Today, the agent was known by the nickname of "Voodoo."

Under Walter Washington's Administration, or lack of it, the city's finances diminished to the point of no return. City officials made little or no effort to collect income or property taxes from the blacks, and depend on the Federal government to pay the enormous costs of this welfare community. While billions of dollars flew through Walter Washington's hands, he repeatedly sought more funds by demanding that Congress levy a "commuter tax" on residents of Virginia and Maryland who work in the District. They finally did this, many years later. The immediate effect was to drive out the white doctors and lawyers who have offices in the city, depriving it of the last vestige of white civilization. In response, they appointed a committee to check on the city's finances.

They reported that it would cost $40 million to audit the city's books, and that they were in such a state of chaos that even then the resulting figures would be meaningless. On one item alone, that of parking meter coins, it was found that one hundred million dollars of meter revenues had disappeared and been stolen during Washington's administration. The city hired a private firm to collect coins from meters with an armoured car. The city has no one who can be trusted to collect coins from the meters.

In his first term as Mayor, Washington hired a well-known white liberal as Deputy Mayor, to placate those who feared he would set up an all-black administration. A few months later, the Deputy Mayor's daughter shot and killed a man she was robbing to support her dope habit. Her father resigned and went to California, where his family's life style would be less noticeable. The daughter was placed on probation, of course. Washington then hired an all-black city government, with the result that there was chaos in every department of the city, with all black faces in all the offices.

This heady atmosphere has resulted in some violent and mentally unbalanced blacks attaining high positions in Washington.

In any event, arrests are rarely made and convictions are almost unheard of in Washington. Most D.C. residents do not report burglaries to the police, because they know that no action will be taken on their complaints.

Instead, they invest heavily in guard dogs, expensive locks and other forms of protection.

This writer was refused a parade permit by the D.C. Police Dept. to honour the memory of the U. S. sailors massacred by Israeli terrorists on the U. S. S. Liberty during the Six Day War. Yet they, allowed the blacks to set up Resurrection City and do twenty million dollars' worth of damage to public land in the District of Columbia! D.C. Police spend most of their time issuing parking tickets to tourists who do not realize that the meters are never maintained and usually do not work.

The tourist drops in a coin, the flag jumps up, and as he walks away, the flag slowly sinks back to red violation. When he returns, he has a ticket.

The true horror of Washington, D. C., is that it is a microcosm of what is happening to all of America. Few citizens realize that the vast, dictatorial Federal bureaucracy came into being solely to take advantage of the "slave" mentality of the blacks. In his plantation orientation all the blacks' problems are taken care of by "Ole Massa" in the Big House. Despite his emancipation, he continues to expect all of his problems to be taken care of by others. Meanwhile, white Americans looked after their own problems. When F. D. R.. took office, he brought with him a horde of Jewish Zionists like Felix Frankfurter who saw that the way to enslave all Americans was to launch national "social" programs to take care of the government's short comings. Social security, welfare and medical bills were foisted on the American people solely because the blacks could not handle these problems for themselves. A Federal dictatorship has been created in DC which takes the earnings of white citizens' and "redistributes" it. This dictatorship now makes war on every sector of private life. Private schools have virtually been outlawed; clubs, churches, and private businesses exist only at the pleasure of Big Brother.

This Federal dictatorship did not exist before 1932, and was created solely because of the failings of the black's ability to look after himself.

In retrospect, it will be seen, perhaps too late, that it is the presence of the black which has destroyed the fabric of American society, just as De Tocqueville correctly predicted more than a century ago. The black cancer spawned in Washington has now invaded all of our cities, leaving nothing but devastation in its wake.

Washington D. C. with its miles of desolation and its black terrorism of white citizens is under present conditions, the future of America.

THE LINDBERGH MURDERS
HAUPTMANN WAS INNOCENT
THE PROSECUTION AND DEFENSE
COMBINED TO FRAME HIM

Why did Charles Lindbergh perjure himself to send an innocent man to the electric chair? Would the arrest of the murderers of the Lindbergh child have prevented the entry of the United States into World War II? Why did "Editor and Publisher", the house organ of the journalism industry, note on the Hauptmann trial, "**No trial in this century has so degraded the administration of justice.**"?

These questions are raised, but not answered by a painstaking examination of the Lindbergh kidnapping in "Scapegoat" by Anthony Scaduto. Published two years ago, it proves that Hauptmann was innocent and that he was convicted solely by suborned perjury from the Jewish prosecutor, David Wilentz. Scaduto found the paybook of Reliance Property Management and photographed the page showing that Hauptmann was working in New York on March 1, 1932, when the baby was kidnapped. Wilentz not only hid the paybook in police files where it remained for forty years, but got the timekeeper to testify in sworn testimony that Hauptmann had not been hired until March 15! Wilentz had an eighty-seven year old New Jersey neighbor of the Lindberghs, Amandus Hochmuth, testify that at one p.m. on the day of the kidnapping, Richard Hauptmann drove up to him, told him his name, and said he was looking for property in the area. Yet Social Security records showed that Hochmuth was legally blind from cataracts and was also senile. **At the time of Hochmuth's testimony, Wilentz was concealing the Reliance paybook which** proved that at the very hour that Hochmuth claimed Hauptmann was conversing with him outside the Lindbergh home, he was actually working in New York!

When J. Edgar Hoover learned that the Jewish prosecutor Wilentz was manufacturing evidence and preparing a horde of perjured witnesses to testify in the Hauptmann trial, he hastily withdrew the cooperation of the FBI in the prosecution. Foreseeing a complete debacle, he remarked to his associate, Clyde Tolson, "Goddamit, I don't know if Hauptmann is going to jail, but I'm sure Wilentz will." Governor Hoffman of New Jersey later wrote in *Liberty Magazine* that J. Edgar Hoover informed him that he and the FBI had formally withdrawn from the case on October 10, 1934. This was three weeks after Hauptmann's arrest, when Hoover's agents reported to him that Wilentz and his chief co-conspirator, the Jew Col. H. Norman Schwartzkopf, head of the New Jersey State Police (Schwartzkopf means "blackhead" in German; [father of General Schwartzkopf of Gulf War fame]) were concocting a completely phony case against Hauptmann. Despite Hoover's hunger for publicity, he was forced to sit on the sidelines throughout the most famous trial in American history. However, the FBI tour in Washington ever since has included a lengthy discussion of the Hauptmann case, with great emphasis on the role played by the FBI agents in the locating and arrest of Hauptmann. Actually, the arresting force included one FBI agent and nine New York and Jew Jersey policemen. Of course the tour guides never inform the gaping public that Hoover refused to participate in the trial because all of the evidence presented by Wilentz, with the exception of the ransom money, was completely phony.

Historians tell us that the First World War was triggered by the assassination of Archduke Ferdinand. It was not until the Scaduto book appeared that this writer realized that the Second World War actually began on March 1, 1932, when the Lindbergh child was kidnapped and ritually murdered. It was a year and a half later that the Jewish leader Samuel Untermyer formally declared war on Germany in his speech of August 7, 1933, before the International Jewish Boycott Conference in Amsterdam, Holland. Yet that war had begun when the murder of the Lindbergh child ensured the election of Franklin D. Roosevelt and the enthronement of the Jewish power in the United States.

For more than two years, the Scaduto revelations have ticked away like a time bomb, threatening to topple the unholy combine of Jewish officialdom and the Jewish-controlled press which holds power in the United States. Because of its ramifications, it has been ignored by the press, of which Scaduto was a member in good standing, having been a reporter for the Schiff-owned *New York Post*. Instead of winning a Pulitzer prize for his brilliant journalistic research on the Hauptmann trial, Scaduto has been relegated to limbo, and his great work on this case is never mentioned. He has no idea of the real forces at work, and apparently has never heard of ritual murder. Indeed, he naively ascribes the Lindbergh kidnapping to a plan by the Mafia to force Lindbergh and other pilots to stop reporting sighted stills seen in their mail runs! In fact, Lindbergh had never reported but one still, which he merely noted in his flight log, and did not even report it to the authorities!

It becomes the task of this writer to answer the questions raised by the Scaduto book. Why did the world's most famous hero, Charles Lindbergh, cooperate with the murderers of his child and perjure himself to send an innocent victim to death? A typical gentile, he was putty in the hands of the wily Jew, Wilentz, who quickly converted him into a robot-like shabez goy, repeating only what he had been told to say. The facts are a matter of record. On the night of April 2, 1932, Lindbergh had accompanied his go-between, Dr. Condon, known as Jafsie, to St. Raymond's Cemetery in New York for the payment of the $50,000 ransom. Lindbergh had remained in the car while Dr. Condon carried the ransom money into the cemetery. He was unable to see the kidnapper, who finally whispered to Condon, "Hey Doctor." This hoarse whisper, some three hundred feet from Lindbergh in the closed car, was barely heard by him. He testified at the Bronx grand jury indictment of Hauptmann that he positively could not identify Hauptmann's voice! These grand jury files remained sealed for more than forty years, until Scaduto obtained access to them. During the Hauptmann trial in New Jersey, Wilentz became fearful that the parade of perjured witnesses he and Schwartzkopf had suborned, as well as the clumsily manufactured evidence against Hauptmann, was having little effect on the jury. In fact, the testimony of senile witnesses like Hochmuth was prejudicing them in Hauptmann's favor. One of his star witnesses was Albert Osborn, the famed handwriting expert, who positively identified Hauptmann as the man who wrote the ransom notes. It was this same outfit of *Osborn and Osborn* which more recently positively identified Clifford Irving's forgeries of Howard Hughes' handwriting as being "unquestionably genuine", thus enabling Irving to defraud his publisher of $300,000.

To understand Wilentz' predicament, we should realize that he was a typical Jewish fraud and loudmouth. Although he was prosecuting the most publicized case in American history, Wilentz had never before tried a criminal case of any case! Like most Jewish officials, he had not been elected to the office of Attorney General of the State of New Jersey, but had been appointed by Gov. Harry Moore as a political payoff after he had persuaded a number of Jews to switch their votes! If he could get a conviction against Hauptmann, he was assured he would become the first Jewish Governor of New Jersey, and perhaps follow Woodrow Wilson's example in moving from that office into the White House. Since he had nothing to connect Hauptmann with the kidnapping and murder of the Lindbergh child but the possession of the ransom bills, he and his fellow Jew, Schwartzkopf, enlisted the state police in manufacturing a phony ladder and other evidence, and rounding up a group of perjured witnesses who would place Hauptmann at the scene of the crime. Because more than a dozen persons were involved in Wilentz' conspiracy, it was inevitable that J. Edgar Hoover and other officials would be warned of what Wilentz was doing. It was even more imperative that Wilentz convict Hauptmann in order to protect the real murderers, the Jews who actually kidnapped and ritually murdered the baby. As a Jew, it was his duty to his tribe not only to erase all leads to the true killers, but also to prevent the public from learning any details of the nature of the crime, a Jewish ritual murder. This was the real reason that Wilentz had taken the unprecedented step of a state attorney general personally taking over the case, which otherwise was even more inexplicable since he had no experience in organizing and directing a criminal prosecution. Traditionally, a state attorney general would remain in the state capitol, and would select a prosecutor who would personally report to him on the developments in the case. Yet all of the hundreds of reporters at the trial unquestionably accepted the explanation that "political ambition" was the sole reason for Wilentz' unusual behavior.

Seeing that the case was going against him, with the possibility that Hauptmann would be freed and that investigators might then discover the true murderers, Wilentz was forced to play his last card. He had a hurried conference with Lindbergh in his office.

"*Mistuh Lintbug*," he said hoarsely (a New York University graduate, Wilentz usually was well spoken, but like many Jews, when agitated, he reverted to a thick Yiddish accent) "*Mistuh Lintbug, this monster is going to be set free ... unless*," He turned away from Lindbergh and suddenly whirled back towards him, his outstretched forefinger almost poking Lindbergh in the eye, "*unless you go out there and tell the jury that Hauptmann's voice is the man you heard in the cemetery!*"

"But I can't do that," protested Lindbergh. "*You know I e already testified before the grand jury that I can't identify Hauptmann's voice.*"

"*That doesn't matter,*" Wilentz reassured him. "*Those grand jury records are sealed. No one will ever see them. Besides, Reilly* [Hauptmann's lawyer] *doesn't know about it.*"

"*It doesn't seem right, somehow,*" said Lindbergh.

"*You know that this man murdered your child,*" said Wilentz. "*I know it. But that jury still doesn't believe it. You're the only one who can convince them. You must decide now. Is this man going to pay the penalty for his crime, or not?*"

A typical goy in the hands of the clever Jew, Lindbergh agreed. Coached by Wilentz, he returned to the courtroom, and testified, "*I heard very clearly a voice coming from the cemetery ... In a foreign accent,... That was Hauptmann's voice.*"

Reporters in the courtroom noted that as Lindbergh spoke, the wife of the accused, Anna Hauptmann, stared directly at him as her lips moved to form the words, "You lie."

Adela Rogers St. John who was William Randolph Hearst's resident sob sister, wrote that afternoon, "Watching Lindbergh today in this ordeal I cannot believe he would swear away the life of any man unless he was sure. Automatically, I looked at the jury, even before I looked at Hauptmann. Yes."

Adela Rogers St. John knew that Lindbergh had just condemned Hauptmann to death. She did not know that he had previously testified the opposite to the grand jury, or that he had been suborned to commit perjury by Wilentz, as had so many other witnesses in this case. However, her unusual credentials should have told her something was wrong. The daughter of a brilliant attorney named Earl Rogers, she had grown up in the courtroom, and was famous for her instincts as to whether a witness was telling the truth, and how a jury would vote. Most importantly here, she did not say that she believed Lindbergh's testimony. She said the jury believed it, which they did.

Wilentz had achieved one vital goal; he had turned the trial into a circus. Hundreds of reporters and thousands of spectators had swarmed into the little town of Flemington, New Jersey, and tried to batter their way into the Hunterdon County Courthouse. Wilentz's opponent in the case, Ed Reilly, had from the beginning played Wilentz's game. Inexplicable at the time, it now seems to have been no accident. Big Ed Reilly, known as the Bull of Brooklyn, had defended more than two thousand clients, most of them accused of murder. Many of them were mobsters, for whom he won acquittals, earning fabulous fees in the process. Now fifty-two years old, he looked sixty-five. Red-faced, with a tremendous paunch and thinning hair, he had been an alcoholic for years. He had spent several million dollars in high living, and was paying alimony to four wives. He was nearly bankrupt, and his law practice had dropped alarmingly. Yet this was the man whom an unusually generous William Randolph Hearst had hired to defend the penniless Hauptmann, for a fee of $300,000! It was well known that Hearst wanted a conviction. He was haunted by the fear that one of his children would be kidnapped, with a probable demand for a million dollar ransom, which he would have difficulty in paying. He had already relinquished control of the Hearst newspapers to a Jew, Richard Berlin. Few people knew that the Hearsts themselves were Jewish, the original name having been "Hirsch". This fact gave further dimension to Hearst's interest in the case. He had forbidden any reporter to ever mention the words "Jewish ritual murder" in any story. Thus he had a common bond with Wilentz in seeing Hauptmann convicted. This meant that Reilly's lackluster conduct of the case was due to more than his failing memory and his alcohol blurred speech. Reilly had refused to cross examine Hochmuth about his 87 year old memory or his loss of eyesight. He was famed as "the Bull of Brooklyn", a man who could tear any witness' testimony to shreds with a few sardonic thrusts, yet not a single prosecution witness was attacked by him.

Hearst himself had abandoned his wife and children to live with a cheap showgirl. As a result, he was no longer received in polite society, and he was reduced to entertaining the Jewish offal of the silver screen in his palace of San Simeon. His granddaughter, Patty Hearst, became the nation's second most famous kidnap victim. After some weeks of intimacies with her captors, a group of degenerate Negro men and lesbians, she lost all desire to return to a normal life.

Although Hauptmann knew that all of Wilentz' witnesses were perjuring themselves, in cluding Lindbergh, he never had an inkling that he had been set up with Reilly as his attorney. The $300,000 fee proved to be a profitable investment for Hearst, as his accountants later found that the additional revenues generated by the coverage of the trial totalled more than eight million dollars!

Although Hauptmann's entire defense consisted of his story that he had legitimately acquired the ransom money, not knowing this was the result of a crime, Reilly did nothing to develop witnesses or evidence which would corroborate this story, nor did any of the hundreds of reporters who swarmed into Flemington. Yet forty years later, Scaduto was able to find reams of evidence corroborating every detail of Hauptmann's claims. He had for several years been a partner with a Jew named Isidor Fisch, buying, trading and selling furs and other commodities in a small way with their very limited capital. He had no idea that Fisch was a notorious confidence man. One of Fisch's coups had been to take Al Capone for twenty thousand dollars, but instead of winding up in the bay, he had slick talked Capone until the supposedly vicious thug had laughed and said, "Oh, hell, forget it." On December 6, 1933, Fisch owed Hauptmann more than five thousand dollars. On that day, he sailed to Germany, undeterred by the news that the country was in the grip of an extremely anti-Jewish movement. Before he left, he assured Hauptmann that he had no cause to worry about the debt. In any case, he wanted to leave a box of his effects with Hauptmann. This box contained part of the ransom money. Hauptmann put it away without examining it. In March of 1934, Fisch was reported to have died of tuberculosis in a Leipzig hospital, although this is a disease which usually takes many months even years to develop. In any case, most doctors in Germany were Jews, and the report was a fake. Hauptmann was never informed of it. Fisch survived the Second World War and emigrated to Israel, where he died in a kibbutz in 1969.

When Fisch did not return, Hauptmann opened the box. He saw the ransom money. Not knowing that Fisch had set him up, he began to spend part of it, offsetting the $5,500 Fisch owed him. However, he did keep meticulous notes of money taken from the box, indicating that he expected Fisch to return for an accounting. Unlike Hauptmann, Fisch had been definitely linked to the Lindbergh household, for he had been seen a number of times with a twenty-eight-year-old English girl, Violet Sharpe, who worked there as a maid. After the police questioned her about the kidnapping, on June 10, 1932, she was found dead at the Morrow household. A can of potassium cyanide was nearby. There was no record of its purchase by anyone in the household, and it could not be traced to any store in New Jersey. No one had ever seen it or knew what it was used for. Schwartzkopf's police promptly ruled the death a "suicide", and made no attempt to trace the cyanide, after deciding that Violet Sharpe herself had brought it there. As she was the only person in the household who could identify the kidnappers, there is little doubt that she was murdered and that Schwartzkopf's police were guilty of collusion in covering up the murder.

Throughout the trial, the news media conditioned the American people to accept as a fact Hauptmann's guilt. Newsboys screamed on the street corners of the nation. "Burn Hauptmann". One reporter, Eddie Mahar, persistently described Hauptmann in his daily stories as "the Nazi monster", even though he knew that Hauptmann had no connection with any political groups in either Germany or the United States. The Hauptmann trial became a national sounding board for the newly inaugurated "hate Germany" campaign which was to herd American gentile youths to Europe to die for the Jews in profitable slaughter. The trial was being held in New Jersey only a few miles away from the spot where Jewish saboteurs were to set fire to the *Hindenburg*, a German Zeppelin visiting the United States on a peaceful goodwill mission. Every Jew in America cheered at the newsreel photos of the German crew dying a horrible death in the exploding Zeppelin. It is now obvious that if Wilentz had not successfully directed the course of the trial away from Fisch and the other Jews who had committed the ritual slaughter of the Lindbergh child, Roosevelt would never have been able to involve the United States in the Second World War. **The arrest of the Jewish murderers would have caused a nationwide current of feeling against the Jews, and would have invoked national sympathy for Germany's struggle to become "Judenfrei".**

Convinced by Lindbergh's testimony, the jury brought in a unanimous verdict of "Guilty". Hauptmann was sentenced to die in the electric chair. Throughout the trial, his wife had been warned to stay out of the hall when Lindbergh was coming into the courtroom, as he dared not face her. He told the bailiffs he would never enter the courtroom until they assured him that Anna Hauptmann had already gone in and was seated.

Several Christians, aware that Hauptmann had been railroaded, now began a desperate struggle to save his life. At their own expense, and with no personal involvement in the case, they sought only to work for justice. One of these men was Ellis Parker, former chief of detectives of Burlington, New Jersey, and considered one of the most brilliant and incorruptible detectives in America. Having known Lindbergh's father-in-law, Dwight Morrow, for some years, he went to Morrow and told him how Wilentz had faked the evidence. He asked only that Morrow persuade Lindbergh to ask for a commuted sentence to life imprisonment while he gathered evidence on the real killers. Morrow's health was failing rapidly, as he had been overcome by the horrible death of his grandson and the resulting publicity. Nevertheless, in June of 1935, he summoned Lindbergh for a confidential talk. "Charles," he said, "you must ask the Governor to commute Hauptmann's sentence, at least for the time being."

"Never," replied Lindbergh, "he must pay the full penalty for his crime." "I didn't want to tell you this," said Morrow, "but Hauptmann is innocent." "I heard the evidence against him," said Lindbergh.

"It was all faked," said Dwight Morrow. "I know that from an unimpeachable source."

"But the money!" exclaimed Lindbergh.

"The money was real," said Dwight Morrow, "but Hauptmann was set up. Can't you understand? He wasn't the man in the cemetery."

"But I identified him," said Lindbergh.

"Any lawyer knows your testimony was worthless," said Dwight Morrow. "Reilly should have invoked the doctrine of familiarity. In a capital crime, you can't identify a voice you have heard on only one occasion. Yet Reilly didn't challenge your testimony. Do you know why?"

"No," said Lindbergh.

"I do," said Dwight Morrow. "He was paid to see that Hauptmann would be convicted. Any competent attorney would have had your testimony stricken, and the jury would have been told to disregard it."

"Even if that's true," said Lindbergh, "I can't take back my testimony."

"You don't have to," said Dwight Morrow. "Just ask for a commutation of the death penalty. I've never asked you for anything, Charles, but I must ask you, in the name of Heaven, to do this. I don't have much time left, and I don't want to see another death added to those of young Charles and Violet Sharpe. Call the Governor today."

"I won't do it," exclaimed Lindbergh. "Why, I've look like a fool!"

"Please," said Dwight Morrow, half rising from his bed.

"Never!" exclaimed Lindbergh.

Dwight Morrow fell back in complete collapse, and died. Lindbergh never mentioned this conversation to his wife, claiming that his father-in-law died without speaking.

[and this death-bed conversation was related to us how?]

Ellis Parker now enlisted the aid of the newly elected Governor of New Jersey, Harold Hoffman. When he was shown the evidence of Wilentz's perfidy, Hoffman began a frenetic campaign to have Hauptmann freed. Schwartzkopf and Wilentz blocked every move he made. J. Edgar Hoover admitted to him that he had withdrawn from the case, but refused to let Hoffman use the FBI files which showed that the evidence against Hauptmann had been faked by the New Jersey State Police. The press launched a nationwide campaign of ridicule against him. The condemned man wrote a despairing letter which was printed in *Liberty Magazine*. Hauptmann said of those who had framed him, "their suffering, their agony, will be greater than mine. Mine will be over in a moment. Theirs will last as long as life itself."

Governor Hoffman told Wilentz that if he ever dared to run for public office, he would expose his handling of the Lindbergh trial. Wilentz settled down to practice corporation law; soon, he was earning five hundred thousand dollars a year. Much of his work consisted of handling business matters for the Mafia. He represented the Mafia leader Anthony Rosso in a series of multi-million-dollar deals. Eventually, he had his revenge on Governor Hoffman. He and other Jews framed Hoffman for income tax evasion. Hoffman had been wont to entertain groups of politicians and journalists at a night spot in Manhattan called *The Pen and Pencil*. Some of his tabs were picked up by an insurance agent who liked to be with celebrities. The Jews called this "unreported income", and Hoffman was convicted.

Meanwhile, Ellis Parker had located the real kidnapper of the Lindbergh child, a man named Paul Wendel. Wendel had been Isidor Fisch's lawyer, and had regularly dated Violet Sharpe, who set up the kidnapping. Wendel's sister lived behind St. Raymond's Cemetery. This was the reason this spot had been chosen for the delivery of the ransom money. Parker had Wendel sign a full confession. When he turned Wendel over to the police, Wendel immediately repudiated the confession and accused Parker of kidnapping him! Parker and his son were convicted under the new Lindbergh kidnapping law, and sent to Lewisburg prison. A few months later, Parker died in prison. His gallant effort to aid Hauptmann had cost him his life.

On March 31, 1936, Richard Hauptmann was electrocuted for a crime he had not committed. To the end, the press, showing its consistent bias, referred to him as "Bruno" Hauptmann. Although his first name was Bruno, he had never liked it, and had been known as Richard Hauptmann throughout his stay in America. The press seized upon Bruno because of its overtones of "brute" and "Brutal", as another instrument to whip up anti-German sentiment. Hauptmann went to his death reiterating his innocence.

As this writer has spent thirty years investigating Jewish ritual murder, the entire handling of the Lindbergh investigation shows the typical reactions of Jews to this crime ... the furious activity of Jewish officials such as Wilentz to cover up all traces of the true murderers, and to find a gentile victim who can be accused of the crime. Was it a coincidence that Richard Hauptmann shared his home in the Bronx with Victor Schuessler? Victor Schuessler was the grandfather of the two Schuessler boys who were murdered in one of Chicago's most famous cases of Jewish ritual murder! The ritual murder of the blond, blue-eyed Lindbergh child was a crime so horrible that it leads one to cry out, "Is there no pity under Heaven?" But, seen in its context, this crime, had it been solved, could have led to the saving of millions of lives in the approaching Second World War. Today, the Lindbergh case is more important to us than ever before, as a symbol round which "the wise and the good can repair", a cross upon our banner behind which we can rally, as did the Emperor Constantine, to march forward once more to bring the benefits of white civilization to a suffering world.

America could not seem to realize that this murder was the high-water mark of the confrontation of the black subterranean satanic forces and the forces of white civilization in modern history. In this encounter, white civilization was found wanting; it sank back, bewildered and defeated, to endure the agony of another world war and the unbridled rule of the satanic Jews over the gentile masses. Destiny had marked both Charles Lindbergh and his father,

Congressman Charles Lindbergh, to become Presidents of the United States. The senior Lindbergh won immortality by leading the battle in Congress against the passage of the Federal Reserve Act, when the Rothschilds imposed their Jewish system as the chains of slavery shackled onto the citizens of America. Logically, the American people should have chosen him as their President. Instead, Baruch and Jewish gold reelected Woodrow Wilson and led us into the mass slaughter of the First World War. When Congressman Lindbergh opposed our involvement in this slaughter for the profits of the Jews, federal agents were sent to his home to burn copies of the books he had written opposing the war. One might suppose that his neighbors and constituents, on seeing their champion under attack by the agents of the Jews, would have rallied to his defense. Instead, they believed a whispering campaign against him, reasoning that since he had been attacked by "federal agents", he must be some sort of super criminal. Congressman Lindbergh was defeated for re-election. Instead of backing his courageous stand, his wife left him, preferring to live independently and earn her own living as a school teacher.

The attack of the agents on their home left a permanent scar on the young Charles Lindbergh. This fear was aggravated by the insecurities he developed when his parents separated during his adolescence. Overcompensating for this, he threw himself into the study of mechanics, and resolved to devote his life to flying. Soon he had his own plane. One of his first assignments was to fly his father around the state on a new campaign to regain his seat in Congress. The Jews sabotaged his plane, and he crashed, but due to his great skill, he brought the plane down without injuring himself or his father. The crash put an end to his father's hopes of a successful campaign, and he died a broken man. It was then that Divine Providence selected the young Lindbergh as the new champion of America. In this light, his incredible feat of flying alone across the Atlantic becomes more understandable. Handsome, shy and inarticulate, he had become a familiar figure at the nation's airports, but no one would have thought of him as an international celebrity or as a national leader. Nevertheless, he found financial backers who put up the money for his flight across the ocean. As he prepared for his entry onto the world stage, everyone believed he was setting off on a suicidal mission. The Jew Zolotow, in his biography of Billy Wilder, claims that a cynical reporter, not wishing to see young Lindbergh die a virgin, paid a prostitute to spend the night with him before his takeoff. He claimed that this accounted for Lindbergh's overwhelming fatigue and drowsiness during much of his flight. A more likely explanation is that the Jews put drugs in his thermos, and concocted this out of character explanation for his planned disappearance. We should not forget that he was taking off from Long Island, a stone's throw from the world headquarters of international Jewry, the bankers whom his father had nearly thwarted. From his own account, in his book, "WE", he seems to have been unconscious during much of the flight, but his plane was borne up by Divine Providence, and instead of plunging into the ocean as the Jews had planned in wreaking their revenge on his family, his survival and future role as Leader was ensured.

Nothing less can explain the hysterical outpouring of joy which greeted him when he landed at Le Bourget field. He had already been given up for dead, and for the rest of his life he would be known as "Lucky Lindy". Others nicknamed him the "Lone Eagle". Instantaneously, he became the most famous hero in the world. Because Movietime News filmed his takeoff, his flight also inaugurated the era of sound in films.

All of Lindbergh's predecessors who had attempted to fly the Atlantic Ocean had vanished into the water. All of them had better equipment and were better financed than Lindbergh, yet this drugged youth in his tiny plane succeeded where others had failed. The Divine Plan was in operation. Lindbergh's succeeding years including the kidnapping and murder of his first-born son, also illustrate the workings of the Divine Plan. He returned home to worldwide acclaim, with a ticker tape parade down the financial center of the world, Wall Street. Everything had been prepared for him to embark on his world mission as the leader of his race. The government requested that he make goodwill missions to many countries. On one of these missions, he met his future wife, Anne Morrow.

Dwight Morrow, Lindbergh's father-in-law to be, had been a member of the famous Wall Street law firm of Simpson, Thacher and Bartlett, when the great J.P. Morgan himself, struck by Morrow's burgeoning reputation, asked him to draft the legal provisos of the Panama Canal treaties. Morrow's work on these treaties was superb. For many years, the Communists have sought to abrogate these treaties, but to the present day they have been unsuccessful. Convinced of Morrow's capabilities, Morgan summoned him to his office and informed him that he was to be a full partner in J.P. Morgan Co., with an assured income of one million dollars a year. After several years with J.P. Morgan, he amassed a fortune and went into public life, becoming a candidate for the Senate, and was later appointed Ambassador to Mexico. When Lindbergh came on his goodwill mission to Mexico, he was a guest at the Embassy. Here he met Morrow's daughter, Anne, who had confided in her school diary that her one ambition in life was "to marry a hero". Although Lindbergh, as shy as ever, paid little attention to her, she arranged future meetings, and soon they were married.

Lindbergh's marriage to the daughter of one of the world's leading international bankers is one of the keys to the mystery of his life. It explains his lifelong silence about the Federal Reserve System, despite his father's courageous opposition to it, an achievement of which any son should be proud. Overnight, the penniless flier had become a worldwide hero and a member of one of the world's most influential families. This financial security was intended to provide a platform from which he could proceed on this Divine mission and carry on his father's work against the Jewish monetary lords. Instead, Lindbergh became moody and irritable, spurning the adulation of the American people. His wife abetted his reaction by encouraging him to retreat into the pleasant and secluded lifestyle of the very rich. Throughout their life together, Anne Lindbergh persisted in leading the lifestyle of a typical suburbanite, with a large staff to maintain her home while she wrote lightweight "philosophical" books propounding a vaporous Junior League attitude towards the real problems of the world, from which she was comfortably insulated by her inherited fortune. Her writings which would never have been published for anyone with a less famous name, were ecstatically received by the Jewish publishing world in New York, who extolled her airy pleadings for more "brotherhood" and "understanding".

Charles Lindbergh's escape from the world of reality was to be short-lived. Even while he was soaring across the Atlantic, subterranean forces were at work which would bring him lifelong sorrow. In New York, the misshapen Franklin Delano Roosevelt was already gathering about him the crew of diseased cripples who would inaugurate a Jewish dictatorship in the United States. As the year of 1932 dawned, they had succeeded in capturing the Democratic Party, and the road to the White House was unencumbered. Herbert Hoover, the likely Republican candidate, had already been saddled with full blame for the Great Depression, which had been caused by classic gold movements of the Jewish international bankers. Suddenly a threat appeared on the horizon. A panicky subordinate informed FDR that the Republican Party leaders, despairing of re-electing Herbert Hoover, had made overtures to Charles Lindbergh to accept the Republican nomination. In fact, his father-in-law, Dwight Morrow, one of the Republican party leaders in New Jersey, had suggested to him that he should seek the nomination, but he had refused. FDR's crew did not know this, and they were appalled at the possibility that the handsome blond world hero would oppose them. There would not even be an election; he would simply be elected by acclamation, as the ancient Roman emperors had been. The crippled Roosevelt would roll his wheelchair back to his mother's estate in ignominious defeat, destroying the plans for world dictatorship of the sinister crew of Communist degenerates, Frankfurter and Bela Moskowitz, who had made his meteoric political rise possible. Something must be done, something so drastic that Lindbergh would abandon all thought of public office. We must now ask, "Would the Jewish conspirators, who had sent federal agents to wreck the Lindbergh home, sabotaged his plane, and drugged his thermos, actually murder a helpless child in the furtherance of their plans?" Let history ask this question of the Lindbergh child, Violet Sharpe, Richard Hauptmann, Ellis Parker and Dwight Morrow, all of whom were put to death in this conspiracy.

THE FOUR HORSEMEN OF THE APOCALYPSE

Propagandists for Israel, Hargis, Graham, Falwell and Robertson, pose as Christians

One of the oldest legends in history is the story of the Four Horsemen of the Apocalypse, who appear just before some great catastrophe, as a warning to all the world. From time immemorial, the Four Horsemen have stood for War, Famine, Pestilence, and Death. Today, in these apocalyptic times, the Four Horsemen appear before us as prominent television personalities, masquerading as Christian patriots while they carry out their stealthy task of propagandizing for the State of Israel and the maintenance of the power of the biological parasite over its Christian host nations. These Four Horsemen are Billy James Hargis, Billy Graham, Pat Robertson, and Jerry Falwell.

Each of these men has made his reputation as a preacher of "fundamentalist Christianity". Amazingly enough, the most fundamental belief which each of them propounds is that we must "love" the Jews, and we must support the bandit State of Israel in its massacres of Arab women and children in Israel's peace-loving neighboring countries. So terrible is the personal tragedy of each of these Four Horsemen that it illustrates with merciless clarity the apocalyptic or endtime situation into which we have been moved. We must understand from the awful manner in which these men have been destroyed that it is a true presage of the Apocalypse. Now, what is the Apocalypse? It is from the Greek word *apokalypsis*, meaning "the Unveiling", or "the Revelation". The national prominence of these four Jewish propagandists presages the temporary rule by the Prince, of Evil, who is also known as Satan,

Belial, and the Anti-Christ (may his reign be short!), and the Four Horsemen of the Apocalypse warn us of the coming, of war, famine, plague, earthquakes and death. In "Paradise Lost", John Milton wrote, IV. 2, "That warning voice which he who saw the Apocalypse, heard cry in Heaven cloud."

To understand why these four men, who between them rake in some three hundred million dollars a year, presage the Coming of the Apocalypse, we have to know their origins, and who put them in a position of power from which they could bamboozle three hundred million dollars a year from well-meaning Christian Americans to finance their propaganda for the State of Israel. It has long been common knowledge since the incorporation of the three major national television networks that each of them was owned, operated and completely controlled by Jews, and that no Christian patriot would be allowed to appear on any of the Jewish networks to preach the True Doctrine of Our Lord and Saviour Jesus Christ, "who had walked in fear of Jewry, for they sought to kill Him." How then, did these supposed Christian patriots gain admittance to the private preserves of world Jewry, the American television system? It is well known that the Jew, in his natural function as a biological parasite, must not only control the thoughts of his host people if he is to survive, but he must also establish their thought patterns and maintain supervision of them. Thus, the gentiles, or host people, are taught to respect and obey the smaller, weaker parasitic organism who is taking his sustenance, making him ill, and slowly destroying him. The entire host-parasite relationship flouts the most basic law of nature, the instinct of survival and of self-preservation. The Jew, being numerically weaker, must, if he is to survive, train the host to tolerate his presence, and to allow him to control the host. The first step is to destroy the host people's native leadership, the Alfalfa Bill Murrays and Ezra Pounds who warn their people against the poisonous presence of the jew. The Jew then recruits from the weakest and most depraved of the host people a new ruling class, known as the "shabez goi", or "Sabbath gentile cattle". These servile and contemptible people live well as long as they do the bidding of the Jews, but at the first objection to some particularly dastardly deed which the Jews demand that they carry out against their own people, they are immediately cast down and destroyed. The shabez goi always have in their degenerate backgrounds a "Panama", a sexual or financial scandal which the Jews use as a hold over them. The "new class", or shabez goi, are the epitome of the living lie, with their insidious conspiracies on behalf of the government of the parasites. In their world, the virtues of manliness, strength and honor are ridiculed and despised. This explains why Hargis, Graham, Robertson and Falwell were allowed to appear on national television to influence and control millions of people in the host nation. To overcome the criticism that all of the television networks were owned and controlled by Jews, even including the Public Broadcasting Service, whose President is a Jew, we were suddenly notified of the establishment of a "Christian Broadcasting Network". At last, or so it seemed, the Christians of America would have their own Christian television network on which they could observe the tenets of the Christian religion. They could escape the filth and the Communist propaganda of the Jewish networks. Or so it seemed. And when the CBN began its daily broadcasting, what was its daily message? We must love the Jews. We must support the State of Israel in all its depredations and its immoral devastation of the Holy Christian Shrines in the Birthplace of Our Saviour. We must help the Jews, and we must, above all, avoid the greatest sin, the sin of "anti-Semitism", whatever that is. Even the Jewish networks do not broadcast as blatantly pro-Jewish propaganda as the Christian Broadcasting Network.

To further understand why these Four Horsemen were promoted by the Jews to their present positions of affluence and prominence, we must remember that for many years, the principal "religious" agency which the Zionists and the Communists used to maintain thought control over the American people was the National Council of Churches. In "The Rockefellers", by Peter

Collier and David Horowitz, p. 155 n, we are told that "In 1950 the Federal Council of Churches merged with twelve Protestant missionary agencies to form the National Council of Churches, with Rockefeller providing the initial capital to fund a wide-ranging study of organizational structures for the new group and donating a large parcel of land near Riverside Church for its headquarters." Although no figure is given, the Rockefellers funded the National Council of Churches with many millions of dollars.

A classic shabez goi operation, the National Council of Churches was staffed by impeccably groomed graduates of Ivy League colleges, many of whom married into the Rockefeller family or its immediate executive group. One Rockefeller trustee, Secretary of State Dean Rusk, was forced to give his white daughter in marriage to a strapping black buck, the final humiliation for this old Southern family. From the outset, the thinly veiled missionary goal of the National Council of Churches was to destroy the white race. In the United States, this was to be done by forced integration of the races in their schools, churches and homes, and in the first step towards this goal, it was necessary for them to murder the Chief Justice of the Supreme Court of the United States, Fred Vinson, to overcome his opposition to forced school integration. In Africa, every white settlement was to be destroyed or to be brought under black domination. To this end, the National Council of Churches purchased arms for the most vicious black guerilla groups throughout Africa, and trained them to massacre white settlers without mercy.

By 1980, most of the goals of the National Council of Churches had been achieved. With the exception of a small white enclave in South Africa, the white settlements in Africa had largely been exterminated in a well-planned and executed program of racial genocide. But the NCC had come under much criticism for its program of arming the murderous black guerillas, and for its well-publicized programs in the United States promoting drug use, homosexuality, Communist fronts and forced racial integration. It was time for the NCC to retreat under attack, and for new front groups to be formed and financed by the Satanic forces. If the National Council of Churches had been so successful in achieving its goals, would not an even more fundamental Christian front be even more useful in promoting the program of Satan? Certainly there were plenty of shabez goi wretches to be found who would be glad to do anything for money. The new "fundamentalists" sounded very good in their initial programs. They preached against drug usage, homosexuality, abortion and fornication, in short, everything which the previous Rockefeller front, the NCC, had stood for. It seemed that a new era had begun, an era in which the Christmas of America would rejoice in the celebration of the most basic tenets of their religion. Alas, it was not to be. The "fundamentalist Christians" always wound up their preachments with the universal admonition, "We must be good to the Jews. And we must always support the State of Israel."

When the American people, in all their majesty, rose up in November 4, 1980, and voted out of office many of the most degenerate of the Satanic stooges in Washington, expressing their righteous indignation and disgust with the most notorious of the shabez goi at the polling booths, the Rockefellers' new stooges, the "fundamentalist Christians" immediately tried to seize credit for the victory. In fact, the Israeli stooges had little direct impact of the election, the principal drive having come from the NCPAC which had raised funds from American patriots, and had spent them in a well-managed campaign to oust the pro-Israeli traitors in Congress, the McGoverns, Churches and Bayhs.

Let us look more closely at our Four Horsemen of the Apocalypse, whose programs are designed to prevent the Holy Shrines of Christ from being taken from the Jews and returned to Christian hands. First is the notorious Billy James Hargis, a confidence man so smooth that he even managed to get sizeable donations from the late patriot H.L. Hunt, until Hunt's agents discovered Hargis' unsavory practices. Hargis always needed plenty of money to finance his expensive sexual debauches. This "patriot" had a penchant for committing perverse sexual acts with handsome white boys. Being under constant threat of exposure, he needed to expend large sums of money in order to continue his filthy pursuits. He insured a constant flow of money to his "religious" work by acting as an unregistered agent for the State of Israel. He repeatedly exhorted his Christian followers to defend the State of Israel, and to uphold the "right" of the Jews to expel or massacre the Arab families who had owned the land for thousands of years. Despite his personal predilection for white youths as his sexual partners, Billy James Hargis also embraced the Rockefeller doctrine of racial integration, and he used his preachments of "fundamental Christianity" to persuade his followers to adopt hordes of mulatto, black and Asiatic illegitimate children and bring them to the United States to further pollute our nation.

Although Hargis' sexual perversions were well known, and were even the subjects of stories in such national magazines as *Time* and *Newsweek*, the man was so utterly without shame that he refused to get off his lucrative gravy train. Instead, with the full approval of his Jewish backers, he has continued as a full time fund raiser, ignoring the national exposes of his notorious personal habits, a typical shabez goi.

The second of our Four Horsemen of the Apocalypse, Billy Graham, has been even more shameless in his promotion of Israeli political goals than Billy James Hargis. Billy Graham, as a young, struggling preacher, suddenly was promoted into national prominence. How did this happen? Billy Graham and his ambitions came to the attention of William Randolph Hearst (Hirsch), the publishing tycoon. Without giving any explanation for his action, Hearst despatched a terse note to his editors, "Puff Graham". This order went out to newspapers all over the United States which were owned by Hearst. With this backing, Billy Graham became an overnight sensation. He soon began to lard his preachments about Christianity with many strange and unfounded statements about the Jews. He was the first Christian in the United States to publicly advance the Biblical claims of the Jews to the Holy Land, claims which were prepared for him by the Anti-Defamation League of B'Nai B'Rith, with whom he has always worked very closely. Graham's claims ignore the entire history of the Jewish people, the Zionist settlers being direct descendants of a tribe, the Khazars, who lived in central Russia and who had never had any connection with Palestine. Benjamin Freedman first exposed the geographical origin of the Khazar Jewish Zionists some thirty years ago, and his work was fully documented by a famous Jewish intellectual, Arthur Koestler, in "The Thirteenth Tribe".

Although Billy Graham's passionate love for the State of Israel was never matched by his concern for the United States, he has become an elder statesman who is preparing to retire with his millions to his palatial mountain estate in North Carolina. As Graham's successor as the leading Israeli stooge, the Jews have been grooming Rev. Jerry Falwell, of Lynchburg, Va. Like Graham, Falwell was recruited from the Anglo-Saxon heartland of America, the Southern Appalachians. He came from what is known as a "rough" background. His father and uncle, twin brothers, operated roadside "tourist cabins" on the outskirts of Lynchburg. As was customary in the nineteen thirties, these cabins came complete with prostitutes, liquor and gambling. During a quarrel over the division of the lucrative "take" from these operations, Falwell's father shot and killed his brother. Because he had been paying off local law enforcement officials who allowed him to operate these enterprises, Falwell escaped punishment for his crime. He later died an alcoholic. Young Jerry Falwell, (*Newsweek*, Sept. 15, 1980) was to have been named Valedictorian of his high school class, but was denied the distinction after school officials learned that for an entire year he had been lunching with bogus tickets. His schooling stood him in good stead after he began to rake in a million dollars a week with his television program, "The Old Time Gospel Hour". In 1973, the Securities Exchange Commission charged him with "fraud and deceit" in selling $6,600,000.00 in church bonds. An out of court settlement provided that Falwell would turn over supervision of his financial operations to a group of businessmen. The head of the SEC who had launched the investigation into Falwell's operations was a Jew. Falwell got the message. He soon became known as an enthusiastic supporter of the State of Israel, and there were no further investigations into his financial operations.

Jewish Week, Feb. 10, 1980, headlined "TV Evangelist Denounces Misguided Foes of Israel. 'Christian' Supporter. Dr. Jerry Falwell, Christian evangelist who supports Israel and contributes to the Jewish National Fund ... He spoke at the Jewish National Fund headquarters at 42 East 69th St. (New York City) on the occasion of an announcement that a Jerry Falwell Forest was to be created in Israel. Falwell ... denounced anti-Semitism and declared that anyone who wishes to destroy Israel 'stands against God' ... Falwell said that he loves Israel and the Jewish people because God loves them and that the enemies of Israel and of the Jewish people are enemies of God." One can only wonder if the contributors to Falwell's "Christian work" know that he contributes money to the Jewish National Fund. In his own paper, *Moral Majority*, Falwell proudly published a photograph of himself visiting with the world's arch-terrorist, the notorious mass murderer and Prime Minister of Israel, Menachem Begin.

The fourth of our Four Horsemen of the Apocalypse, Pat Robertson, claims that he had only $1.75 in his pocket when he founded the Christian Broadcasting Network. He has managed to parlay that stake into millions of dollars a week, a splendid office building, and the other appurtenances of national prominence and affluence. Like the other Four Horsemen, Robertson's Christian

Broadcasting Network repeatedly exhorts his listeners to love the Jews and to support the State of Israel. His political stance is more understandable when we learn that he is the son of the late Senator A. Willis Robertson, (D. Va.). A loyal and lifelong supporter of the Byrd machine in Virginia, Robertson was a Congressman until he was named the successor to the famous Jewish stooge, Senator Carter Glass, who had been totally senile and unable to answer a rollcall for eight years. Not only was his mental condition considered to be no handicap by his Jewish masters, but they even reelected him to another term! The Byrd machine, of course, was operated by Harry Byrd's mentor, Lewis Lichtenstein Strauss, a partner of the international Jewish banking house, Kuhn, Loeb, Co., the American representative of the Rothschild family interests. Byrd named Robertson as his successor to the chairmanship of the prestigious Senate Banking and Currency Committee. In this post, Robertson faithfully carried out the desires of his Jewish banking masters. Should we wonder that his son found that public support for the State of Israel would bring in a million dollars a week?

The public activities of these Four Horsemen of the Apocalypse should serve to warn us of approaching war, famine, and pestilence. Let us be courageous and hold fast to our true Faith in Our Lord and Saviour Jesus Christ, and let us not be misled by these propagandists for the State of Israel.

Other Books by Eustace Mullins

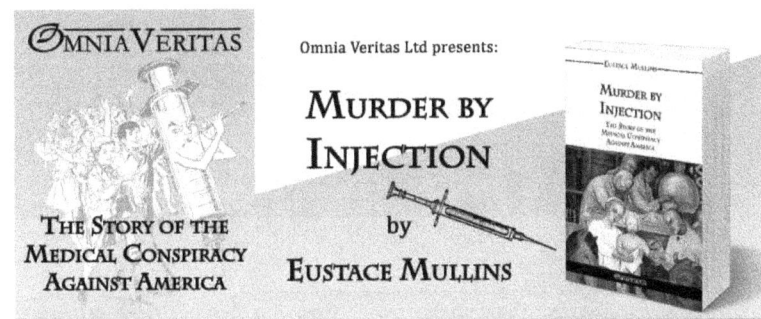

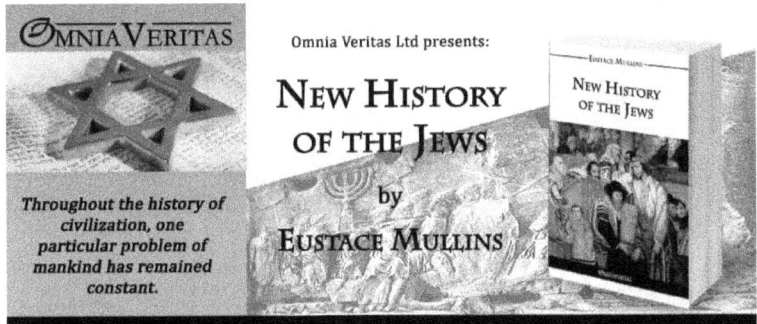

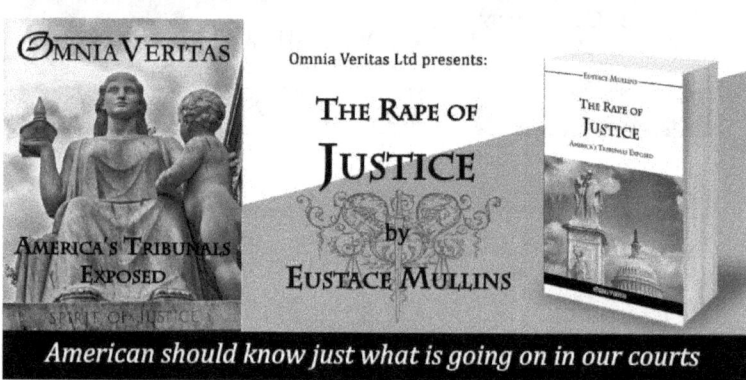

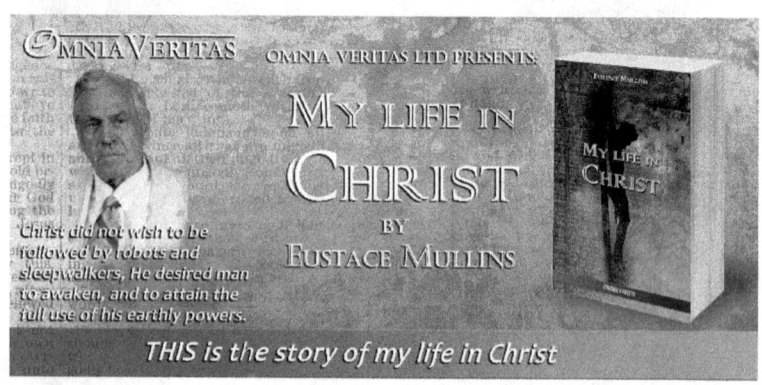

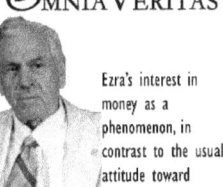
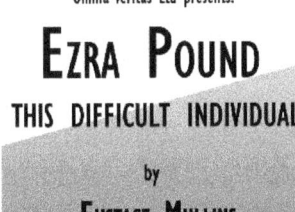

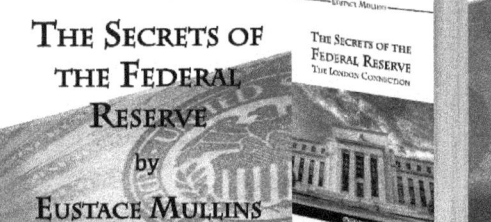

www.omnia-veritas.com

www.ingramcontent.com/pod-product-compliance
Lightning Source LLC
Chambersburg PA
CBHW050124170426
43197CB00011B/1707